Tírghrá

Tá an leabhar seo mar cuimhneachán ar na 364 poblachtánach atá ar an Roll of Honour. Fuair na fir agus mná seo bás, baill Óglaigh na hÉireann, Cumman na mBan, na Fianna Éireann agus Sinn Féin, thug siad a raibh acu ar son saoirse na hÉireann.

Ní raibh siad ag lorg ar phribhléid ná buntáiste agus gan aird a thabhairt ar íobairt phearsanta, chuir siad a saol í ngeall don phoblacht.

Tá an leabhar seo tiomnaithe ar chuimhne ár gcairde caillte, agus ar na clanna a d'íompair an chailliúut trom seo le dínit agus le bród.

Is fianaise beag í, na leathanaigh seo, ar an ard-mheas atá ag poblachtánaigh sa ghaile agus thar lear ar chomradaithe caillte s'againn agus ar na clanna.

Ireland's Patriot Dead

This book is in the memory of the 364 Republicans whose names are on the Roll of Honour. These men and woman, Volunteers in Óglaigh Na h-Éireann, Cumman Na mBan, Fianna Éireann, and members of Sinn Féin gave their lives in the cause of Irish Freedom.

They did not seek favour or glory, and irrespective of personal sacrifice, pledged their lives in service of the Republic.

This book is dedicated to their memory, and to their families, who have borne loss with dignity and pride.

Tírghrá would like to thank everyone who contributed in the compilation of this book. We are forever in their debt. Tírghrá also regrets that some photographs and other information were unavailable.

These pages are a small testimony of the high esteem in which Republicans at home and abroad hold our fallen comrades and their families.

Réamhrá

Tírghrá

**Ní thig leat Éire a chloígh
Ní thig leat fonn saoirse mhuintir na hÉireann a mhúcadh.**

Pádraig MacPiarais

Níl rud ar bith níos tabhactaigh ná saoirse. Téann an foilseachán seo 'Tírghrá' amach ag an am céanna leis an ómós náisiúnta ar an 13ú Aibreann do chlanna n mball d'Óglaigh na hÉireann agus do Shinn Féin a maraíodh sa troid ar son saoirse na hÉireann.

Ba mhaith liom coiste 'Tírghrá' a mholadh agus gach aon duine a bhí páirteach in eagrú agus cur i láthair na hocáide seo atá gan reamhshampla, tiomsú leabhrán 'Tírghrá' san aireamh.

Tá an ómós s'againne le haghaidh clanna ár mairtírigh poblachtacha. Tá saol na mairtíreach poblachta agus clanna na mairtíreach poblachtach á gcomóradh agus á gceiliúradh san fhoilseachán seo. Is mar ómós dóibh a thugaimid an bronnadh uathúil dóibh. Tá sé mar aitheantas agus mar léirthuiscint dá gcaillteanas mór agus dá ngrá gan leithleachas. Is comhartha é dár ndiongbháilteacht saoirse, cóir agus síochán a bhaint amach do mhuintir na hoileáin seo.

Is teacht le chéile stairiúl é seo nach bhfacthas a leithid a riamh, an chruinniú seo le clanna poblachtacha ó na 30í, 40í, 50í agus 60í in ómós a thabhairt dóibh uilig, na fir agus na mná uile a fuair bás sna treimhsí éagsúla den streachailt agus do na daoine a chuaigh amach i 1916 agus arís sna 1920í chomh maith.

Ach tig an cuid is mó den fhreastal ó chlanna na bpoblachtánach marbh de tríocha bliain anuas, na 70í, na 80í agus na 90í.

Is taifead suntasach é 'Tírghra', cineal de 'who's who' dár mairtírigh den treimhse seo – an chéim is faide den troid ar son neamhspleachais agus aontais na tíre seo, agus atá ar leanúint go fóill.

Tá liosta fada na ndaoine taobh istigh den "Roll of Honour" an cuimhneachán agus tá sé mar mheabhrúcháin ar an íobairt a d'fhulaing na céadta clanna poblachtacha.

Tá 364 ainmneacha, ar an liosta seo. Bhí an cuid aba mhó acu ina fir agus mná óga, gan pósadh nuair a chailleadh iad, ach ina measc bhí gníomhaithe ní ba shine, athracha agus máthracha, chomh maith le mic agus iníonacha, agus b'fhéidir dornán de seanathracha agus seanmháthracha san aireamh.

Tá siad uilig anseo, i leathanach i ndiaidh leathanaigh de griangrafanna agus beathaisnéisí gairid. Ba ghnáth daoine iad siúd uilig, baill Óglaigh na hÉireann agus

Sinn Féin. Mar gheall ar na hamanna agus na cúrsaí mar a bhi siad thart orthu fuair siad an neart inmheánach, an diongbháilteacht agus an misneach le seasamh in aghaidh éagóir agus cos ar bholg agus le cearta is saoirse a héilimh do mhuintir na hÉireann.

Bhí an fis acu, chonaic siad thart ar an cogadh, thart ar na céadta de gabháil na tire seo agus bhí siad ábalta meon phobhlachtach Tone, Mac Piarais agus Uí Conghaile a bhreith agus le seasamh suas ar son na fírinne agus cóir, ar son saoirse agus comhionnanais.

Dúirt Bobby Sands é nuair a scríobh sé sa dán 'The Rhythm of Time' fá dtaobh den neart inmheánach sin a threoir agus a stiúr é féin agus a chomradaithe, fir is mná, frid an agóid pluide agus an stailc níocháin. I dtaca liom féin de 'an rud inmheánach seo' atá le fáil i ngach uile solas dóchais agus nach n-aithníonn teorainn na spás agus a screadann as súile na dtíoranach, labhrann sé thar ceann a bhfuil le cuimhniú insan leabhrán seo agus na saolta a ndéanaimid comóradh orthu.

You cannot conquer Ireland.
You cannot extinguish the Irish passion for freedom.

P.H. Pearse

There is nothing more important than freedom. This publication 'Ireland's Patriot Dead' accompanies the national tribute on 13th April to the families of IRA Volunteers and Sinn Féin activists who were killed in pursuit of Irish freedom.

I want to commend the Tírghrá Committee, and everyone involved in organising this unprecedented occasion, including the compilation of Ireland's Patriot Dead.

Our tribute is to the families of our republican dead. It is for the families whose loved ones we commemorate and whose lives we celebrate in this publication. The unique presentation they receive is by way of our tribute to them. It is our acknowledgement and appreciation of their great loss, and their unselfish love. It is an earnest of our commitment to secure freedom, justice and peace for the people of this island.

This gathering hosted by Tírghrá Committee, is a unique coming together of republican families from the 30's, 40's, 50's and 60's in homage to the men and women who died in those phases of the struggle and to those from the 1916 and 1920's period also.

But the bulk of the attendance is from the families of the republican dead of the last three decades, the 1970's, 1980's and 1990's.

Ireland's Patriot Dead is a remarkable 'who's who' of our patriot dead from that period - the longest and continuing phase of the struggle for independence and unity of our country.

The number of people contained in this roll of honour and remembrance is a sad reminder of the sacrifice endured by hundreds of republican families.

There are 364 mainly young men and women, mostly single but including older activists, fathers and mothers, as well as sons and daughters, and perhaps a handful of grandfathers and grandmothers as well.

They are all here, in page after page of photographs and short biographical notes.

These Volunteers, Fianna and Sinn Féin activists were ordinary men and women who in extraordinary and difficult circumstances found the inner strength, determination and courage to stand against injustice and oppression, and to demand the rights and entitlements of the Irish people.

They had the vision to see beyond the conflict, beyond the centuries of occupation, and to embrace the republican spirit of Tone, of Pearse and Connolly, and to stand up for truth and justice, for liberty and equality.

Bobby Sands summed up all of this when he wrote in The Rhythm of Time of the 'inner strength', that is 'found in every light of hope' and 'knows no bounds or space' and which 'screams in tyrants' eyes' speaks of all of those we remember in this book and whose lives we celebrate.

> **It lights the dark of his prison cell,**
> **It thunders forth its might,**
> **It is 'the undauntable thought', my friend,**
> **That thought that says 'I'm right!'**

Gerry Adams
13th April 2002

A Personal Reflection

It is an honour and a privilege to have been asked to contribute in some way to this book, the first national publication of its kind.

I had the good fortune to have known many of these men and women honoured in this book, indeed some were good friends as well as comrades. All of them were very warm and very decent human beings who loved their families and the communities amongst whom they lived.

It was this love above all else that drove so many young men and women to take up arms in defence of these communities.

The first person honoured in this book is Fiann Gerard McAuley, a young Belfast boy who was shot and killed while trying to defend his home and the homes of his neighbours from a rampaging Orange mob. Sadly these homes in Bombay Street and in other streets across Belfast were burnt to the ground by Loyalists as the RUC stood by and in some instances joined in. But from those ruins and ashes arose a new and re-invigorated Irish Republican Army. A new phase in a very long and very old struggle had begun.

This book tells the story of that phase of our struggle but it is neither the whole of the story or indeed the end of it.

I had come to know the homes and many of families of Bombay Street very well. My good friend and comrade Tom Williams, God rest his soul, was reared in No.46 by his granny Fay. Tom, like many other young men and women of his day joined the IRA in the middle of another campaign that had begun in the early months of 1939, on the eve of the Second World War.

Ironically, many of those who I came to know in the ranks of the IRA had been radicalised by the poverty of the '30's or their experience of the widespread sectarian pogroms that swept across Belfast in 1935.

Tom was executed on September 2nd 1942 and is remembered to this day right across the country but he was not the only IRA Volunteer to be executed or killed in action during that campaign or the one that followed in the 1950s. Many other brave men were executed, fell in battle, or died on Hunger Strike in the years before and after Tom's death. Many others, men and women, were hounded and jailed on both sides of the border and in England and endured great hardships for the cause of freedom. These were difficult times to be a Republican.

Both of the campaigns sadly ended inconclusively. As executions, arrests and continuous harassment took its toll on a dwindling number of Republican activists, what was left of the IRA could only bide its time and await the opening of the prison gates and more fortuitous circumstances.

I am proud to have been part of that generation of Republicans. Their sacrifice, their commitment ensured that the spirit of freedom was never entirely extinguished.

In 1969 a new generation of Republicans took up the same cause and as these pages testify, paid a terrible price. Each and every one of them was a cherished family member and friend, and we must remember that each death broke another hundred hearts. We must not, we will not, forget them or their families.

This book tells their story but it is neither the whole story or indeed the end. The struggle must continue until we realise the dreams and aspirations of our fallen comrades.

Fuair siad bás ar son na hÉireann

Joe Cahill

Fiann Gerard McAuley

16th October 1953 - 15th August 1969

Gerard McAuley was born on 16th October 1953. He lived in Colinward Street in the Beechmount area of West Belfast and attended St John's Primary School before he moved on to St Thomas's Secondary School. While at Secondary School his great interest in outdoor activities became evident. He was particularly interested in fishing, hurling and Gaelic football for which he had won a number of medals.

The Loyalist onslaught, backed by the RUC and 'B' Specials, saw the present phase of the conflict break out in 1969. It was around this time that Gerard had secured employment as an apprentice cloth-cutter.

Gerard was shot dead in Waterville Street on 15th August 1969 while defending the Clonard area from sectarian attack by rampaging Orange mobs. He was the first Republican activist to lose his life during the present phase of Ireland's freedom struggle.

Gerard was buried in Milltown Cemetery. His funeral cortege was given a guard of honour by his comrades in Na Fianna Éireann.

Óglach Liam McParland

9th August 1926 - 6th November 1969

Liam McParland was born in Omar Street, off the Falls Road, on August 9th 1926. He was educated at St Finian's Primary School which he left, at the age of 14, to become an apprentice cabinet maker with the Co-op Furniture Company on Donegall Street.

During his early years, he joined Fianna Éireann, taking a great interest in the Irish language, dancing and culture. From the Fianna he joined the IRA.

During the 1950s campaign, he was arrested by the RUC and interned in Crumlin Road Jail. Despite being imprisoned, Liam continued the struggle by organizing escape attempts and Irish language classes. He was released in 1961, after four years' internment, and immediately reported back to the Republican Movement for active service.

When civil strife erupted in 1969, Liam, then living in the Whiterock area, was a member of 'B' Company, 2nd Battalion IRA. Whilst on active service on October 19th 1969, Liam was fatally injured in a car accident. He died as a result of his injuries on November 6th 1969.

Liam McParland was subsequently buried in the Republican Plot in Milltown Cemetery, being the first Volunteer to be interred there in the present phase of the liberation struggle.

It has always been a Republican tradition for a volley of shots to be fired over the graves of Volunteers killed while on active service. However, the then Army leadership, in the days leading up to the split, refused him this honour. Two Volunteers, though, ignored this order and, unbeknown to most people, the shots were fired, in secret, over the grave.

Óglach Henry McIlhone

27th August 1937 - 27th June 1970

Henry McIlhone was born on 27th August 1937 at 55 Baker Street in the Pound Loney area. He attended St Comgall's School, Falls Road, and when he left, at the age of 14, like most young lads of that time, he went to work in the local mill. In 1953, at the age of 16, Henry went to England in search of better employment, but stayed only five years. He returned on New Year's Eve 1958, where at a local dance he met his future wife, Sue Weir from Sheriff Street, Short Strand. They married the following year and had five sons: Paul, Henry, Colin, Kevin and Stephen.

Just back from England, Henry first found employment as a window-cleaner and then general labouring before working as a scaffolder, progressing to the job of rigger at which he worked at the time of his death. He had no specific favourite pastimes, although he did enjoy placing a bet on the horses and dogs, going dancing and having a few pints of beer with friends. He was a popular figure in the Short Strand, making friends extremely easily. In fact, he often used to joke with his wife that although he was a 'Falls Road man', and she was born and reared in the Short Strand, he knew more people in the area than she did.

Henry fell victim to the very bigotry and sectarianism that he opposed when, on 27th June 1970, he was shot dead during a gun-battle with Loyalists who attacked St Matthew's Chapel.

Although not a member of the IRA, Henry McIlhone was included on the Republican Roll of Honour as a mark of respect to a great Irish man by Republican comrades who fought alongside him in the defence of the Short Strand on that historic day.

Óglach Joe Coyle

22nd June 1925 - 27th June 1970

Volunteer Joseph Eamon Coyle was born in Derry's Bogside on 22nd June 1925. He had two sisters and three brothers.

Joe was a pupil at Rosemount Boys' School. Like his father and brother he became a yellow button man at Derry Quay, and was a member of the Transport and General Workers Union.

He met and married Joan in August 1953 and lived at 20 Eden Place, Bogside, where four of their nine children were born. Due to poor housing conditions they were moved to Creggan and settled at 21 Rathkeele Way. Joe was a keen gardener growing vegetables and flowers which he shared with his neighbours. His other hobby was his aviary where he bred budgies. In the late 1960's Joe was very much involved in the Civil Rights Movement, and took part in protest marches all over the north. Also in 1969 as a member of the Republican Movement he defied an order by the RUC and with 5,000 others marched in Derry to commemorate the Easter Rising of 1916.

In 1970 the British Army and RUC were attacking Derry's Bogside. On the 26th June as the fighting raged on, Joe and republican comrades, preparing to resist British incursions with the only means available, were in Tommy McCool's house in Dunree Gardens. In the early hours of the 27th there was an explosion followed by a raging fire. Joe, Tommy McCool and two of Tommy's daughters died in this tragic accident. Tommy Carlin died a short time later.

Óglach Tommy McCool

31st May 1927 - 27th June 1970

Tommy McCool came from 16 Moore Street near the bottom of Bishop Street. Quiet and modest, he played Gaelic football and was also a member of the Owen Roe O'Neill Flute Band. In 1953 he married Josie O'Hagan. They moved to England a short time later where Tommy found work on a construction site.

They returned to Derry a couple of years later and he worked as a labourer on building sites. He was involved in the IRA campaign in the 1950's and in December 1957 he was arrested at the family home in Moore Street and charged with possession of guns, ammunition, grenades, explosives and a copy of the then banned United Irishman. He refused to recognise the court and was sentenced to 12 years in jail.

Tommy was released under an amnesty in 1962 when the IRA ended their campaign. During the next few years, Tommy worked in building sites in the city and when the Civil Rights Campaign began, was deeply involved once more in the struggle. He was instrumental in founding the Provisional IRA in Derry.

On Friday June 27th 1970 there was serious rioting as a result of Bernadette Devlin's arrest and Tommy, with his comrade Joe Coyle, left for Tommy's home in Dunree Gardens, Creggan, to make petrol bombs. There was an explosion in the kitchen and Tommy, Joe Coyle and two of Tommy's children, Bernadette and Carol died. Another Volunteer, Tommy Carlin, died later from injuries he sustained in the blast.

Óglach Tommy Carlin

1st October 1915 - 8th July 1970

Volunteer Tommy Carlin was a very well known man. Some say that he knew half of Derry and the other half knew him. Even today, almost 31 years after his death, people still mention to his family that they knew him and sometimes accompany this with a bit of a yarn.

When Tommy's family gather at the usual 'get-togethers', his memory will almost always be spoken of, even if only briefly. The times when he used to make and sell toffee apples and clove rock from the kitchen; the pile of thrupenny bits that he kept on the top of his old wardrobe, seemingly out of reach of the wanes, but nonetheless always given to them anyway. In today's terms, Tommy was an enterprising man, in a working class sort of way, full of ideas on how to turn the next shilling.

Politically, he got involved in everything; Action Committees, Defence Associations and the IRA. But he'll probably be remembered best for flying the Tricolour from his bungalow home on Central Drive every Easter from 1950 until he died in 1970.

At the first Easter March held by the Republican Movement in Derry, in 1970, Tommy marched as a member of the IRA Colour Party. Spoken of as a founding member and life-long Republican, he had great spirit. Even as he lay dying from the severe burns caused by the explosion and fire, he managed to retain this sense of humour, joking that the bandages that encased his hands made them look like boxing gloves.

For his family, Tommy's death left a huge hole that nothing could fill.

The Carlin Family

Óglach Jimmy Steele

8th August 1907 - 9th August 1970

Jimmy Steele joined Na Fianna Éireann at a very early age. After the Treaty split, Jimmy continued to assist the IRA. He was first arrested in 1923, being taken from his home and detained for a period.

In 1924 he was again arrested and held for several months. During the 1924/25 re-organisation of the Army, Jimmy, along with Anthony Lavery, was appointed to re-organise Na Fianna Éireann.

Jimmy was re-arrested several times over the following years including being sentenced to several months imprisonment in 1933. Following the abortive Campbell College raid, the IRA convened a court-martial to examine matters arising from the raid. Twelve men, including Jimmy, were arrested and charged with 'treason', when the area where the court-martial was being convened, was sealed off by the RUC. Jimmy was sentenced to five years penal servitude.

After his release in 1940, Jimmy married Anna Crawford. In December 1940 Jimmy was captured and sentenced to ten years in jail. In January 1943 Jimmy escaped from Crumlin Road jail along with three of his comrades. His period of freedom was short lived. While back in jail, he continued to write for 'War News', 'An tOglach' and 'The Critic'. Eventually, in 1950, he was released from prison. He was the last Republican Political Prisoner to be released.

He was interned in 1957 for three years and upon release he once again reported back to the Army, helping to re-organise the Movement during the Sixties. Jimmy spent over 20 years of his life in prison for his ideals. When he died, aged 63, he was still active in the ranks of the Movement.

Óglach Michael Kane

2nd January 1935 - 4th September 1970

Michael Kane was born in 1935 and was educated at Star of the Sea School. When he left school he took up the trade of French-Polisher and at the time of his death he was, along with his brother, preparing to set up a furniture business.

He was a typical youth of his generation and enjoyed socializing with his friends. An all-round craftsman, he was extremely gifted with his hands and had the unusual hobby of making miniature jewellery boxes.

Michael came from a Republican background. His grandfather, Jack Coogan was an IRA Volunteer who was killed in Valentine Street in the 1920's.

In 1969, at the outset of the present phase of the struggle for national independence, Michael joined the ranks of Óglaigh na hÉireann. He was a committed and highly respected volunteer and when he died, while on active service, on 4th September 1970 near Newforge Lane in Belfast, he was the second member of the 3rd battalion of the Belfast Brigade to be killed.

He was sadly missed by his family, friends and comrades throughout the City.

Óglach Peter Blake

8th August 1952 - 27th October 1970

Peter Blake was born on 8th August 1952, the youngest of ten children, and lived at Benares Street in Belfast. He was educated locally at St John's Primary School before moving on to St Thomas's Secondary School located on the Whiterock Road, West Belfast. Upon leaving school he found work as a van driver. However, he gave this job up at the start of the present phase of the struggle, as he believed that he was making himself vulnerable to Loyalists, and soon found employment in the Franklin Laundry on the Springfield Road where he worked until his death.

In 1969, after witnessing the burning of Bombay Street, he joined the ranks of Óglaigh na hÉireann where he played an active role in defending nationalist areas from the pogroms being carried out by the loyalists and their associates in the Crown Forces. A 'quiet big fella' with a great sense of humour, he was the typical big softie with a heart of gold and is fondly remembered by all of those that he came into contact with for his telling of jokes and relaxed attitude to life.

In October 1970 he took part in an IRA training camp. As he was returning to Belfast from the camp, his car was involved in a collision with a British Army vehicle near Dungannon, County Tyrone. Peter died as a result along with his comrade Tom McGoldrick.

Peter was a quiet and dedicated Volunteer, and was admired for these attributes by all of those who worked with him.

Óglach Tom McGoldrick

23rd September 1949 - 27th October 1970

Tom was born in 1949 and grew up in Harrogate Street. After leaving school, he began work as an apprentice plumber, his work taking him all over West Belfast. At once he realised that socially and economically, the people of the Falls and Shankill had much in common.

His interest in politics began in 1964 when Ian Paisley threatened to remove the Tricolour from the election offices of Sinn Féin if the RUC did not act. The RUC smashed their way into the offices provoking serious rioting. Tom then began attending Gaelic clubs and Republican socials. He joined Óglaigh na hÉireann in 1966 - at the time of the fiftieth anniversary of the 1916 Rising. He was just 17 years of age but put his heart and soul into the Republican Movement. He was also heavily involved in the Civil Rights Movement and took part in most of the big marches.

At the height of the crisis in August 1969, Tom's instructions were to proceed to Ardoyne and help defend the beleaguered people of this area. The people of North Belfast know themselves how much they owe to Tom and his comrades. Around this time Tom began dating Ann, a girl from the St. James area.

Disillusioned and disgusted at the failure of the then leadership to provide proper defence to nationalist areas, Tom threw his weight behind those prepared to reorganise and rearm. By 1970 he had become a highly respected member of the 2nd Battalion, Belfast Brigade. On 27th October 1970, while returning from a training camp with his comrade Peter Blake, they were involved in a collision with a British Army vehicle in County Tyrone, killing both Volunteers. He and Ann had just decided to marry and were just planning their wedding at the time of his tragic death.

Óglach James Saunders

5th September 1948 - 6th February 1971

Jim Saunders was born at 7 Ardilea Street, Oldpark Road, on 5th September 1948. He attended The Sacred Heart Primary School and St Gabriel's Secondary School until he was 16 years old.

After leaving school he had a number of jobs until, at 18, he found full time employment in the City Bakery as a time-and-motion clerk. He then moved to Milanda Bakeries but was forced to take voluntary redundancy because of the dangers of working in an area that was unsafe for Catholics.

Jim, like many other young men from nationalist areas throughout the six counties, joined the IRA just after the 'Split' in 1969/70. He was a trusted and highly respected member of the 3rd Battalion of the Belfast Brigade.

At a time when Nationalist areas in Belfast were under almost daily attacks from loyalist mobs, the IRA were on the streets in defence of their communities. On the 6th February 1971, Jim, and a number of his comrades, went on to the streets defending their area from yet another loyalist attack, when he was shot dead by the British army.

Jim was one of the first members of the 3rd Battalion to be killed on active service during this phase of the campaign. He died defending the community that he loved and his death inspired many young men and women from his area to join the ranks of Óglaigh na hÉireann.

Óglach Charles Hughes

26th December 1943 - 8th March 1971

Charlie Hughes was born in Servia Street, Belfast on 26th December 1943. He was the youngest of a family of nine children. He went to St Joseph's School at nearby Slate Street.

As a boy Charlie was quiet and likeable, thoughtful and kind to young and old. He was a member of St Peter's Confraternity and was a Pioneer.

Charlie was interested in all aspects of Irish culture from an early age. He came from a Republican background and his uncle, Owen Hughes was shot dead by Loyalists in the 1920's.

Charlie joined the IRA and the National Graves Association. On March 8th 1971, Charlie was shot dead by Workers Party gunmen from a shop in Cyprus Street.

Óglach Tony Henderson

4th April 1950 - 4th April 1971

Volunteer Tony Henderson was born on the 4th April 1950, and attended St. Teresa's Primary School on the Glen Road in Andersonstown. Later he moved to the nearby Christian Brothers' Secondary School. When he finished his school days in 1966, he went to work as an apprentice bricklayer.

Tony was very aware of the seriousness of the situation, that was developing throughout the six counties in the late 1960's, and, when Belfast was engulfed in sectarian violence in 1969, he was quick to join the Republican Movement as it reorganised in defence of the people.

A dedicated, active Republican freedom fighter, Tony Henderson waged relentless war against the British occupation forces. It was while involved in a training exercise at a camp near Portlaoise that this young volunteer lost his life as a result of an accidental shooting.

A member of the 1st Battalion, Belfast Brigade, Óglaigh na hÉireann, Tony Henderson gave his young life in the cause of Irish freedom on his 21st Birthday, 4th April 1971. Tony's remains were brought home to Belfast and were interred with full honours in Milltown Cemetery.

Óglach Billy Reid

1st January 1939 - 15th May 1971

William James Reid was born on 1st January 1939, at Regent Street in the Carrickhill area of North Belfast where he attended the local schools before taking up a trade as a joiner.

Billy had a great interest in cycling, art and music. He played the trumpet and wrote his own songs. He took an interest in the old people of his area and organized social functions for them. He was also a keen boxer and fought for the Holy Family Club.

Having joined the IRA he became a dedicated Volunteer in C company 3rd Battalion of the Belfast Brigade and was instrumental in the organizing and carrying out of many successful operations against the Crown Forces.

On 15th May 1971, Billy and a number of his comrades ambushed a mobile British Army patrol in Academy Street in Belfast city centre. In the ensuing gun battle, two British soldiers were wounded and Billy was shot dead.

One of Billy's comrades was also wounded but he and the rest of the active service unit returned safely to base, despite an intensive follow-up operation by the British Army and the R.U.C.

Billy's memory is immortalized in the song 'The Ballad of Billy Reid'.

"If you think he was right, come and join in the fight
and help to free our land,
for the blood that he shed, and although he lies dead,
in our hearts his memory will last."

Óglach Patrick McAdorey

22nd February 1947 - 9th August 1971

Patrick McAdorey was born on the 22nd February 1947. He was educated at Holy Cross Primary School, Butler Street and St Gabriel's Secondary School, Crumlin Road. After leaving school, Patrick served his time as a wood machinist before joining the Merchant Navy, where he served as an assistant cook.

He returned to Belfast in 1968 just as the present phase of the struggle began. Paddy, like many others who witnessed the pogroms being carried out by Loyalists, with the assistance of the Crown Forces, immediately became involved with the Republican Movement. As a result, like many others, he also fell victim to constant RUC harassment.

Like many young men Paddy loved music, dancing and football. A regular at Ceili dances, he also went to dances in the Ardoyne Hall, St Gabriel's and the Plaza and played football for Kell's Cubs of Flax Street.

On the morning of Internment, 9th August 1971, Paddy lost his young life at the hands of a British soldier in his native Ardoyne, sadly never seeing his only child who was born shortly after his death.

Óglach Seamus Simpson

24th July 1950 - 11th August 1971

Seamus Simpson was born on 24th July 1950 and came from Cawnpore Street, later moving to Glenshane Gardens in the Andersonstown area of West Belfast. He was educated at St Augustine's Secondary School.

After leaving school, Seamus became apprenticed as a fitter at James Mackie's. He later married.

Seamus came from a strongly Republican background; his uncle Pat Simpson was sentenced to life imprisonment for his involvement in the same incident for which Volunteer Tom Williams was hanged in 1942. His brothers Joey and Seany were both sentenced to terms of imprisonment for their Republican activities in the present phase of the struggle.

Having joined 'C' Company of the 2nd Battalion, Belfast Brigade, in 1970, Seamus was active and took part in several successful actions against the forces of occupation.

On 11th August 1971, two days after the introduction of Internment, Seamus was throwing blast-bombs at the British Army, during rioting at Rossnareen, Andersonstown, when he was shot dead.

Óglach Eamonn Lafferty

25th October 1951 - 18th August 1971

Eamonn Lafferty was the second eldest of eleven children, five boys and six girls, born to parents John and Maureen.

Eamonn went to Rosemount Boys' Primary School, just around the corner from his home. After that he went to St. Joseph's Secondary School at Westway. It was then that he first began to take an interest in fishing and hunting. As he neared the end of his four years at St. Joseph's he got himself a job in Doherty's Butchers. He started each morning at 6 am and worked until 8 am returning home to have his breakfast and to start his school day.

On leaving St. Joseph's at fifteen he started work as an Apprentice Baker at Milanda Bakery in the Glen Road, where he served his time. It was whilst working in Milanda that he incurred a back injury, a slipped disc, which meant he had to sleep on a wooden board to ease his back.

It was at this time that Eamonn bought his first motorbike and also his first shotgun. Whilst out hunting, if he shot a goose or duck over water, he would strip off and swim in to get the bird. Eamonn was also a member of the "Knights of Malta" from his early teens.

Then came that fateful day when the army attempted to come into Creggan, up Southway, and from Kildrum Gardens a gun battle raged between British soldiers and IRA Volunteers.

During this battle Eamonn was shot and subsequently died from his injuries. Whilst being taken to hospital the ambulance was stopped on Craigavon Bridge and his friend, who was in the ambulance with him, was arrested and then interned in Long Kesh.

Óglach James O'Hagan

6th June 1955 - 19th August 1971

Jim was intense and serious, but could enjoy himself, and really was no more than a boy, since he was only 16 when he died. Even before his teenage years he would have been remembered 'pasting up' any paper cuttings of the 1916 Easter Rising.

From 1968 on, he attended all marches. His area, the Triangle (Union St.) in the Waterside area of Derry was being demolished and he moved to Clooney Estate. He was active in the Boys' Club in St. Pat's Hall, he took part in club shows and played some sports. He left the Waterside Boys' School in 1967 and went to St. Brecan's Secondary School. It was here he learnt a bit of Irish.

Like many of his friends, Jim progressed from rioting, to defensive work (protecting the Good Shepherd Convent for example) and from there to joining the IRA.

He died on the 19th August 1971, just after Internment, and a day after Eamonn Lafferty. He was accidentally shot and fatally wounded while on active service in the Waterside area. His death shocked everyone and his funeral was very large. The cortege was stoned by loyalists (many of whom would have known Jim) at Irish Street/Rossdowney, and the hearse had to accelerate leaving mourners behind. Many of them missed the actual burial.

Óglach Terence McDermott

10th November 1952 - 2nd October 1971

The McDermott family lived at Tullymore Gardens, in Andersonstown, and Terry was born on 10th November 1952. He attended the Holy Child Primary School and later moved to St. Peter's Secondary School. Following this he attended Lisburn Technical School to study for his City & Guilds qualification in electrical engineering.

Terry went to work as an electrician for Hendron Brothers in Eliza Street, Belfast, while at the same time continuing his studies on a day release basis.

His keen interest in the culture and heritage of Ireland was developed through his love of reading. The treatment of his country and people by the British led Terry to realise that the liberation of Ireland could only be achieved by resistance to oppression.

Terry joined Na Fianna Éireann when he was sixteen, and quickly progressed to become a Volunteer in the ranks of Óglaigh na hÉireann. As a member of the 1st Battalion, Belfast Brigade, Terry was involved in many operations against the British forces.

Along with another IRA Volunteer, he undertook a commercial bombing mission on an electricity sub-station at Harmony Heights, Lisburn, on October 2nd 1971. The Volunteers had placed the anti-handler device and were preparing to leave the area when a cat ran out and triggered the bomb.

Terry's comrade was injured in the explosion, but, being closer to the device, Terry McDermott was killed.

Dorothy Maguire Cumann na mBan

3rd April 1952 - 23rd October 1971

Dorothy Maguire was born on April 3rd 1952 in to a family with strong Republican connections. Her father was one of the four Republicans who took part in the famous escape from Crumlin Road jail in January 1943.

A bright humorous and popular young woman, she was always amusing and outraging her friends with her jokes and pranks.

In February 1971, the Special Powers Act was used to arrest young vigilantes at the barricades for wearing combat jackets, under the pretence that they were 'paramilitary uniforms'. Dorothy, along with Máire Drumm and several other women organised a protest. They dressed in combat jackets, and carrying Hurley sticks, they took the place of the men at the barricades. They became known affectionately as the 'combat brigade'.

In the early hours of October 3rd 1971, after hearing rumours of heavy raids in the lower Falls area, Dorothy, her sister Maura and a number of other comrades, set off in a car, equipped with a siren, to alert the people in the surrounding areas.

With the siren blaring they were passing a number of British Army vehicles when they were raked with gunfire. Both Dorothy and her sister Maura were shot dead and their comrades were seriously injured.

Maura Meehan Cumann na mBan

18th June 1940 - 23rd October 1971

Maura Meehan was a mother of four young children when she was shot dead by the British Army on 23rd October 1971. From a staunch Republican family, her father Ned was among the group of Republican prisoners who escaped from the Crumlin Road Jail in January 1943, it was no surprise that she would choose to join the Republican Movement.

A loving mother to her children, she was highly regarded and respected member of her community. Although only a member of Cumann na mBan for a short time before she was killed Maura was extremely active. She was among a number of women who despite being occupied with parenthood, found the time to take an active part in the struggle.

On one such occasion, in the early hours of 23rd October 1971, during a period of heavy raids by the British Army and the RUC, Maura, along with her younger sister Dorothy Maguire, took to the streets to alert the locals that the raids were taking place.

As they drove through the area with a warning siren blaring from their car, British soldiers opened fire killing Maura and Dorothy and injuring the other two occupants of the car.

The sacrifice of Maura Meehan and her sister Dorothy was the inspiration for many of the women volunteers who subsequently joined the ranks of Cumann Na mBan and Óglaigh na hÉireann.

Óglach Martin Forsythe

19th December 1951 - 24th October 1971

Martin Forsythe came from the Turf Lodge district in West Belfast, and was a Volunteer in the 1st Battalion, Belfast Brigade, Óglaigh na hÉireann.

Born on the 19th December 1951, Martin was educated at St. Paul's Primary School, and later at St. Thomas's Secondary School. On leaving school, Marty, as he was known to his friends and comrades, went to work for Ross's Mill, and the Ulster Foundries. He was still employed there at the time of his death on active service.

Marty joined the IRA in 1970, and was an active and dedicated Volunteer, respected by all who knew him. On October 24th 1971, he took part in an operation to bomb the Celebrity Club, a well-known nightspot in Belfast city centre. Having planted the device, the active service unit was leaving the premises when RUC Special Branch men who, unknown to the Volunteers, were in the building, opened fire.

Marty Forsythe was shot and wounded. One of his comrades, Cumann na mBan Volunteer Pat Murray, was also shot in the back, seriously injuring her spine. As Volunteer Marty Forsythe lay bleeding from his wounds, members of the RUC Special Branch moved in and shot him dead.

Volunteer Marty Forsythe was buried alongside his comrades in Milltown Cemetery, Belfast.

Óglach Michael Crossey

22nd November 1971

"Michael Crossey, my brother, was one five sons and five daughters. We were born in Derrymacash just a few miles from Lurgan. Life at home was not any different than that of any other large family in the area except that we all knew tragedy when we were young. Our brother Aidan was shot and wounded by the B Specials.

As time passed we all gradually left home to go to work. Michael by 1968 was working for Goodyear. He started off working nights and after a while went onto shiftwork. He had a great interest in trying to better conditions for his fellow workers. He became a member of the TGWU and became a shop steward.

He had many friends. One of them recalled to me how he, his wife, Michael and his girlfriend would spend many of their week-ends in the pub where he liked nothing better than a good sing song. They would often go to the Red Hills and meet up with other friends for a night's 'craic'.

Michael was a quiet fellow who spent a lot of his time reading, mostly books about his native Ireland. As time went on he left Goodyear and started work for Peter Kelly in Lurgan. He seemed to enjoy his work there. Like most of the young Nationalist people in Lurgan he would join in the marches against internment. It was during this period that his brother-in-law was 'lifted' and was later to become known as one of the 'hooded men'.

Michael was killed on 22nd November 1971 at the age of 21 years. When we think of him now we see him as he was then, just the same quiet, laughing young man."

Óglach Tony Nolan

25th April 1949 - 8th December 1971

Tony Nolan, known always as 'Hooky' was from the Markets area of South Belfast where he was born on the 25th April 1949. The fourth in a family of six children he attended Gloucester Street Primary School and later St Augustine's Secondary School on the Ravenhill Road.

When Tony left school he inherited a docker's button from his father that would have ensured him a steady job and income working in Belfast Docks. Instead, he chose to work in the local Fruit Market, selling fruit from his mother's stall. He was a well known face in the busy Market and, with his long dark hair and thick moustache, he was quite a distinctive character.

Hooky's pastimes included snooker and football and, like most young Belfast men of his generation, he attended weekend dances. His usual haunts were the Jazz Club beside the Markets and the Maritime Club in the city centre.

Hooky was on active service, on stand-by in a call-house in the Markets area, when he was killed as a result of an accidental shooting on 8th December 1971.

He was 21 years old and had only joined the IRA a few short weeks before he died, so tragically, a short distance from his own home.

Óglach Charles Agnew

10th December 1935 - 17th December 1971

Charlie Agnew was born in 12 Railway Street, Armagh, on 10th December 1935. He attended St Patrick's Primary School in Banbrook Hill until he was 11 years old. During these formative years, Charlie was a promising pupil, managing to gain entrance into St Patrick's College where he was to further his education. Charlie, however, had other ideas, and after a relatively short time he was expelled for truancy. In 1958 Charlie met Mary Nixon, a Tyrone girl, whom he married two years later in 1960. The couple had four children, two boys named Patrick and Eamonn, and two girls named Teresa and Cathy.

Charlie was an active member of the Harps Gaelic Athletic Club, and a staunch supporter of the County Armagh football team. But despite this firm allegiance to Armagh, Charlie was constantly teased by friends as he was married to a Tyrone woman. Friends and family were especially amused by the antics in the Agnew house on match days, when Mary would hang a huge Tyrone flag out the front window. Charlie decide that something had to be done, and after many arguments the couple reached a compromise, the Tyrone flag was hung to the rear of the house while the Armagh flag took pride of place at the front.

Charlie's initial ties with Republicanism were forged when he joined na Fianna Éireann at just eight years of age. This connection was maintained until his death on 17th December 1971. On the day of his funeral he was honoured with a full Republican burial, with many comrades from the North Armagh Brigade in attendance. When the cortege left the street where Charlie had previously lived, a British foot patrol was passing by. Upon noticing the Tricolour on the coffin they stopped, formed up and presented arms - Charlie was still keeping the British army on their toes! The graveside oration was read by Charlie's lifelong comrade and fellow Republican Liam McDonagh.

Óglach Martin Lee

25th December 1953 – 18th December 1971

When you sit down to write about someone you were born and reared with it is amazing how hard it is to remember them the way they were. Martin to me and the rest of the family was just the baby of the house. I remember reading reports of his death and his age was given as between eighteen and twenty; in fact Martin died a week before his eighteenth birthday.

Being the youngest in the house we had all hoped Martin would carry on with his studies, having the ability to do so. But he was having none of it, and when he left school he followed me into the bricklaying trade. Sadly he only got two and a half years of his time done.

Martin's greatest passions were fishing, shooting and Gaelic football, and like all other teenagers he had a great interest in getting wheels on the road. His first venture was to buy a second hand scooter. Everything was O.K. until the first morning of the frost when he came off his bike. After this first spill the machine was parked and sits in the garage until this present day.

I can't remember if Martin ever passed his driving test but I do know he had made the Ballymaguigan Senior Football team. His last ever game for the club was winning the first ever Derry Intermediate Football final. Spectators of football said Martin would have been one of the great Ballymaguigan players; this is something we will never know just as we will never know how he would look today in his forty-ninth year.

Martin died on 18th December 1971, alongside his comrades Johnny Bateson and Jim Sheridan while on active service in Magherafelt.

Óglach John Bateson

1st October 1951 – 18th December 1971

John George Bateson was born on the 1st of October 1951 at Aughacarnaghan, Toomebridge, County Antrim. He was the fourth child of Paddy and Mary Bateson. He had three older brothers, Patsy, Jimmy and Eddie and two younger brothers Finbar and Peter. He also had four younger sisters, Ann, Dolores, Mary and Clare. He had a distinctive grey streak in his hair that earned him the nickname 'Magpie'.

He attended Carlane Primary School where he started at the same time as his brother Eddie who was 13 months his senior. He left Carlane when he was eleven years old and went to St Olcan's Secondary School in Randalstown. He was a diligent student but decided to leave school at 15 years of age to go to Magherafelt Technical to train to become a mechanic. By this time his family had moved back to their native Balymaguigan and Johnny began an apprenticeship with Adam H Irwin in Antrim before gaining full employment with John McGlone in Ballyronan.

Johnny was a keen Gaelic footballer and played with his local team, St Trea's in Ballymaguigan where he won a junior championship medal in 1969 and an intermediate championship medal in 1970. He was a sharp forward in all senses of the word – sharp with his tongue and his fists but equally when it came to pace and scoring goals.

He loved stockcar racing and, being a mechanic he loved to compete in local races with his old bangers. As a young man growing up in the late 1960s - early 1970s he enjoyed going to dances with his brothers and his friends. With his long hair, the style of the day, he was unhappy when he had to get his hair cut to do best man at his brother Jimmy's wedding in December 1970.

Johnny was a highly respected Volunteer with the South Derry Brigade of Óglaigh na hÉireann when he was killed in an accidental explosion on the 18th December 1971.

Óglach James Sheridan

13th January 1951 – 18th December 1971

James was born on 13th January 1951, the second of eight children born to Hugh and Maureen Sheridan. Better known as Jim, he was educated at St. Trea's Primary School, St. Pius X Intermediate School and Feldon House Belfast College of Technology, now known as University of Ulster, Jordanstown.

He qualified as an Electrical and Mechanical Engineer and worked at Dublin Airport for a period of time, and then changed his job to work for a local man nearer home. Jim was an avid reader, especially history books and the bible. As a child going to Donegal to his grandparents' house, he always came home with history books.

He had a great interest in the local football club, St. Trea's. Although he did not play football himself as he suffered from asthma, he went to all other functions, and worked at the building of the new hall.

Jim had a very high regard for the older generation - listening to their stories and frowning on the use of foul language in their presence; Jim made them feel special, and in return he was noted for his politeness and caring nature. He was a serious person, yet full of fun and loved singing or pretending to play the drums to his favourite soul music.

Jim was one of the first volunteers in the newly organised South Derry Brigade, he died along with his comrades Johnny Bateson and Martin Lee in an accidental explosion in Magherafelt on the night of December 18th 1971.

Jim Sheridan is buried in Newbridge Graveyard.

Óglach Gerard McDade

22nd November 1950 - 21st December 1971

Gerard McDade was born at the family home in 17 Oakfield Street, in the Ardoyne area of North Belfast, in November 1950. There were five boys and two girls in the family, which was very musical, and Gerard was no exception with a reputation as an accomplished singer.

Gerard was educated at Holy Cross Primary School on Butler Street before moving on to St Gabriel's Secondary School on the Crumlin Road were he showed a talent for football.

Gerard came from a Republican background so it was not surprising that he became a Volunteer of Óglaigh na hÉireann, joining the Movement in March 1970 and becoming an extremely active freedom fighter.

On 21st December 1971, just six weeks before his only child was born, Gerard McDade was coldly murdered by British soldiers, who shot him in the back in his native Oakfield Street in Ardoyne.

Gerard's brother James also joined Óglaigh na hÉireann, playing an active part in bringing the War to the British before dying in an accidental explosion while placing a bomb in Coventry, England.

Óglach Jack McCabe

24th July 1916 - 30th December 1971

Jack McCabe joined the IRA in Shercock, County Cavan in the early 1930's. He went to England and was based in the Manchester area during the IRA's bombing campaign at that time. He was arrested in England and sentenced to 20 years Penal Servitude during which he engaged in a hunger strike on the Isle of Wight. He was released from Parkhurst in December 1948.

Jack played a very active part in the IRA's operation 'Harvest' in the 1950s and was involved in the famous raid against Omagh barracks in County Tyrone during which the IRA engaged the British army in a firefight. Jack managed to get out of the Omagh area after the raid, only to be captured on the Donegal border by the RUC.

Jack played a leading part in the current phase of the freedom struggle from August 1969. Subsequent to the burning of Belfast's Bombay Street, Jack with other Republicans from the 26 Counties retrieved weapons which had been dumped since the 1950's campaign and smuggled them into the Six Counties. He was a key figure in the IRA's developing bombing campaign against British targets in the North. He was killed by an accidental explosion in Dublin on 30th December 1971.

His tragic death ended an involvement in the IRA which spanned four decades.

Jack is buried in Killane Cemetery, Shercock, Cavan.

Óglach Danny O'Neill

15th September 1951 - 7th January 1972

Danny O'Neill was born on the 15th September 1951 and lived in Clonard Street in West Belfast. He attended St Mary's Grammar School on the Glen Road and after leaving school found work as an insurance clerk. There was a strong Republican tradition in the O'Neill family, Danny's aunt, Bridie O'Neill was imprisoned in Armagh during the IRA campaign of the 1950s. Danny's father, Billy, was interned in Long Kesh at the time of his son's death.

In 1969, while still in his teens, Danny was to witness at first hand the naked sectarianism of the Northern statelet when loyalist mobs, encouraged by the forces of the State, launched attacks on nationalist communities throughout Belfast. The pogroms left Danny's native Clonard area ablaze and like so many of the other young people of his generation, these events had a profound effect on the young teenager.

It was at this time that he made the decision to join the ranks of Óglaigh na hÉireann. Quiet and unassuming by nature, he became a highly respected and enthusiastic Volunteer who was to take part in many successful operations against the Crown forces. On the 3rd January 1972 Danny was on active service in Oranmore Street in his native Clonard area. He was in a car with two other comrades, when they came under gun attack by members of a British Army mobile patrol. Danny, who was a back seat passenger was shot and seriously wounded.

He was taken out of the area by his comrades. He received first aid before the decision was made because of the seriousness of his injuries, to take him to hospital. He died a few days later on 7th January in the City Hospital.

The death of such an experienced volunteer was a severe blow to his comrades but his selflessness and dedication proved to be an inspiration to those who followed in his footsteps.

Fiann Michael Sloan

30th July 1956 - 11th January 1972

Michael Sloan was born on 30th July 1956 and attended St Thomas's Secondary School. A typical young lad of his generation he had many interests, but his main pastime was playing soccer.

Growing up in the heavily fortified area of West Belfast, the young Fianna boy had witnessed the wrongs of partition. Like many of his peers, who should only have been interested in football and teenage hobbies, he became a member of the youth wing of the Republican Movement in an attempt to play his part in the struggle for national independence.

On 11th January 1972 Michael was on active service when he was killed as a result of an accidental shooting during an arms training lecture. He was 16 years old.

Fiann Eamonn McCormick

29th May 1954 - 16th January 1972

Eamonn McCormick was born in the Ballymurphy area of West Belfast on 29th May 1954. His parents, who had moved to Ballymurphy in 1950, had four other children, two boys and two girls. Eamonn was the first-born in their new home and was a true Ballymurphyman!

He was educated at St Aiden's Primary School and St Thomas's Secondary on the Whiterock Road, where he showed a keen interest in all forms of sporting activity and played for the schools hurling and football teams. He was a member of the Rossa Gaelic Athletic Club teams that won the Minor hurling and football leagues in 1970/71, and was selected for the County Antrim Minor panel.

After leaving school Eamonn found work in a timber yard but was forced to leave due to intimidation from loyalist co-workers.

During the frequent attacks on the Ballymurphy area by the British Army and Loyalists, Eamonn would be at the forefront in resisting these attacks on his community. On Hallowe'en night in 1971 when loyalists were attacking St Peter's School he was among a number of local people who were attempting to quell the attack, when he was shot and seriously wounded by a member of the British Army.

A bullet had pierced his liver and shattered his spine, causing paralysis from the waist down. Eamonn died from his injuries on 16th January 1972.

Óglach Peter McNulty

6th February 1925 - 26th January 1972

Peter McNulty was born in 1925, the son of Paddy McNulty and Mary Ann Rooney who were married in Leitrim chapel by Fr Quail in 1911. He had six brothers and two sisters. The McNulty family were a highly respected farming family with strong republican traditions and it was little wonder that Peter went on to become a dedicated volunteer.

In the McNulty home were numerous Republican pictures depicting the history of the Irish struggle. Mary Ann was the proud owner of a book presented to her by Padraig Pearse when he adjudicated at Feis An Duin. Peter was heavily involved in the 1950's campaign and was a leading example to those young men and women who followed in his footsteps. A man of few words but plenty of action, on one occasion Peter was arrested by local RUC men as he left Mass in Castlewellan and given a severe beating but not before he had downed a few of his assailants first.

A great friend of JB O'Hagan, Peter had many comrades from throughout the 32 Counties. Former Prisoners from across the length and breadth Ireland were often heard speaking of his courage during the long nights of incarceration in the cages of Long Kesh. At the start of the present campaign Peter went off to the border to be in the thick of the action but later returned to spread the action to the South Down area. On his return in the early 1970s he was the driving force behind many very successful operations in South Down.

On the 26th January 1972, Peter was on active service when he lost his life during an attack on Castlewellan barracks. His commitment to the Republican Movement not only in South Down but throughout the 32 counties was sorely missed but he will always be remembered for his leadership qualities and his quiet determination.

Fiann Gerard Donaghey

20th February 1954 - 30th January 1972

Gerard Donaghey came from the Bogside area of Derry. Following the deaths of his mother and father in 1965/1966 he was brought up by his sister Mary and brother Paddy. They moved from Wellington Street to an upstairs flat in Meenan Square and following a short spell at the Derry Tech, Gerry got a job as a helper on a beer lorry with Carlins at Clooney Terrace.

He had cousins in the Ballymacarret area of Belfast and was affected by the way Catholics in Belfast were being treated. He joined the Na Fianna Éireann early in 1971 and in April of that year he was arrested and charged with riotous behaviour, which then carried a mandatory sentence of six months in prison. He had not been involved in rioting and this trumped up arrest was enough to convince Gerard to go full-time with Republicanism. He went on the run, spending a lot of time in the South, where he attended training camps and did fund-raising work for the nationalist community in the North.

During the summer of 1971 his sister was evacuated, along with many others, to a Free State Army camp in Blessington, Co. Wicklow and he visited her there. Following Internment and the shooting dead of Volunteer Eamonn Lafferty in Derry, Gerard travelled back to Derry. He ended up in prison in October of that year and spent some months in Crumlin Road Gaol. He was released in December 1971.

Gerard was shot dead by British Paratroopers on 30th January 1972, Bloody Sunday.

Óglach Phelim Grant

19th September 1939 - 5th February 1972

Volunteer Phelim Grant was the fifth child of Patrick and Margaret Grant, Ballynamullan near Toome. His father was a retired farmer and he lived in Toome all his life, while his mothers' family was originally from Maghera, Co. Derry. He was born on 19th September 1939 in Randalstown; he had four brothers and three sisters. He was christened Felix after his uncle Felix, who had been an active Republican all his life. Phelim attended Carlane Primary School until he was 14 years of age. After leaving school he went to live with his uncle Paddy and aunt Josie McCloskey in Ballyduggenan. He helped on their farm and in later years he purchased a digger and worked with the local farmers in the area, this he really enjoyed as he loved a bit of craic and telling yarns.

He had a keen interest in Gaelic football; he played football for the local club Erin's Own G.A.A. and supported them in competitions. Phelim was to be seen at most of the local ceilis. On Sunday 30th January 1972 a local G.A.A. club was holding a ceili, Phelim was asked to attend this ceili by some of his friends, he replied, "How could anyone enjoy themselves when thirteen of our fellow Irishmen have been murdered by the British Army!" This was a typical comment of this dedicated Irishman who was to lose his own life six days later.

During the 1966 Easter Rising celebration he was a member of one of the organising committee in the Toome area and in 1968 he became involved in the Civil Rights Movement. When the long march from Belfast to Derry was blocked by loyalists in Randalstown, Phelim and a few friends went to Randalstown and helped transport the marches to Toome, he joined the march and was caught in the Burntollet ambush. All of these events influenced his decision in becoming a Volunteer in the North Antrim Brigade.

Sadly on 5th February 1972 at he age of 32 he and his comrade Charles McCann died in a accidental explosion in Ballyginnif. They were buried in the Republican Plot in Cargin graveyard. Phelim is best remembered as a good-humoured, quiet and discreet Republican.

Óglach Charles McCann

30th October 1944 - 5th February 1972

Charles McCann came from the Ardoyne area of North Belfast, although his family originally came from the Toomebridge area. His parents only moved to Belfast during the war so that his family might find work. Charles was the second eldest of fifteen children born to James and Margaret McCann, three of whom died in infancy and are buried in Randalstown graveyard.

He moved back to Toomebridge where a large number of his relatives lived, and lived with his uncle Henry on the Shore Road at Toome. He was a plasterer by trade like his father, and also a keen sportsman, having played in goals for Ardoyne GAA Club. He was a very good singer.

Charles had only been living in Toome for two years prior to his death and during that time he had become a member of the South West Antrim brigade. It came as a huge shock to his family and the people of the Ardoyne community when they heard of his untimely death, because Charles was so well liked and quite unassuming in his manner. Very few people knew of his involvement in the Republican Movement.

Charles died in an accidental explosion when he and a comrade returned to make safe an unexploded device on a sandbarge prior to workers arriving. He was twenty-eight years of age when he died.

Both Charles and his comrade Phelim Grant are buried at Cargin Chapel just outside Toomebridge.

Óglach Joseph Cunningham

22nd June 1945 - 10th February 1972

Joseph Cunningham was born on 22nd June 1945 at 55 Verner Street, in the Markets area. He was educated at St Patrick's Primary School, Holywood and later at the Christian Brothers' School, Oxford Street and St Malachy's College, Antrim Road.

Joseph's hobbies were golf and Gaelic Football, which he played for St Malachy's GAC. He was a popular character in dockland, where he worked as a docker. He married and he and his wife, Sally, had two children. Although his family had no connections with the Republican Movement, they were definitely Republican in outlook. Joseph joined the IRA in November 1969 when 'E' Company was formed in the Rathcoole Estate, a predominantly loyalist area, where he had lived for a number of years. He was a dedicated Volunteer and would not think of asking others to do what he would not do himself.

On 10th February 1972, Joseph was killed on active service. The operation was to execute a major in the UDR who worked as a director in a factory located on the Church Road, adjacent to the O'Neill Road in Newtownabbey. Joseph and a number of other Volunteers waited in a car on the O'Neill Road, which in itself exposed them to the danger of being discovered by mobile patrols of British soldiers and RUC who often toured the area. In the event, two RUC landrovers arrived, blocking off exit routes from the road, with their occupants immediately taking up firing positions and shooting at the Volunteers' car.

Joseph opened fire with a Thompson machine-gun allowing the other Volunteers to withdraw on foot across the fields which led into Rathcoole. He managed to get only one short burst from the Thompson before it jammed, but this was enough to allow the others to make good their escape. The RUC returned fire and, unable to get the Thompson back into operation, Joseph took cover at the side of the car. The RUC, realising his dilemma, closed in, and Joseph was shot twice, once in the head from close range.

Fiann David McAuley

16th December 1956 - 19th February 1972

David McAuley was born and reared in the Ardoyne area of North Belfast, where he attended St Gabriel's Secondary School on the Crumlin Road.

As a young boy growing up in an area that had seen the brunt of the sectarian nature of the State, he had witnessed at first hand the effects of discrimination and inequality. He had also witnessed the almost daily attacks on the homes of his friends and neighbours.

It was as a result of this sectarianism and oppression of his community that David made the decision to join the Republican Movement when he was only twelve years old, entering the ranks of Na Fianna Éireann.

He was a young lad beyond his years and was a highly respected member of the youth wing of the republican Movement, held in deep regard by his comrades both, young and old.

Fiann David McAuley died as a result of an accidental shooting on the 19th February 1972. He was given a Republican Guard of Honour at this funeral.

Óglach Gerard Bell

4th May 1953 - 21st February 1972

Gerard Majella Bell, from Seaforde Street, Short Strand, was born on 4th May 1953. He was educated at St Matthew's Primary School, Seaforde Street, before moving on to St Augustine's Secondary School on the Ravenhill Road.

On leaving school, in 1968, Gerard, or 'Dinger' as he was best-known, found work as an apprentice plumber with Crowes of Corporation Street.

A boisterous though mild-mannered young man, with a distinctive, infectious laugh, Dinger's spare time was mostly spent playing football and handball, or just having the craic with his friends on the street corner.

Dinger was deeply interested in Ireland's history and, as a teenager of the late '60's, witnessing the corrupt and sectarian nature of the Orange State, he decided to abandon his career and carefree life and join the IRA. This he did in 1971 and, after taking part in numerous successful military operations against British forces, he gave his young life on active service at the youthful age of 20, when he fell victim to an accidental explosion while on active service on 21st February 1972.

His death came as a shock to many in the community who were unaware of Dinger's involvement with Óglaigh na hÉireann.

Gerard's elder brother, Jim, was subsequently shot dead by loyalists in East Belfast not far from his home in the Short Strand, on 1st September 1993.

Óglach Gerard Steele

23rd July 1944 - 21st February 1972

Gerard Steele, from Thompson Street, in the Short Strand, was born on 23rd July 1944, the sixth child in a family of ten children.

Nicknamed 'Nailer' from an early age, Gerard was educated at the nearby St Matthew's School in Seaforde Street. He left school in 1958 to work in the abattoir in Graham's Place at Bridge End, where he worked until the early '60s when he got a job as a lead painter in Belfast Shipyard. Later he became self-employed, working with his father cleaning windows. He was an introverted young man, quiet in his own way but at the same time enjoying a practical joke or two.

When not working, Nailer's time was spent playing handball up against the gable wall of Anderson Street or at the corner of Clyde Street.

Gerard's family were deeply Republican - his uncles 'Keeler', Phil and Terry McCullough were all well-known Belfast Republicans from the '50s campaign and were interned on the Alrawdha prison ship in Strangford, County Down. Gerard himself joined the Republican Movement in mid-1971.

He lost his life fighting for Irish freedom when, along with his three comrades, Volunteers Gerard Bell, Joseph Magee and Robert Dorrian, he fell victim to an accidental explosion after aborting a commercial bombing mission on 21st February 1972.

Óglach Robert Dorrian

13th October 1943 - 21st February 1972

Robert Dorrian, from the Short Strand, was born in the Markets area on 13th October 1943. He attended St Comgall's School, Eliza Street, and on leaving school at the age of 14 found employment as a roofer.

He married Betty McLarnon in 1965 and moved to live in the Short Strand. They had four sons, one of whom was knocked down and killed by a British army jeep as he played close to his home in Altcar Street.

In late 1971, Rab Dorrian joined 'B' Company, 3rd Battalion, Auxiliary IRA, where he proved to be a dedicated Volunteer.

Becoming more and more active in the local Auxiliary unit, and increasingly acknowledged and highly regarded by his comrades for his courage and commitment, Rab was soon accepted into the IRA.

He died along with three comrades - Gerard 'Dinger' Bell, Gerard Steele and Joe Magee - on Monday, 21st February 1972 while on a commercial bombing mission.

Having arrived at their target with their bomb primed and ready to be placed in position, the four Volunteers for some, as yet undiscovered reason (possibly, as some believe, the presence of enemy forces near the target), aborted their mission and began a withdrawal along the Knock dual carriageway. En route the bomb exploded, killing the Volunteers instantly.

Rab was buried with full military honours and, along with his three other comrades, his remains lie in Milltown Cemetery.

Óglach Joseph Magee

9th September 1940 - 21st February 1972

Joseph Magee was born in 1941 in Bow Street, Pound Loney and was educated at St Colmgall's School on the Falls Road. He left school in 1955 and found employment as a steel fixer. In 1965 he married Jemima Fitzsimmons and they had three children, Margaret, Sharon and Joseph.

In 1969 Joe and his young family were intimidated out of their home in Richardson Street, Ravenhill Road and had to seek refuge in Jemima's mother's house in Arran Street, Short Strand, living there for six months before getting a house of their own in Lisbon Street.

When the sectarian Orange state exploded in 1969, Joe's was a regular face on the street corners, manning the barricades against Loyalist attacks.

His decision to join the Republican struggle came in early 1972 around the time of Bloody Sunday. He lost his life at the age of 31, on February 21st 1972, when a bomb, which he and three comrades were transporting away from an aborted bombing mission, exploded.

Óglach Albert Kavanagh

17th April 1953 – 4th March 1972

Albert Kavanagh was from Cavendish Street and he was born on 17th April 1953. He was educated at St Paul's Primary School and at St Malachy's Grammar School.

When he left school he found work as an apprentice compositor. In his spare time he took an active interest in his local community, becoming a founder member of St Paul's Youth Club, Cavendish Square.

Albert joined the IRA in 1969. Although his family had no connections with the Republican Movement, his mother's parents have strong Republican sympathies. For the next three years Albert was a dedicated fighter for the cause of Irish Freedom.

On March 4th 1972, Albert and a comrade had planted a bomb at a factory on the Boucher Road, when two RUC men appeared on the scene. The RUC opened fire at once and the two volunteers ran off towards a high wire fence to get away. Albert stopped and put his hands up. His comrade clambered over the fence and was shot trying to get away. As he lay wounded one of the RUC men ran up and emptied his revolver into his body. Miraculously, he survived.

Albert, still standing with his hands raised in surrender was cold bloodedly shot in the head and chest by the other RUC man. His body was left lying there where he fell for over two hours.

Óglach Gerard Crossan

1st May 1952 - 9th March 1972

Gerard Crossan was born on the 1st May 1952, the fourth child in a family of seven. He began his life in Beechmount Bungalows, then, in 1969, his family moved to Cavendish Street. He was educated in St John's Primary School and later St Thomas's Secondary School on the Whiterock Road.

He was fun-loving by nature and was the type of person to have a smile for anyone - no matter who they were. Always ready to help people in need he was fond of sport and was a keen footballer. An avid supporter of Glasgow Celtic he also enjoyed motorcycle racing and often travelled to the Dundrod circuit to watch the races. When he left school he started work as a bricklayer and helped with the re-building of Bombay Street after the street was demolished during the loyalist pogroms of 1969. He enjoyed bricklaying and had high hopes for the future.

It was also around this time that he realised the need for an armed defence of nationalist areas and he made the conscious decision to join Óglaigh na hÉireann.

He got married in 1970, during the Falls Road Curfew, and moved with his new wife to Annadale Street in the New Lodge Road area.

He continued with his Republican activities in the Clonard area and it was here on 9th March 1972 that Gerry and three of his comrades were killed in an accidental explosion while on active service.

At the time of his death he and his wife had two young children.

Óglach Tony Lewis

4th April 1955 - 9th March 1972

Tony Lewis was born on 4th April 1955. He lived at 27 Bombay Street in the Clonard area of West Belfast, an area which bore the brunt of the loyalist pogroms in 1969.

Tony was educated locally and when he left school he soon found work as an apprentice butcher. He enjoyed playing both hurling and football, turning out for Cumann an Phiarsaigh and winning medals for both.

Although merely a boy of 14 at the time, he played an active part in the defence of the Clonard area during the 1969 pogrom. No doubt it was his experiences which led him to join Na Fianna Éireann in that same year, becoming extremely active in that organisation. Tony displayed great courage and determination in defending the Clonard area once again in 1971 during the Internment riots. He later joined the ranks of Óglaigh na hÉireann.

On 9th March 1972, Tony lost his life, dying in an accidental explosion in Clonard Street, close to where he had grown up. Three of his comrades were also killed in the same explosion.

Óglach Sean Johnston

12th September 1952 – 9th March 1972

Sean Gerard Johnston was born on 12th September 1952 and he lived at Cawnpore Street, Belfast.

Sean attended St Gall's Primary School and St Thomas's Secondary School. From a strong GAA family, he played football at school level and for Clonard GAC, as well as boxing in the famous Star Club on the New Lodge Rd. John also won an Ulster Schools table tennis championship doubles title along with Dessie Reynolds.

Sean was 'well got' in his local area, where his ready wit and sense of humour, not to mention his talent as a wind up merchant, kept friends and comrades on their toes, and helped raise moral when times were hard.

A devout Catholic, Sean's faith was very important to him. He was particularly close to Fr. Egan, who was based at Clonard Monastery, and who heard his confession on the morning of his death.

Sean made the decision to join the Army in 1969 and took part in actions across Belfast against the forces of occupation, going on the run to evade capture. On March 9th 1972 he and three of his comrades, Gerry Crossan, Tony Lewis and Tom McCann were killed in an accidental explosion in Clonard Street.

Óglach Tom McCann

20th January 1952 - 9th March 1972

Tom McCann was born on the 20th January 1952 and lived in Waterford Street in the Clonard area of West Belfast. His father, Tom senior, was originally from Co Fermanagh and was a lifelong Republican. Tom was the eldest in a family of eight; five girls and three boys, and attended St Paul's Primary School in Cavendish Square and St Thomas's Secondary School on the Whiterock Road.

Tom was a good athlete and played football and hurling for St Paul's and Clonard. He also had a trial for the Antrim County Minor hurling team. When he left school he found work in the Shipyard as a welder. This was to be short-lived however, as he was forced to leave work due to constant intimidation from loyalist co-workers, who on one occasion, dipped him in lead paint. Not one to remain idle he quickly found a new occupation when he began work as a textile screen printer in Silk and Rayon Printers in Waterford Street. Well liked throughout his area he was always well presented whether socialising or out on an operation with his local unit of Óglaigh na hÉireann.

He was always smiling, not only because it was his nature but also because he was quite obsessive about dental hygiene and loved to show off his pure white teeth. His sisters hated it when Tom got into the bathroom before them, because they'd have to wait ages and when he finally emerged he'd grin and ask "how do I look?" Considerate by nature he would let his parents know when he would be late home; he was also a frequent Mass goer and had attended Mass and received Communion on the morning he was killed.

He joined the Republican Movement sometime in 1966 and was a dedicated Volunteer whose entire life was devoted to the struggle for Irish national independence. He died in an accidental explosion alongside three of his comrades in Clonard Street on the 9th March 1972 and was buried on St Patrick's Day.

Óglach Colm Keenan

12th August 1953 - 14th March 1972

Colm's student days at St. Columb's College were enlivened by his passionate support for the various liberation struggles of the period. For Colm there was no difference between the Vietnamese, South African and Palestinian People's struggle for freedom, the world-wide student revolts and the age old battle for a 32 County Irish Socialist Republic.

Colm was ever present at Civil Rights demos and when the RUC and Loyalist gangs attacked the Bogside on August 9th 1969, Colm was one of those who helped repel the invasion. As state violence intensified, Colm joined the IRA. The rest of his life he devoted to the cause, while never losing his love of music, nor neglecting his budding talents as a poet.

Colm Keenan, despite his youth, was one of the most active, effective and daring volunteers in the Derry Brigade. Not a single day passed in Free Derry but Colm and his comrades would be in action. Shortly before his death, Colm was temporarily blinded in an audacious landmine attack on a British Army armoured convoy on Elmwood Terrace. He could have gone away to recuperate, he could have sought leave of absence, but within days of his sight returning, he was back on active service.

On the night of March 14th 1972, Colm and his friend and comrade Eugene McGillan were in a house in Dove Gardens. A major gun battle erupted outside when senior British Intelligence Officers, in Derry for the Widgery Whitewash, decided to visit the Bogside. Unarmed Colm and Eugene stepped outside. Both men were shot and fell beside each other. Colm died instantly from a gunshot wound to the head, Eugene died on his way to hospital.

Óglach Eugene McGillan

22nd April 1953 - 14th March 1972

Eugene lived in Rathowen Park in Creggan and had six brothers and four sisters. As a teenager he always enjoyed a bit of craic. He was first on the dance floor and last off, in places like 'Borderland' and the 'Embassy'. He really fancied the style in the 1970's. He liked Neil Diamond and his favourite song was 'Sweet Caroline', for reasons only his closest friends know. He also had the girls in the Ben Sherman factory getting him free shirts which he gave out to his friends.

Eugene was a refrigeration engineer with a local firm, where Mitchel McLaughlin was his foreman. Eugene drove a grey mini van for the firm which he used most Saturdays to take people to visit relatives in Long Kesh in the early '70's.

Out of a group of eight friends seven joined the Republican Movement. Unknown to his closest friends Eugene was the first to join. Later it was revealed that he joined about 6 months before Bloody Sunday and had taken a leading part in many operations.

Eugene was a very good friend of Colm Keenan, and they used the same billet in the No-Go area. During a gun battle Eugene and Colm stepped outside, both were unarmed and were shot dead by British soldiers. Eugene's last words were, "How's Goodly?" (Goodly was the nickname we gave Colm). This sums up Eugene, always thinking of his friends.

Fiann Sean O'Riordan

28th October 1958 - 23rd March 1972

Sean O'Riordan was born in Oranmore Street, off the Springfield Road, on the 28th October 1958. His parents Jack and Flo had five other children, three girls and two boys. He attended St Gall's Primary School where his talent for sporting activities, particularly hurling and football was first spotted - he was also a good swimmer. He had represented Springfield in the juvenile GAA league and had won medals for his swimming.

Easy going by nature, he made friends quickly and enjoyed life to the full. With a keen interest in the Irish language, he won a scholarship to the Donegal Gaeltacht when he was 12 years old. He never brought any trouble to his family, who were all proud of his achievements.

Like many of the young men of his generation he was politicised at a young age and, having witnessed the corrupt and sectarian nature of the Six County State, he joined the Republican Movement.

Sean O'Riordan was shot dead by a member of the British Army at 8.45pm on the 23rd March 1972 in Cawnpore Street not far from his family home. He was 13 years old.

As a member of Na Fianna Éireann he is buried in the Republican Plot in Milltown Cemetery.

Óglach Patrick Campbell

15th July 1955 - 25th March 1972

Patrick Campbell, from Ballymurphy in West Belfast, was born on 15th July 1955. He received his education at St Aidan's Primary School before he moved on to St Thomas's Secondary School on the Whiterock Road. In 1970 he left school and found work as a bread-server.

Patrick's family had a long history of involvement in the freedom struggle; his granny, Cassie Lynch, a Republican, was brutally murdered by Black and Tans while she nursed her child on her knee - the child also died from injuries and shock. Years later a second cousin was interned on the 'Al Rawdah' prison ship. It came as no surprise then, to family or friends, when Patrick, or 'Peachy' as he was nicknamed, joined Na Fianna Éireann in 1970.

Picked up in the internment swoop of August 1971, he was taken to Girdwood Barracks and later to Crumlin Road. Peachy, however, was not interned. He did, though, become a constant victim of harassment by the British forces, who regularly raided his house to arrest him. In one particular case, every single member of his family was taken into custody.

Undeterred by this constant abuse, Peachy's commitment grew daily and in early 1972 he decided to leave Na Fianna Éireann to join the ranks of Óglaigh na hÉireann.

On 25th March 1972 he was shot dead while on active service at the junction of Springhill Avenue and the Springfield Road. He was only 16 years old.

Óglach Samuel Hughes

26th February 1955 - 7th April 1972

Samuel John Hughes was born on 26th February 1955, the youngest boy of seven brothers and two sisters and he got on very well with all of them. When Sammy was 8 years old his family moved to 52 Bawnmore Park, Mill Road, where he lived until his death in 1972.

Samuel attended the Star of the Sea Primary School and then Stella Maris Secondary School. He left school at 15 and joined Abbey Meat Packers as an apprentice butcher. Each week he would eagerly await his wages so that he could rush off and buy the latest "gear" and head down to the local disco.

Despite his love of dancing he was a shy boy who did not like having his photo taken and a result of this, his family have nothing but a few of Sammy's baby photos.

With many other young people Sammy joined the Republican Movement after the Bloody Sunday murders in 1972. On 7th April of that year, Sammy told his mother that he was going to town to buy some clothes.

Around 2.00pm there was a loud explosion in some garages at the end of the estate. Sammy's family thought he was safe in town but sadly he had not got there and was killed in the premature explosion along with two of his best friends, Jackie McErlean and Charles McCrystal.

Sammy was buried together with friend Jackie in Our Lady's Acre.

Óglach Charles McChrystal

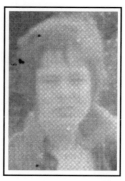

1954 - 7th April 1972

Charles McCrystal was from the Bawnmore area of Newtonabbey, on the outskirts of North Belfast. His parents Joe and Annabel had a large family of thirteen children and Charles was their youngest son. He attended Stella Maris Secondary School and it was here that he was able to develop his interest in football. His other sporting passion was fishing.

Charles was a very quiet natured young man - the type of person who never brought any trouble to his parents' door, and, unlike many of his peers, he never drank or smoked. When he left school he worked as a milk delivery man and would have to rise at the break of dawn each morning to do his deliveries.

Growing up in the Nationalist Bawnmore estate he witnessed discrimination, oppression and the complete unwillingness of the British Government and their Unionist allies to treat Catholics as anything other than second-class citizens.

He made the decision to help right some of the wrongs inflicted on his friends and neighbours and joined the ranks of Óglaigh na hÉireann. He was determined and committed to help end this oppression.

On the 7th April 1972, Charles was on active service with his comrades Samuel Hughes and John McErlean in Bawnmore Park near his own home. All three Volunteers were killed when the bomb they were preparing exploded accidentally.

Charles was 17 years old when he died.

Óglach John McErlean

21st August 1954 - 7th April 1972

John McErlean, or Jack as he was known, was born at 21 Mary's Place, Whitehouse on the 21st August 1954. He was the eldest of a family of five brothers and three sisters born to his father, Jack senior, and his mother Kathleen. When Jack was ten years old the family moved into a house on the new Bawnmore Estate.

He was educated at the Star of The Sea Primary School, Greencastle and Stella Maris Secondary School. On leaving school he attended Feldon House Training Centre to train as a mechanical engineer. He received a City and Guilds Certificate for this, which his parents received a few months after his death.

He had an easy going and laid back manner and his great hobby was making model aeroplanes and warships. He enjoyed discos and attended the local one in the Fountain Hall, Whitewell Road, where he was supposed to be going on the night he was killed.

On Friday the 7th April 1972, Jack left his home in Bawnmore at 1.55pm to join his two friends Sammy Hughes and Charlie McCrystal. They went to a lock-up garage at Bawnmore Grove and at 2.05pm an explosion ripped through the garage. Jack and his two comrades were killed instantly as a result of the accidental explosion.

On the 11th February 1974, one year and ten months after his death, Jack's 18-year old sister Margaret was travelling to work with a number of friends when Loyalists ambushed their car. Four of the occupants were injured, including 16 year old Thomas Donaghy, who died on the way to hospital, and Margaret, who died a week later on the 18th February 1974.

Óglach John Starrs

20th March 1953 - 13th May 1972

John Starrs was only 19 years old when he died on active service on the streets of Derry, a member of 'B' Company of the Bogside's 1st Battalion. John had lived at Hamilton Street in the Brandywell area with his parents and brothers. By the time of Bloody Sunday he was a soldier and a trained marksman in the Free State Army. When he learned of the massacre on his own streets, he decided that his abilities would be put to much better use back home, and like many other young Derry people he joined the IRA, where he quickly made a reputation for himself as an able and fearless Volunteer.

On Saturday 13th May 1972 John was part of a four-member IRA unit out "floating" in search of British Army patrols. Armed with two .303 bolt actions rifles, a .30 Garand and a Sterling sub-machine gun, the unit searched for targets around the periphery of the Bogside, before deciding to split up. Arriving at the William St./Chamberlain St. junction in early afternoon, John and a comrade readied themselves for action.

As they prepared their weapons, John was shot in the chest by British soldiers hiding in the top floor of a nearby shop. As his comrade bent to help him, he too was shot in the arm. As bullets danced around them, sympathetic bystanders, regardless of their own safety dragged both men and weapons away. John's comrade was spirited away to hospital in Letterkenny, but young John Starrs lay dead.

John was buried with full military honours in one of the biggest republican funerals ever seen in his native Derry.

Fiann Michael Magee

8th October 1958 - 13th May 1972

Michael Francis Magee, from Ballymurphy, was born 8th October 1958. He attended St. Thomas's Secondary School. His hobbies were football and fishing. A typical teenager in many respects he enjoyed the company of his peers and was well-liked by all who knew him.

Like a large number of young men in his native Ballymurphy he joined the ranks of Na Fianna Éireann in an attempt to play his part in the struggle for national liberation.

Hundreds of young men and women from throughout the country, having witnessed and been victims of British injustices, were politicised from a young age and were forced to make decisions that would not normally have been made by teenagers.

Fiann Michael Magee was on active service on the 13th May 1972 when he was accidently shot dead. He was just 15 years old.

Óglach Edward McDonnell

20th November 1942 - 28th May 1972

Eddie McDonnell, from Kilmood Street, Short Strand, was born on 20th November 1942, the fourth child of a family of seven children. He received his education at St Matthew's School, Seaforde Street, and although passing his technical examination, which guaranteed him a place in the Belfast Technical College, decided instead to give up schooling to follow in his father's footsteps and become a butcher. He found a job in the abattoir at Stewart Street in the Markets area, and while there joined the ITGWU.

Eddie, whose mother Mary comes from a staunchly Republican background, first became involved shortly after the 'Split' in 1970, when he joined the newly-formed Sean Martin/Sean Treacy Sinn Féin Cumann. Along with Harry 'Ducksy' Crawford, he helped to build the old Republican Club in Seaforde Street.

According to his family, football was his main pastime but they are quick to agree with Eddie's friends that the sport he excelled in was making people laugh. He was gifted with a lightening wit, which he would use at every opportunity to slag friend and foe alike. He also had a great singing voice and a vast repertoire of songs but it was his rendition of Mary from Dungloe (his own personal favourite), which, when called upon to sing at local functions or parties, brought the house down.

A member of the Auxiliary IRA since mid-1971 he joined Óglaigh na hÉireann just after internment. Forced to lead a life on the run from then onwards, Eddie took part in numerous engagements with the British forces. He and three comrades died in an accidental explosion in Anderson Street on 28th May 1972, while preparing to leave on a bombing mission.

Four civilians also lost their lives in this explosion. They were: Harry 'Ducksy' Crawford, John Nugent, Mary McGreevey and Geraldine McMahon.

Óglach Jackie McIlhone

4th August 1954 - 28th May 1972

Jackie McIlhone from Clyde Street, Short Strand was born on 4th August 1954, the fourth in a family of six. He attended St Matthew's Primary School, Seaforde Street and later St Augustine's Secondary School, Ravenhill Road. On leaving school in 1970, 'Jake' as he was better known found work as an apprentice welder only yards from his home in Sam Watson's Engineering Works in Thompson Place.

Although an extrovert in character, Jake was a lad of simple pleasures. His pastimes included football, playing cards and listening to pop music (Slade and T-Rex being his favourite groups). He always looked forward to the weekends when being fashion conscious, he got himself 'done up' and went off to a disco.

His main interest, however, was Republicanism. When the local slua of Fianna Eireánn was formed in 1970, Jake, eager to combat the enemy, joined up. He got his first taste of action when he acted as an ammunition runner during the June 1970 gun battle around St Matthew's Chapel. He stayed with the Fianna until shortly after Internment when he joined the Auxiliary unit of the IRA, progressing into the ranks of Óglaigh na hÉireann in early 1972.

Jake died at the age of 17, in an accidental explosion in Anderson Street on May 28th 1972.

Óglach Joseph Fitzsimons

13th July 1954 - 28th May 1972

Joey Fitzsimons was born on 13th July 1954, the sixth child in a family of eighteen. He went to St Matthew's Primary School and St Augustine's Secondary School, where he excelled in Technical Drawing and Art. On leaving school, he found a job as a process operator for a photographic firm and later he worked as a casual labourer for McGrattan's fruit merchants.

Always cheerful and full of energy, Joey's main pastimes were football and music, learning how to play the accordion at a very early age. Joey came from a Republican background. His grandfather, Paddy McLaughlin, was an IRA Volunteer in the 1930's and his cousin, Francie Fitzsimons, died on active service in October 1976. In 1969, Joey, who had just turned 15, was already on the barricades which appeared in all nationalist areas following the 1969 loyalist pogroms. He helped to found the local James Connolly Slua of Fianna Éireann in early 1970 and was in action as an ammunition-runner during the gun-battle around St Matthew's Chapel in June of that year.

Shortly after Internment, in September, Joey was charged with riotous behaviour and sentenced to six months imprisonment in Crumlin Road Jail. Released on the morning of the funeral of his comrades killed on the Knock Dual carriageway, Joey had only just finished delivering Mass cards from the POW's in Crumlin Road to the bereaved families when he reported back for active service with the local IRA unit. In one particular incident, Joey was fired on and wounded in the arm by paratroopers who had stumbled upon him and other comrades of an IRA active service unit when they were about to carry out a commercial bombing attack in Belfast city centre. He returned fire enabling himself and his comrades to retreat to safety.

He lost his life in an accidental explosion at the age of 17 on 28th May 1972 in Anderson Street, while preparing to go on a commercial bombing mission.

Óglach Martin Engelen

19th October 1953 - 28th May 1972

Martin Engelen was born on 19th October 1953, in the Short Strand, the youngest of a family of eight brothers. Martin attended St Matthew's Primary School, Seaforde Street (where he first got the nickname 'Big Min', which everyone, even the enemy forces, knew him by), and then St Augustine's Secondary School, Ravenhill Road. A motor-car fanatic, Martin left school in 1968 and found employment as an apprentice motor mechanic with Gaydor Auto Electricians, but being the only Catholic employed there he was forced to leave due to sectarian harassment.

A quiet, unassuming person, whose only other pastimes, apart from cars, were a bet on the horses or a game of cards on the street corner. Martin, who was often slagged by his friends for his lack of confidence and nerves while in female company, showed no absence of either when, in early 1971, he joined the ranks of Óglaigh na hÉireann.

A fine example of his courage and, to a lesser extent, of his dry sense of humour was displayed in early 1972 during a concerted bombing operation in Belfast. Martin was instructed to place a hoax car-bomb on the Albert Bridge in East Belfast. He had only travelled a short distance when the car he was driving broke down. Martin calmly got out and started to push the car towards its destination. A passing mobile RUC patrol spotted him and stopped to investigate. Still remaining calm and hoping that none of the patrol recognised him, Martin told them that the car was out of petrol and asked for their assistance in pushing it to the side of the bridge. The unsuspecting RUC men obliged while Martin, excusing himself to fetch a can of petrol from a nearby garage, bade them a hearty farewell.

A deeply committed and dedicated IRA Volunteer, Martin was killed on 28th May 1972 in an accidental explosion in Anderson Street, Short Strand.

Fiann Joseph Campbell

15th July 1955 - 11th June 1972

Joseph Campbell was born on 15th July 1955 and received his education at St. Columbanus' Primary School and St. Gabriel's Secondary School where he obtained certificates in mechanical engineering.

Like many of the young men of his generation, he had first hand experience of the discrimination and inequality that existed in his community and made the conscious decision to do something about it. He joined the Fianna in late 1970 when he was 15 years old.

A typical teenager, he loved to hang around with his friends and enjoyed the normal every day things that teenagers get up to. But his life was cut short when on 11th June 1972, Joseph was shot dead by British occupation forces.

He was the first member of Fianna Éireann to die in the Ardoyne area during this phase of the struggle.

Óglach Tony Jordan

2nd June 1952 - 28th June 1972

Tony Jordan, from Carrigart Avenue, in Lenadoon, Belfast, was born on 2nd June 1952. He first attended St. Joseph's School, in Slate Street Belfast, and later at St. Thomas's Secondary School on the Whiterock Road.

After leaving school, Tony had several short periods of employment in different occupations, including one with Eason's stationary company in Belfast city centre.

Tony Jordan was a very energetic young man who enjoyed cycling, swimming and camping, and was also fond of acting.

In 1970 Tony joined the Republican Movement, and proved to be a dedicated Volunteer. In June 1972, a bilateral truce was declared between the IRA and the British government. Only hours later, on the 28th June, Tony Jordan and his comrade, Volunteer John Finucane died as a result of a car crash on the Falls Road, while they were on active service. Tony Jordan was buried in Milltown Cemetery, Belfast.

Tragedy was to strike the Jordan family a second time, when young Volunteer Pearse Jordan was murdered by the RUC on 25th November 1992, on the Falls Road in west Belfast, not far from where Tony had died twenty years earlier.

Óglach John Finucane

1st January 1951 - 28th June 1972

Throughout the conflict in the six counties, many families paid a high price for their commitment to freedom, justice and peace. The Finucanes were one such family.

John Finucane was born on 1st January 1951 and attended St. Finian's Primary School on the Falls Road and St.Peter's Secondary School, Whiterock Road. After leaving school, John worked for Andrew's Flour Mill in Percy Street. He married his wife, Sue, in 1972 and they had one son whom they named Patrick Pearse.

John had joined the Republican Movement in 1970, and after the introduction of internment in 1971, he was held for a period on the prison ship, Maidstone, and in Long Kesh and Magilligan prison camps. The family were to become no strangers to prisons. His brother Seamus was to become one of the youngest internees, and would later receive a 14-year prison term.

Another brother Dermot was sentenced to 18 years, but was one of the 19 POWs who successfully escaped from H7 Long Kesh in 1983. The British authorities failed to get him extradited to the six counties. Patrick Finucane, John's brother and the solicitor who championed the rights of the prisoners through the courts, was murdered by loyalist gunmen at his home in February 1989.

Volunteer John Finucane, Belfast Brigade Óglaigh na hÉireann, died in a car crash along with his comrade, Volunteer Tony Jordan on June 28th 1972 only hours after a bilateral truce had been called between the IRA and the British government. Both Volunteers were buried in Milltown Cemetery, Belfast.

Óglach Denis Quinn

13th May 1943 - 3rd July 1972

Denis Quinn, aged 29, was originally from Meenagh Park in Coalisland. On 3rd July 1972 he died as a result of an accidental shooting while on Active Service. The East Tyrone Brigade of Óglaigh na hÉireann issued a statement at the time saying he had died when a weapon was accidentally discharged as a unit prepared to go out on patrol.

His friends and true comrades laid Volunteer Denis Quinn to rest in Coalisland Cemetery.

Denis is remembered locally as having been a great fisher and huntsman who had a love and respect for nature. He was often seen out around the Loughshore, and had a reputation as a skilled and well-equipped hunter. Socially he enjoyed the craic with others from the Coalisland and Stewartstown areas, but Denis was dedicated to his wife and young daughter. His wife was expecting their second daughter at the time of his death and his death was a terrible blow to his family and the area.

"If by my tomb some day you careless pass,
A moment grieved by coming on my name,

Then let your grief, be it a single tear,
Upon your cheek in tender sorrow fall,
Forget where I did fall: keep only dear
The deeds for which you loved me overall."

'If you should pass'

Dora Sigerson Shorter

Óglach Julie Dougan

20th August 1945 - 8th July 1972

Julie Dougan was born in Portadown and was brought up on the fringes of the 'Tunnel' district. Like many others in the late sixties, she was involved in a number of the original Civil Rights demonstrations, campaigning for equality and justice. She subsequently became involved in the Republican Movement, becoming an active Volunteer with Cumann na mBan.

A victim of constant harassment from the Crown Forces and the subject of death threats from the UVF, Julie narrowly escaped death following a gun attack on her home in Ballyoran Park. Shortly after that incident, she moved to County Monaghan where as an active Volunteer and continued with her Republican activities on both sides of the border. In the early 1970s the Nationalist communities in North Armagh were coming under constant and sustained attack from the British Army, RUC and their Loyalist allies, especially in the 'Murder Triangle.

Julie could have chosen to remain in the South, but decided to return to her native North Armagh. While on Active Service, the car in which Julie was travelling with another Volunteer was involved in an accident in Oban Street. Julie was taken to hospital in Belfast where she died from her injuries on 8th July 1972. Her remains were brought to her mother's home in Portadown's Thomas Street, where members of Na Fianna Eireánn formed a Guard of Honour.

However even in death, Julie Dougan, her family and community were to become a target for Loyalists. In the early hours of the morning of July 10th, in spite of Crown forces surveillance, several UVF gunmen took up position directly across the street and sprayed the wake-house with gunfire. Julie was eventually laid to rest in the Republican plot in St. John's Cemetery, Drumcree.

Fiann John Dougal

22nd December 1955 - 9th July 1972

John Dougal was born on 22nd December 1955 and was from the Springhill Avenue in Belfast. He went to St. Gabriel's Primary School where he was well liked by his classmates and developed a reputation as a bit of a joker. It was during his time at St. Gabriel's that he developed a keen interest in Irish history. After St. Gabriel's he attended St. Peter's Secondary School and upon leaving took a job at Casey's Betting Shop.

John had many interests as a boy, but particularly loved working on old cars, usually belonging to his mates' parents. He also had a great love of motor bikes and longed for the day when he would be old enough to afford one of his own. Sadly that day never came.

It was during one of the many gun battles that marked an end of the truce in 1972 between the IRA and the British Government that John lost his life. On Sunday, 9th July 1972, British soldiers backed by Loyalist gunmen attacked the Ballymurphy Estate. In the ensuing battle, John was killed along with five local civilians. Those killed alongside John were; Patrick Butler, Angelo Fionda, Margaret Gargdin, David McCaffetry and the local Priest, Father Fitzpatrick, who was killed outside a house near the Corpus Christi Church.

Óglach Louis Scullion

5th June 1945 - 14th July 1972

Louis Scullion, from Unity Walk, was born on 5th June 1945. He was educated at St Patrick's, Bearnageeha. Louis was always a very boisterous person, full of life and energy. As a boy he was very interested in gymnastics and was often picked out for exhibitions. He was also fond of animals and spent a lot of his spare time working with them. His main interest was darts, a game at which he excelled.

Louis joined the Republican Movement in 1970, after witnessing the heavy sectarian attacks on his own Unity Flats area by the RUC and loyalists. He became the victim of constant harassment by both the RUC and the British army. On one occasion, he was tied to a lamp post by RUC men and savagely beaten.

Louis's cousin, also named Louis, was a life-long Republican who was given a Republican funeral after he died of cancer in 1983.

The British Army had often threatened Louis that they would kill him and on 14th July 1972, at 1:45am, they carried out their threat. Louis was walking into Unity Flats when a British soldier shouted to him. When Louis turned around he was shot four times. There were two people with Louis, one of them from the Loyalist Sandy Row area. At the inquest, they gave evidence that Louis was unarmed at the time and that he was shot for no known reason. The coroner brought in a verdict that Louis had shot himself four times in the chest!

None of the British soldiers concerned were ever charged with the cold blooded murder of Louis Scullion.

Óglach James Reid

23rd May 1945 - 14th July 1972

James Reid was born on 23rd May 1945, the second son of James and Rachael Reid at 166 Brompton Park, Ardoyne. He had three brothers and two sisters and he attended Holy Cross Primary School in Butler Street, and St Gabriel's Secondary School on the Crumlin Road, where he was better known to his friends as 'Bimbo'. He was a keen footballer and a handball enthusiast.

On leaving school, at the age of 15, Jim worked for short periods at a number of different jobs, but like so many others at this time he was unable to find steady employment. Thus he was forced to go to England in order to find work.

He came home for a short period in 1969 when his younger brother was shot and wounded by Loyalists in the Ardoyne area before returning home for good in February 1972. Within a few shorts weeks of his return he joined the local unit of the Auxiliary IRA. He was a staunch and committed Republican whose uncle, Stephen Gibbons, was a member of the IRA during the '40s and '50s campaigns.

On the night of 14th July 1972, Jim was killed during a gun-battle with the British Army while on active service in Estoril Park, close to his Ardoyne home.

Óglach Tobias Molloy

23rd March 1954 - 16th July 1972

Tobias Molloy was 18 years old when, returning from his girlfriend's home in Lifford, he was struck above the heart by a rubber bullet fired by the British Army. The British propagandists were quick to claim that Tobias was shot while taking part in a riot but these claims were disputed by local eyewitnesses who were adamant that he was nowhere near the riot and was shot down in cold blood, without reason.

Local youths helped carry the injured Tobias to Lifford hospital where he was pronounced dead on arrival.

As his body was being taken home from across the border, accompanied by hundreds of mourners, it was attacked by British soldiers as it passed by their army base. Mourners were forced to fight their way through as they were attacked with batons and rubber bullets, some of which hit the hearse that carried the dead Fianna boy's coffin.

The funeral, which was attended by thousands of people from the West Tyrone area, stretched over five miles to the Donneyloop graveyard in Donegal. As the remains reached the cemetery it was surrounded by hundreds of Free State soldiers and Gardaí, who were there under of the auspices of preventing an IRA tribute, a tribute that had already been paid before Tobias's remains had left his hometown.

Tobias Molloy is survived by his mother Mary, brother Patsy and wider family circle who, along with his friends and comrades in the Republican movement in West Tyrone, remember him with pride.

Óglach Joseph Downey

23rd April 1949 - 21st July 1972

Joe Downey, from the Markets area, was born on 23rd April 1949, the eldest son of Joe and Sheila Downey. He attended Gloucester Street Primary School, off May Street, and when he left school in the mid-60s, went to work as a casual labourer in the Low Docks in Belfast city harbour.

His hobbies included football, handball and snooker. Joe made the headlines in the daily papers when he shouted 'Up the IRA!' at Orange marchers as they passed over the Albert Bridge, past the Markets area, chanting sectarian songs and slogans. The Orange marchers were ignored, while Joe was set upon by the RUC, arrested, charged and subsequently sentenced to six months imprisonment for 'incitement'.

To the nationalist community in the Markets area, his treatment epitomised the sectarian nature of the Orange state. His treatment focused their attention on the corrupt and biased nature of the state's sectarian laws and the forces which were charged with upholding them.

Joe joined the IRA, only weeks before his death occurred in Cromac Street in his native Markets area. On 21st July 1972, Joe was shot dead by an unknown sniper as a gun-battle raged with the British Army and Loyalists.

Óglach Seamus Cassidy

23rd January 1950 - 28th July 1972

Seamus Cassidy was born on the 23rd June, 1950 and lived at 5 Ardilea Drive in the Ardoyne area of Belfast. He attended the Holy Cross Primary School for boys and then went on to St. Malachy's College on the Antrim Road.

Seamus was known for his quiet good nature and took all things in his stride. He was a happy go lucky fellow and never had cause to give his family any trouble. He showed quite an interest in fashion and style and was known to be quite particular about his appearance. He had a great interest in the sport of Billiards and had his own cue and often went to the 'Hibs', Herbert Street to play a few games with mates. As a child he loved football and could often be found playing in the street with his friends. While at St. Malachy's College, Seamus developed an interest in swimming and ultimately swam for the College. After his school day he held a paper round which he worked at throughout his school years.

Upon leaving school Seamus took to work on the boats but this did not last long as he missed his home and wanted to return. He briefly took work in England and Wales, but with things back home worsening, felt he had to return. After returning home he worked with his uncle as a pipe stresser until his death.

Seamus joined the Republican Movement and quickly became a well respected member of Óglaigh na hÉireann. It was on the 27th July 1972 in North Belfast, while sitting in his car outside the Starry Plough bar on the New Lodge Road, that he was shot in the head by British Occupation forces. Mortally wounded, he was taken to hospital where he then died on 28th July 1972.

Óglach Seamus Bradley

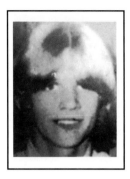

16th July 1953 - 31st July 1972

Seamus Bradley came from the Creggan Estate and was one of a large family. He was a very happy go lucky young man, with a smile and a charm that meant he was always surrounded by girls. Seamus worked as a labourer with a local building firm and was fond of music and dancing.

Seamus joined the IRA and was a member of 'B' Company, 2nd Battalion and was involved in a lot of active service activity throughout late 1971 and 1972. His brother Robert was killed by a British Army armoured car in 1972.

On the night of 31st July 1972 he was on the streets of Creggan when the British invaded the no-go areas, in what the British Government called Operation Motorman. Seamus was captured, alive, at about 4a.m. and his body was delivered by British soldiers to the local morgue at 7a.m. He had been shot four times and had bled to death. His body was covered in extensive bruising. British soldiers claimed that they had shot a gunman carrying a machine gun. They said that they shot him twice.

British soldiers raided his home the next morning and told his father as they were leaving that his son was in the morgue.

Seamus was buried with full military honours despite the British Army laying siege to the wake house and harassing people who came to pay their respects.

Óglach Robert McCrudden

13th September 1952 - 3rd August 1972

Robert James McCrudden was born in Ward Street in the Lower Falls area, West Belfast, on 13th August 1952. In 1967 the family moved to the Springhill area and in 1971 they moved again, this time to the Springfield Road.

Young Bobby went to school at St Joseph's Primary School on Slate Street and later attended St Gabriel's Secondary on Britton's Parade. After leaving school he obtained work as a barman. It was around this time that he began to take an interest in Irish history and Republicanism. He then joined 'F' Company, 2nd Battalion, the local slua of Na Fianna Éireann, and within a couple of months was accepted as a Volunteer in 'B' Company, 2nd Battalion, Belfast Brigade, Óglaigh na hÉireann.

Bobby was a dedicated and active IRA Volunteer and took part in several operations. He died on active service on 3rd September 1972, when he was shot while behind a house in Hooker Street. He was wounded in the neck by a British soldier who was on sentry duty in an observation post in the Flax Street Mill. The British soldiers, who claimed that they had seen someone pointing a rifle at them, immediately sealed off the entire area, preventing an ambulance from reaching the dying Bobby McCrudden for an hour and a half. He was taken to hospital but died of his wounds shortly after his arrival there.

Óglach Colm Murtagh

1st April 1954 - 9th August 1972

John Colm Murtagh was born in Daisy Hill Hospital on the 1st April 1954, and brought up by his parents Peter and Maureen. He had three sisters, and three brothers. He was educated at St Clare's Convent, Abbey Primary - where he passed the 11 plus - and Abbey CBS before finishing at St Joseph's. When he left school at 16, he found employment with Ulster Textiles, dyeing yarn.

Colm enjoyed swimming, handball and pole-vaulting, but his favourites were motorbikes and cars. He was also a keen Gaelic footballer, playing for the Abbey team which won the McMahon Cup in 1968. His family history was steeped in Republican tradition. His paternal grandfather Peter and great uncle James both served in the 4th Northern Division IRA during the Civil War.

At the beginning of the present phase of the campaign in 1968, Colm acted as a steward at marches and rallies. The introduction of Internment hardened his attitudes and it was then he decided to participate in the freedom struggle, and joined Óglaigh na hÉireann. In April 1972, he was arrested in Monaghan in possession of a gun and sent to Mountjoy where he eventually got bail. From then on, he was constantly on the run from the British and Free State authorities. He took shelter in a number of safe houses and operated from these. His girlfriend Marian Rickard from O'Neill Avenue spent as much time as possible with him. They were deeply devoted to each other and a testament to that is the fact that Marian and the Murtagh family have remained in constant contact.

On the first anniversary of Internment, Colm was tragically killed in an accidental explosion on the Dublin Road, Newry. Such was his bravery, he threw himself on top of the bomb, which was about to explode, saving the lives of a number of comrades and civilians. Colm is proudly remembered by all his family, friends and comrades.

Óglach Michael Clarke

2nd September 1949 - 11th August 1972

Michael Clarke was from Ballymurphy and he was born on 2nd September 1949. He went to Slate Street Primary School and further at St Peter's Secondary School.

During the riots of 1969 he was among the first to lend assistance to the people who had been driven from their homes. He witnessed the savage attack on the people of Ballymurphy after the bombing of Kelly's Bar by Loyalists. He decided that the only form of effective resistance was by armed struggle, so he joined the 2nd Battalion, Belfast Brigade, Óglaigh Na hÉireann.

He was killed on August 11th 1972 alongside Cumann na mBan volunteer Anne Parker. They were transporting a bomb and it exploded accidentally. The intended target was a large store in North Howard Street. As the street was crowded with shoppers, the Volunteers decided that rather than jeopardise the safety of civilians, they would abort their mission. The bomb exploded in their car as they were travelling away from the store on its return journey back to base.

Michael was a popular Volunteer and always eager and willing to learn any new skills.

Óglach Anne Parker

30th June 1954 - 11th August 1972

Anne Parker of Whitecliff Crescent, Ballymurphy, was born on 30th June 1954, and came from a large family of six brothers and four sisters. Her great grandmother was a cousin of Michael Collins. She was educated at St Kevin's Primary School and St Rose's Secondary School.

A happy-go-lucky and fun loving young woman she had witnessed her community under attack from a foreign power and their domestic allies and made the decision to join the Republican Movement when she became a member of Cumann na gCailini in February 1972 before progressing to Cumann na mBan in April 1972.

An active member of Cumann na mBan she and her comrade IRA volunteer Michael Clarke were on active service on the 11th August 1972 when they were forced to cancel the bombing mission because of the risk to civilians in the area. As they were driving away from the area, the bomb accidentally exploded and both Anne and her comrade were killed. She was 18 years old at the time of her death.

Óglach Patrick Hughes

1st October 1937 - 22nd August 1972

Patrick (better known as Patsy) Hughes was born on the Quarter Road, Camloch on 1st October 1937 and was reared on the Derramore Road, Bessbrook. His parents Michael and Elizabeth, had five other children: Michael, William, Richard, Lilian and Philomena.

At sixteen, he joined the British Army. He met his wife to be, Theresa Halligan, originally from Caledon, Co Tyrone at a dance in Armagh and a year later they were married. Patsy and his young wife were then posted to Germany, North Africa and Kenya. They had seven children altogether: Michael (an IRA Volunteer who was shot dead by the British Army in October 1974), Kate, Elizabeth, John, Angela, Lorraine and Patricia. After nine years, Patsy opted out of the British Army for the sake of his family. They lived in the pre-fabs on the Deramore Road for seven years before moving to Main Avenue in the new Derrybeg estate. With the troubles flared, Patsy got involved in the local vigilante group for the protection of his family and community. As an ex-British soldier, he was appalled by the actions of the British Army now occupying his country. He could not stand by and watch, so he volunteered to join the ranks of Óglaigh na hÉireann and fight for his country's freedom. His love of animals, gardening and DIY was his cover for involvement in the IRA. His military knowledge and experience proved invaluable to his comrades.

On Tuesday 22nd August 1972, Patsy volunteered to take the place of another Volunteer and tragically died in an accidental explosion on the Dublin Road, Newry. Two other Volunteers, Oliver Rowntree and Noel Madden, were killed along with Patsy. The community was shocked, not only to learn of Patsy's death, but also of his involvement with Óglaigh na h-Éireann. He remained 'clean' to the end, arousing the suspicions of no-one. Patsy was a dedicated Volunteer in the ranks of Óglaigh na hÉireann and shared his Republican beliefs among a few fellow comrades. His memory has instilled confidence and courage in IRA units ever since.

Óglach Oliver Rowntree

22nd July 1949 - 22nd August 1972

Oliver Plunkett Rowntree was born on 22nd July 1949 along with his twin brother Colman (also killed in action some years later). He came from a family with deep connections to republicanism. His father James and mother Dolores had another nine children Cecilia, Dolores, Maria, Denise, Alex, Kieran, Seamus, Enda and Bronagh (deceased).

He started his schooling at St Clare's Convent, moving to the Abbey Primary, then onto the Abbey Grammar. He had a very successful academic career which finished at Trinity College, Dublin. Oliver became heavily involved in the Civil Rights movement, always prepared to do what was asked of him. In his early teenage years, he joined Na Fianna Éireann. A fluent Irish speaker, he was as proud of his culture as he was of his Republicanism. His hobbies included playing snooker, billiards and football - he was a member of the John Mitchel's GFC. He also had a great interest in cross-country running, being a member of the Shamrocks running club.

In the early 70s, Oliver had to go on the run for a spell. He was arrested in the South, charged with possession and remanded to Mountjoy Prison. But the evidence was flimsy and he was released. Having joined the IRA some time earlier, he believed fervently that only a full time commitment from a dedicated Army could bring about the objective of a 32 county, socialist republic. He was opposed to republicans fighting each other, believing that the "Official" IRA which was active then had a part to play fighting the common enemy militarily. As a consequence, a dual operation was planned where one group detonated a landmine while the other exchanged gunfire with the British Army. On 22nd August 1972, Oliver was killed in an accidental explosion at the customs station on the Dublin Road. Two other comrades died along with him as well as a number of civilians.

Thousands of people turned out for his funeral at St Mary's graveyard. In a unique tribute to a courageous Volunteer, two sets of firing parties fired over his coffin, one from his beloved Óglaigh na hÉireann, the other from the "Official" IRA.

Óglach Noel Madden

2nd January 1954 - 22nd August 1972

Noel John Madden was born on the 2nd January 1954. His mother Mary and father John had three children, Aidan, Fiona and Julia. He was educated at the Abbey Primary School and St Joseph's Secondary School on the Armagh Road. Like the vast majority of students, Noel left school at 15 to seek employment. He found employment as an apprentice painter and once he was qualified many local firms sought his services because of the quality of his work. A popular young man, he enjoyed life, particularly his social life at weekends, when he would attend the local dances and discos. As a pastime, he loved fishing. A natural daredevil, he once walked over the mud at the 'Ramparts' when the tide was out and struggled for three hours to get back on shore.

When he was fourteen, the Civil Rights Movement organised a massive demonstration in Newry. Suffering from massive social deprivation and discrimination, it wasn't a hard decision for the youth of Newry to join the ranks of the Irish Republican Army to fight for a better society for all. When the British Army was introduced onto the streets of the North, people like Noel realised that only a military offensive would bring the British to the negotiating table. Internment was the last straw.

As part of an Active Service Unit, Colm took part in several attacks. A comrade, Colm Murtagh who died in an accidental explosion had a major impact on him and other Volunteers like himself. Less than a fortnight after his untimely death, Noel was to die in similar circumstances. On 22nd August 1972, along with two fellow comrades, Patsy Hughes and Oliver Rowntree, he was killed at the Customs Station on the Dublin Road. Several civilians also died tragically.

Noel's death was a shock, not only to his comrades but also to his family who were unaware of his involvement with Óglaigh na hEireánn. His family, friends and comrades remember him with pride.

Óglach James Carlin

26th August 1932 - 26th August 1972

Jim Carlin was a married man with four children. He was a well-known character in the South Down area and many doors were open as a result of the respect that local people had for him. His easy manner meant he blended easily into the local homes where he is fondly remembered for his good humour and wit.

Jim could talk his way through anything and his charm and charisma got him out of many a tight hole. On one occasion Jim and a comrade drove into a British army checkpoint with a car loaded with explosives. Keeping his cool, he calmly slipped the revolver he had stuck in the sun visor, into his waistband and with a cigarette in his mouth struck up a conversation with the unsuspecting Brit, offering him a drop of the 'hard stuff' to keep the chill away. The Brit gratefully accepted and waved Jim and his comrade through the checkpoint.

He was a close friend and comrade of Volunteer Peter McNulty and was devastated when he was killed. He was not deterred however and re-dedicated himself to continuing the fight that took the lives of so many comrades. On 26th August 1972 Jim Carlin lost his life while on active service as a result of an accidental explosion.

Óglach Martin Curran

3rd October 1950 - 26th August 1972

Martin (Dickie) Curran was born the second child of a family of five on the 3rd October 1950. He lived most of his short life in the Downpatrick area and attended the local Primary and Secondary school. After leaving school and with limited prospects of a job like so many other young Nationalists growing up in the six counties, Dickie decided to go to London for a while.

However, while he was in London Dickie watched the unfolding drama of the Civil Rights campaign of the late 1960s and decided he had to come home and play his part. On his return he joined the Civil rights movement in Downpatrick and struck up a close relationship with Leo O'Hanlon. Dickie soon realised that the injustices the Civil Rights movement were striving to resolve were simply a consequence of British mis-rule in Ireland and that the root cause of the conflict was the continued occupation of Ireland by a foreign power.

Dickie was determined to play his part in removing the root cause of the conflict and soon afterwards he met Jim Carlin and joined the local unit of the IRA. Dickie went on to prove himself to be a dedicated Volunteer and it was with great sadness that local Republicans learned of his death, on active service along with that of his colleague Jim Carlin, at the Downpatrick Racecourse on the 26th August 1972.

Óglach Michael Joseph Quigley

3rd September 1952 - 17th September 1972

Michael was a sincere and honest person everyone loved being around. Michael enjoyed impersonating people which had us all in stitches lots of times. When party times happened he would sing "Boulavogue" or "Slievenamon" for our mother and father who were very proud of him. The funny thing was every time there was a knock at the door it was always for Michael. Our mammy would answer the door and whoever would ask for 'Mickey' she would say 'there's no 'Mickey' here but there's a Michael,' leaving the people with red faces.

Michael was a printer, working for the Commercial Paper Company, Guildhall Square, making labels for, among others, Mundie's Wine. We would always smell ink from him when he arrived home from work. Michael was a keen and competent footballer.

Michael saw the cruelty and injustice of the British Army being here and torturing and murdering innocent people in Derry and he could not sit by and let Orangeism and British Army tactics kill our hearts and families. One of his closest friends was Vol. Eugene McGillan.

Michael was always working hard and saving, and was able to pass his driving test first time and buy a wee car. He was going steady with a girl called Marion, whom he loved very much and they made plans to get engaged at Christmas 1972 but tragically Michael's life was snatched away by British Army murderers.

Because of his consciousness about personal security, a lot of Mickey's friends both in and out of the IRA ranks did not know of his involvement in Óglaigh na hÉireann.

Fiann Joseph McComiskey

12th September 1954 - 20th September 1972

Joseph McComiskey, from Ardoyne, was born on 12th September 1954. He went to school at St Patrick's on the Antrim Road.

His interests were football, handball and woodwork, for which he had a unique talent. Joseph was also a member of the Ardoyne Band for a short while.

Because his parents suffered from ill health; his father had long-term paralysis and his mother had poor health; Joseph had to assume a great deal of responsibility for the family from an early age. He adopted the parental role for his three young brothers and his young sister.

It was this strong sense of responsibility towards the Irish people that led to his joining Fianna Eireánn at the start of the present phase of the National struggle.

Joseph died on September 20th 1972, just one week after his 18th birthday.

Óglach Jimmy Quigley

28th May 1954 - 29th September 1972

Jimmy Quigley from Cyprus Street in the Lower Falls was born on 28th May 1954. He attended St Peter's Primary School and later St Peter's Secondary School in Brittons Parade. Jimmy was still attending St Peter's when he died.

From an early age, Jimmy had an insatiable interest in the Gaelic language and Irish History, subjects on which he spent many long hours of study. He joined Fianna Eireánn in 1969 at the age of 14. In July 1970 he was arrested, charged with riotous behaviour and sentenced to six months in St Patrick's Boys Home, Glen Road.

On his release Jimmy continued his Fianna activities and was accepted into the ranks of the IRA shortly before he was arrested and interned in early 1972. His period of internment was spent on the Maidstone prison ship, which was moored in Belfast Lough and also in Magilligan Prison Camp in Derry. He was released in July 1972.

Jimmy was 18 when when he died, and was studying for his 'A' Levels.

On September 29th 1972, whilst lying in wait in an attic room above a chemist's shop at the corner of Servia Street and Albert Street, Jimmy was taken unawares when British troops entered the street on his blind side and opened fire on him.

Within minutes, Jimmy's IRA comrades exacted their revenge on the enemy forces when they shot dead a British soldier stationed in the entry behind the chemist's shop.

Óglach Daniel McAreavey

16th May 1951 - 6th October 1972

Daniel McAreavey was born in the Castlereagh area on 16th May 1951. He went to school at St Peter's Primary School and later to St Peter's Secondary School, Whiterock.

When he left school he worked for two years as a chef for NIR on the Belfast-Dublin train. He spent one year working in the Conway Hotel and he also worked in Mooney's in Cornmarket for a couple of years.

From an early age Danny had a great interest in everything Irish: the music, culture and language. In 1972 he joined the I.R.A. and became a very active Volunteer.

On 6th October 1972, the local IRA unit planned to place a bomb beside a derelict shop, which they had discovered was being used by British Army undercover troops. Danny, armed with an armalite rifle, was acting as cover for his unit when the British Army spotted him and opened fire. He fell to the ground seriously wounded.

Minutes later, in a follow up operation, a large number of British Army troops entered the area. One of their armoured vehicles pulled up beside the wounded Danny. He was shot at point blank range as he lay on the ground. He died from these injuries.

Óglach Patrick 'Maguire' Pendleton

20th August 1948 - 10th October 1972

Paddy, from the Pool area, was the 'Pimpernel' of the Republican Movement. He was introduced to his Beechmount comrades as Paddy Maguire even though his real name was Paddy Pendleton. Born on 20th August 1948, he joined the IRA in October 1969 going on to become an Engineering Officer. He was a good musician and singer, entertaining manys a scoraiocht! He was an active Volunteer which had the British Army raiding everywhere looking for him - and they even had a perfect description of him. He worked part-time in Hynes Bar and when he was p-checked he gave his right name, Paddy Pendleton, he was always let go because he was 'clean'!

Paddy was killed in a premature explosion in a derelict house in Balkan Street in the Lower Falls on October 10th 1972. He was 24 years of age. Two other comrades died with him, Volunteers Joseph McKinney (a nephew of Bingo Campbell) and John Donaghy.

His family erected his headstone and had it engraved with an epitaph with which Paddy would have been proud: 'Greater love hath no man than he lay down his life for God, his country, and its people'.

Óglach John Donaghy

29th January 1953 - 10th October 1972

John Donaghy was born on 29th January 1953. He attended St Peter's School in Raglan Street where he earned the nickname J.D. Although he had many interests, like most young men of his generation, his main passion was football. He also liked to knock about with his mates and go to dances.

Like most of the young men of his generation however, he was growing up during a time of massive unemployment and the obvious discrimination and inequality that existed in the Six Counties. He made the decision to join the Republican Movement when he became a member of Fianna Éireann in August 1971.

He later progressed into the ranks of Óglaigh na hÉireann and was a highly active and respected member of his local unit.

On the 10th October 1972, John was on active service in a house in Balkan Street with his two comrades Joe McKinney and Patrick Maguire when the bomb they were preparing exploded accidentally.

John's death and that of his two comrades came as a severe shock to his family and to his friends and comrades, though they were the inspiration for many who followed them into the ranks of the Republican Movement.

Óglach Joseph McKinney

27th October 1955 - 10th October 1972

Joseph McKinney was born and reared at 1 Milan Street off the Falls Road. He went to the local primary school and then to St Peter's Secondary School.

He left school and went to work in Sawyers in Castle Street, where he was hardworking and liked by his fellow workmates.

Like many people the Falls Curfew and the introduction of Internment in August 1971 had a big impact on him. One of his family, an uncle P.C. Campbell was one of the men who were interned on the prison ship Maidstone, which was docked in Belfast harbour.

Joseph joined the I.R.A. and was a member of the 2nd Battalion. He brought to his unit the hardworking attitude which he had displayed in Sawyers.

On the 10th October 1972, Joseph was on active service in a house in Balkan Street with his two comrades John Donaghy and Patrick Maguire when the bomb they were preparing exploded accidentally. The large crowd which attended the funerals highlighted the sense of loss of these Volunteers in the Falls Road area.

Óglach Hugh Heron

29th April 1935 - 16th October 1972

Hugh Heron was 37 years old when he was murdered by the Staffordshire Regiment in Ardboe Hall car park on the 16th October 1972. He was murdered along with his comrade John Paddy Mullan. Hugh was married to Rita, and the couple had six young children, four sons and two daughters. Hugh is buried in Ardboe Graveyard.

Hugh's daughter in later years wrote of her memories of her father:

"The memories I have of my father are good memories, but it would have been nice to have got to have known him much better. To me the crown forces and the Orangemen are all the one. So, in my opinion they are all to blame for my mother dying young, of a broken heart. We are all very proud of our father, for what he believed in and died for, also his comrades and any man who gave his life for Ireland. My father also had five grandsons and three granddaughters, which he never knew, who are all proud of him from what they hear and I know that he would have been proud of them too. My father and every other man and woman were only fighting to keep England out of Ireland."

Óglach John Patrick Mullan

1st January 1935 - 16th October 1972

John Paddy Mullan was from Strews, The Rock outside Cookstown, County Tyrone. John Paddy had begun his involvement in the struggle for Irish freedom in the 1950's. He was 38 years old when he was killed by members of the Staffordshire regiment in the car park of St. Patrick's Hall, Ardboe, on the night of 16th October 1972. Hugh Heron, a leading member of his local unit was killed in the same incident.

Within minutes of the shooting a local priest arrived at the scene and was told by a British soldier that a car had been stopped nearby and the three occupants taken out for questioning and for the car to be searched. It was during the search that a British soldier said a rifle was pointed at him and he opened fired at the three men, hitting and killing Volunteer Hugh Heron. The other two men then attempted to escape from the scene and when they failed to stop when called upon, the other members of the foot patrol fired again. John Paddy was killed protecting the youngest member of the unit, who managed to escape.

Both members of the Official I.R.A. and their political wing Republican Clubs attended the funerals of Hugh and John Paddy and heard Cathal Goulding, a leading republican of the time, give the oration.

Volunteer John Patrick Mullan is buried in the Rock Cemetery.

Óglach Stan Carberry

19th October 1938 - 13th November 1972

Stanislaus (Stan) Carberry was born on 19th October 1938, in Beechmount. He was educated at St Peter's Primary School.

When he left school he found work as a heating engineer. He got married and then went to live in Bingnian Drive, Andersonstown. Six children were born to the Carberry family and at the time of Stan's death, they ranged in age from ten years of age to 22 months.

Stan joined the Republican Movement after witnessing Bloody Sunday whilst he was working in Derry.

Together with Volunteer Paul 'Basil' Fox, Stan was travelling on the Falls Road when they were stopped by British Army forces at La Salle Drive near Beechmount. The British Army opened fire and though his comrade managed to escape, Stan was mortally wounded.

Stan Carberry died on 13th November 1972.

Óglach John Brady

8th June 1952 - 28th November 1972

John was the sixth child of a family of ten.

Football and snooker were the joys of his life. He was an excellent football player and in his teenage years, took trials to play for Derry Youths, but the troubles came along and that put paid to that. Spurs were his favourite team and he supported them until the day he died.

When John left school he went into the shoe factory in Springtown and remained there until he was made redundant. That same year he and a friend went to Butlins holiday camp in Wales where they had a ball, returning, not wiser, but in excellent spirits, to find the riots in Derry in full swing. Soon after, John joined the IRA.

Throughout these years he played an active role with his unit and, until Operation Motorman, lived as normal a life as possible. After that he was constantly on the run, sleeping in safe houses until the day he died.

I remember there was one special girl in his life and I always felt that he would have ended up with her had things been different. As brothers and sisters we all went out together and the summer of 1972 was one of the best I can remember and the last we had with John, so all these memories remain with us forever.

Tuesday 28th November 1972 was the day John died on active service alongside Volunteer Jimmy Carr, and life was never the same for our family again.

The Brady Family

Óglach Jimmy Carr

3rd April 1953 - 28th November 1972

Jimmy Carr was a great sportsman and liked nothing better than to display his skills during the inter-street matches played around the Wells where he lived up to the early '70s. He also loved music and playing snooker in the "Star."

One of Jimmy's first encounters with state violence was when he and his father were assaulted by the RUC who had attacked the residents and their homes on St. Columb's Wells during 1969. This was just one of the many episodes which Jimmy witnessed that made determined to fight back. Jimmy joined the IRA.

Although Jimmy worked hard as a joiner around the city he was also active in his role as a volunteer. He was always careful to ensure his security was protected. This allowed him to escape the regular "swoops" on republicans, and to take part in active service at any time. During this period Jimmy was one of those Volunteers who carried the war to the heart of the enemy.

On 27th November several members of Cumann na mBan brought a supply of explosives to a house in the Bogside. The next morning of 28th November 1972 Jimmy and John Brady prepared for the operation but shortly after 11am one of the charges went off accidentally and Jimmy and John were killed.

Volunteer Jimmy Carr and Volunteer John Brady were buried in the City Cemetery which were conducted with full military honours.

Fiann Bernard Fox

16th January 1956 - 4th December 1972

Bernard Fox was born in Ardoyne in 1956. He attended St Gabriel's Secondary School, Crumlin Road.

He was always extremely security conscious, very few people were aware of his participation in Na Fianna Éireann. News of his death came as a severe shock to his family.

After the death of his schoolmate, friend and comrade Fiann David McAuley in February 1972, Bernard took part in the guard of honour at David's funeral.

On Monday December 4th 1972, Bernard who had risen to a leadership position in the local Fianna unit was shot dead. Another young man was wounded. They were on stand-by protecting the area from loyalist attacks. They were in a house in Brompton Park and the British Army opened fire, killing Bernard and wounding his friend. The British Army claimed that they had come under fire.

Bernard Fox was aged 16 when he was killed.

Óglach Louis Leonard

22nd July 1946 - 15th December 1972

Louis Leonard had recently married his partner Betty, the couple had an 11 month old son Tony and their butchery business was beginning to take off with Louis devoting up to 16 hours a day working hard to build up the new shop in Derrylin. Louis had everything to live for but on 15th December 1972 he was murdered by unknown assailants, widely believed to be British Forces. Having failed to come home on the night of 15th his family became suspicious and went to investigate. His brothers Hugh and Ciaran and brother in law Tom broke into the butcher's shop through a skylight and found Louis in the freezer room, he had been shot a number of times.

The murder of Louis was never properly investigated and the family were constantly harassed and intimidated by the British Army even disrupting Louis' wake at the family farm in Donagh. On one occasion the family solicitor was taken aside by a member of the RUC and threatened that he should drop any inquiries into Louis' death.

Louis Leonard was a handsome, clean cut young man, described as a local hero who was popular with his customers and in the area generally. Very fit and extremely athletic Louis played centre-half-back for Knock GFC, a team which he captained to honours. In 1994 St. Patrick's GFC's new ground was named Louis Leonard Memorial Park in his honour. The official program stated "Louis Leonard in his short life was an outstanding example of all the GAA stands for" and that it would be "some consolation that the name of this great sportsman and Irishman will be remembered for generations".

Óglach Eugene Devlin

22nd December 1950 - 27th December 1972

Volunteer Eugene Devlin was married with one child when he was killed on active service two days after Christmas Day in 1972. Eugene and a comrade were returning from an arms dump and were in the Head of the Town area of Strabane when they were spotted by a British Army patrol who opened fire without warning shooting both Volunteers. Though seriously injured his wounded comrade was taken to hospital and survived the shooting but Eugene, whose body lay at the scene for over an hour, died from his wounds.

A year after his death, Eugene's comrade refused to recognise the jurisdiction of a British court and from the dock paid tribute to his fallen comrade whose sacrifice he said "was in the pursuit of the noble and just cause of peace in Ireland."

A plaque, in memory of Volunteer Eugene Devlin, was erected close to the spot were he died but this was vandalised by the British army. However, the local residents, including many former prisoners were not going to let his memory fade. They worked hard and oversaw the construction of a plinth which now stands in Drumrallagh Estate, a fitting tribute to a respected member of their community, IRA Volunteer Eugene Devlin.

Eugene is forever remembered with pride by his family and by his friends and comrades in the Republican Movement in West Tyrone.

Óglach James (Junior) McDaid

29th January 1940 - 29th December 1972

Junior McDaid was a hard working family man. He and his wife Patsy had two children, both of whom died very young with cystic fibrosis. They lived in the Shantallow area of Derry.

Junior had many hobbies. He loved singing, playing football, and was instrumental in forming a Glasgow Celtic Supporters Club in Derry.

He joined the Republican struggle early on and was active in the Brandywell area. He later moved to Shantallow to become a member of the 3rd Battalion, Derry Brigade. He was also very active in Sinn Féin.

Junior was reputed to be the best, if not one of the best bricklayers in the city. Two of his finest works were the electricity sub station near Craigavon Bridge at Foyle Road and the Parochial House in Creggan, which he had just completed at the time of his arrest in Donegal on arms charges on 8th May 1972. He subsequently spent time in Mountjoy gaol and the Curragh Military Camp and was Adjutant of republican POW's. He undertook a successful hunger strike with other comrades for political status. Junior sustained an ulcer and was hospitalised for months.

On his release he reported back to Óglaigh na hÉireann the next day 9th December 1972. He was active until his untimely death on 29th December 1972 just 3 weeks after his release.

On the day of the ambush he and two comrades crossed the border at Ballynagard and on their to way to Donegal, they were confronted by undercover British forces who shot him dead. His comrades escaped.

Óglach Francis Liggett

27th January 1948 - 18th January 1973

Frances Liggett was born in Sussex Street in North Belfast on 27th January 1948. His interests included music and football and he was also a keen pigeon fancier. He was third in a family of six, with two older brothers, one younger brother and two young sisters. Francey, as he was known, was very tall and strong and worked as a labourer, rarely being out of work.

In 1972, Francey joined the Republican Movement. After Internment he felt the need to carry on the fight for freedom.

He was killed on the 18th January 1973, whilst on a fundraising operation at a branch of the Northern Bank inside the Royal Victoria Hospital. The Active Service Unit approached the bank and carried out the robbery, getting away with a large sum of money. He was detailed to cover the escape, but was shot dead by undercover members of the British Army during an exchange of gunfire. Because of his courage, his comrades managed to return safely to base.

Maureen and Francey were married just six weeks before he was killed. They had gone out together for most of their teenage years and were a very devoted young couple. They were living next door to Maureen's parents, a well-known Republican family in the area. The people of St James and the surrounding area were devastated by the tragedy.

Francey was a true gentleman, and is still remembered by the people of St James.

Óglach James Sloan

19th June 1953 - 3rd February 1973

Jim Sloan was born on 19th June 1953 and lived at 99 Lepper Street, in the New Lodge area of North Belfast. He attended St Thomas' School on the Whiterock Road in West Belfast and upon leaving school he went on to serve his time as a chef.

At the time of his death, Jim was married, and his son, Jim Junior, was born shortly after his father's death.

Jim senior was shot dead by unknown gunmen on the New Lodge Road on 3rd February 1973 at the age of 19. Five others were killed in the same incident. In all three Volunteers and three civilians died, when the gunmen opened fire from a passing car in conjunction with British soldiers who were based in Duncairn Gardens as part of a co-ordinated attack on the nationalist New Lodge community.

Jim Sloan was buried in a joint funeral with two comrades, Vols 'T.C.' Campbell and Jim McCann who died in the same incident. As the hearses and mourners moved towards the junction of Conway Street and the Falls Road, loyalist gunmen from the Shankill area attacked the funeral, aiming a long burst of gunfire at the funeral cortege. Two of the mourners were injured.

Óglach James McCann

10th May 1955 - 3rd February 1973

Jimmy McCann was born on 10th May 1955 at Hartwell Street, off the New Lodge Road. He was the youngest child and, as such, was greatly loved by his family. Educated at St Patrick's Christian Brothers' School, Bearnageeha, he went on to become an apprentice upholsterer. He worked at this alongside his brother, Hugh.

Friends knew Jimmy as a quiet, unassuming man who was very intelligent and kind. Not a great one for the drink he could, however, enjoy a couple of lagers. He was a keen footballer and a devout Glasgow Celtic supporter.

Jimmy was a staunch trade unionist and socialist and this deep commitment to justice led him to join the Republican Movement in October/November 1971. He was shot and wounded on one occasion before the fateful day in 1973.

On 3rd February 1973 Jimmy and his comrade, Óglach Jim Sloan were at the corner of the New Lodge Road when they were shot by unknown gunmen firing from a passing car. Both Volunteers were unarmed at the time. Óglach Jim Sloan died immediately at the spot.

Óglach Tony Campbell

3rd February 1954 - 4th February 1973

Tony Campbell, nicknamed 'T.C.', was born on 3rd February 1954. He lived in Artillery House on the New Lodge Road and attended the nearby St Patrick's School.

At ten years of age, he joined the Newsboys Club and played football for them; he also took part in their drama group and travelled to England with their 'Black and White Minstrels' troupe to take part in a number of shows and competitions.

Growing up in North Belfast, T.C. would have seen at first hand the failures of the sectarian State and in 1970, like many others in his area, he joined the Republican Movement. There was already a tradition of Republicanism in the Campbell family, one of his brothers was imprisoned for their Republican beliefs and his grandfather, Johnnie Casey, had been interned in the 1920s.

A happy type of person, who enjoyed dancing and meeting people in general, T.C. had been out celebrating his 19th birthday when he was shot dead by British troops, dying on 4th February 1973. Five other people, including two other unarmed Volunteers, were also brutally murdered that same night and they became known as the 'New Lodge Six'.

Tony had been walking along Edlingham Street when the British soldiers opened fire from the Duncairn Gardens area.

Óglach Vivien Fitzsimmons

26th July 1955 - 10th February 1973

Vivien was born in 1955 and lived all her young life with her parents and brothers in Lynn Doyle Place in Downpatrick. As a young girl Vivien attended Assumption Grammar School in Ballynahinch while at the same time working part-time in the local newsagents. From there she went on to study at Belfast College of Business Studies.

As a young Nationalist growing up in the late 60s and early 70s, Vivien was acutely aware of the injustices that were prevalent in the six counties during that time. Like so many young people of her generation Vivien decided that she could not just sit idly by and she made the conscious decision to became involved in the Republican struggle by joining Cumann na mBan.

Those who knew her remember her as a young girl who, while full of life, was deeply dedicated to righting the injustices she saw being perpetrated against her community. She sought to play as full a role as possible in that struggle and it was that willingness to play an active role despite her tender years that saw her at the scene of the fateful explosion that claimed the life of herself and her comrade Leo Hanlon.

Vivien was tragically killed alongside her comrade Leo Hanlon in Castleward Park, near Strangford on the 10th of February 1973 when the bomb they were preparing accidently exploded.

Óglach Leo Hanlon

22nd April 1949 - 10th February 1973

Leo Hanlon was born in 1949 and lived with his wife and young son, Michael at Vianstown Park, Downpatrick. As a young man he overcame many of the injustices faced by people from a Nationalist background and managed, through hard work and ability to become a schoolteacher.

He taught in Portaferry Secondary School and, acutely aware of the discrimination and prejudice faced by his young students, he joined in the battle for Civil Rights and was instrumental in establishing the Civil Rights Movement in Downpatrick.

However, Leo realised that civil rights alone would not bring lasting peace to Ireland and, risking his academic future he made the brave and conscious decision to join the local unit of the IRA.

Just as in his work with the Civil Rights Movement, he brought a passion and determination to his Republican activity and those around him, particularly the younger Volunteers showed great respect for his leadership and vision.

Leo was killed alongside his comrade Vivien Fitzsimmons while they were on active service in Castleward Park near Strangford, at 7.45pm on Saturday 10th February 1973.

His death was a severe loss to the Republican Movement in the South Down area.

Óglach Patrick McCabe

17th May 1956 - 27th March 1973

Patrick 'Pat' McCabe was born on 17th May 1956 in Duneden Park, along with his twin brother Gerard, who tragicaly died at birth. One of 6 children, Pat also lost his mother at the age of 14.

Pat attended Holy Cross Boys' School and St Gabriel's Secondary School, where he excelled at art. He was a studious young man who had considered a vocation with the priesthood.

Pat joined the Fianna at the age of 13, but he was also an active member of St Gabriel's Youth Club and was passionate about Judo.

At the time of his death Pat was training to be a motor mechanic.

On 27th March 1973, at the age of 15, Pat was shot dead by the British Army in Etna Drive, Ardoyne, whilst on active service.

Óglach Edward O'Rawe

1st August 1945 - 12th April 1973

Edward O'Rawe from 7, Garnet Street in the Lower Falls area was born on 1st August 1945. He was educated at the nearby St Peter's School, Raglan Street. He was nicknamed 'Mundo'.

On leaving school he found work as a docker, he became a member of the Irish Transport and General Workers Union. He joined Na Fianna Éireann at about the same time. His hobbies included hurling, which he played for the Michael Dwyer Gaelic Athletic Club.

Having emigrated to England to work, he returned to Belfast in 1969, as the present phase of the liberation struggle was beginning. Mundo joined the IRA in Ballymurphy and later transferred to 'D' Company based in the Lower Falls area.

On April 12th 1973, Mundo was shot dead by British troops. Shortly before the shooting the British Army were photographed searching Mundo and a companion, Sean Rowntree. Both men were unarmed when they were shot.

Óglach Brian Smyth

23rd October 1941 - 17th April 1973

Brian Smyth, of 43 Oldpark Avenue in the Cliftonville area of North Belfast, was born on 23rd October 1941. He was educated at the Sacred Heart School and went on to work as a labourer. He was shot dead while unarmed by British soldiers at Etna Drive, Ardoyne, on 17th April 1973.

It was later revealed by one of the soldiers, Chris Hendley, that he had been ordered to open fire on a group of unarmed men and that the officer in charge, a Major Burt, had concocted a story for the British soldiers to tell the court in order to cover up the murder.

Although there was no evidence of the existence of a weapon, a friend of Brian's was arrested, charged and sentenced for possession of a weapon. Following the revelations by the former British soldier, Chris Hendley, in an article in the Daily Mirror, the British had no option but to release Brian's friend from jail. The British Army's Major Burt, however, was never charged with any offence.

Óglach Tony Ahern

15th November 1955 - 10th May 1973

Tony Ahern was born in Cork in 1955. The Ahern family lived at St Joseph's Park, Mayfield, in Cork City. Tony was the youngest of five brothers. With his friend and comrade Dermot Crowley, Tony went to the North Monastery School and also joined the Clann Eireann Athletic Club. He represented both Club and County in juvenile and youth events in athletics.

Standing over six feet tall with a big physique, Tony was a very determined, committed and mature young man. The events of the late 1960s and early 1970's made an indelible impression on him. Like many other young Volunteers in Cork he was determined to play his part in the struggle for Irish Freedom. He continually pressed the local leadership to go on active service and eventually he left to fight with the IRA in Fermanagh.

The active service unit he was attached to had planted a land mine to target British Forces which had been using the Roslea/Clogh Road. The mine went off accidently and Tony was killed on 10 May 1973. Tony had not yet reached his 18th Birthday. He is buried in Carraigaline, Co Cork.

Óglach Kevin Kilpatrick

26th May 1952 - 13th May 1973

Kevin Kilpatrick was born on 26th May 1952 in County Tyrone where he was to spend his whole life. Kevin was one of six children born to Joseph and Elizabeth Kilpatrick and in his early years he became a pupil of Annaghmore Primary School. On leaving school he began training to become a mechanic, being a natural he successfully completed his apprenticeship in Lyttle's Garage, in Coalisland.

Kevin was a keen sportsman especially Gaelic games and he was a popular playing member of first Clonoe O'Rahilley G.F.C. and then with Derrytresk, Fir na Cnoic.

Those who knew Kevin as a young Volunteer and friend said of him:

"He was some pup, very game, nobody as game as Kevin, not then, not since."

And of his ability for enjoying life and the craic,

"He had a fantastic personality, - a devilish, devilish sense of humour."

Volunteer Kevin Kilpatrick was shot by the Ulster Defence Regiment on the 13th of May 1973 in the Diamond area, Ardboe. He had been on the run from the British forces for just over a year, and it was less than a week before his 21st birthday. He is buried in Clonoe Cemetery.

Óglach Joseph McKenna

November 1948 - 17th May 1973

Joseph McKenna was born in November 1948 in a small kitchen house in Fort Street in the shadow of Mackies Foundry - where no Catholic worked in those days. The son of Louis and Sarah McKenna, he was the ninth of ten children and was educated in the Christian Brothers School, St Gall's, and then went on to St Thomas' on the Whiterock Road. Born with only partial movement in his left arm he overcame this disability and went on to become a French polisher.

From an early age he showed a great interest in Irish culture and politics. In 1970 he got married and along with his wife and daughter he left the Falls to live in George's Street.

The murals that now adorn the walls in Belfast originated with Joseph and his comrades. Joseph was one of the first to paint symbols on gable walls, much to the disgust of the people who owned the gable walls, including Mackies Foundry.

In April 1973, as he walked along the Grosvenor Road on his way to meet his wife in the city centre he was shot from a passing car outside the Oak Bar. Though not fatally injured, his injuries left him a quadriplegic.

He was in the Royal Victoria Hospital for a short time before being transferred to the spinal injuries unit at Musgrave Park. Sadly he died due to complications on 17th May 1973. Ironically his nephew Joseph was born on 17th May 1979, six years to the day after the death of his uncle.

Joseph is buried in Milltown Cemetery alongside his parents.

Óglach Thomas O'Donnell

15th July 1931 - 17th May 1973

Thomas O'Donnell, from the Short Strand in Belfast, was born on 15th July 1931. He was educated at St Matthew's Primary School in Seaforde Street before going on to work as a joiner for George McCann Ltd in Madrid Street in 1946.

At the age of 18 Tom joined the Republican Movement. He was interned in 1957 in the Crumlin Road Jail. Shortly after his release he married Nancy Rooney, on 18th February 1958. They had eight children.

In 1966, Tom started his own building and contracting business. Three years later however, due to his increasing Republican activity, he was forced to go on the run. He was arrested in England along with another Short Strand man, Jim George in 1970. They were held for six months in Brixton Prison on a charge of attempting to procure arms. Eventually the charges were dropped and Tom was able to return home to assist with the massive reorganisation process, which was taking place within the Republican Movement.

Tom's commitment to the Republican freedom struggle was absolute. His dedicated and unselfish manner in carrying out his duties soon guaranteed him a place on the General Headquarters Staff of Óglaigh na hÉireann.

In February 1973 Tom was seriously injured in a car accident near Drogheda while on Active Service. Tom's heroic spirit kept him alive for several months despite his injuries, but he died in Dublin's Richmond Hospital on 17th May 1973.

Óglach Seán McKee

24th January 1956 - 18th May 1973

Sean McKee was born on 24th January 1956. The only son of Bobby, from the Falls Road, and Alice Murray, from the Docks, Sean had a sister named Maureen. He attended Holy Cross Primary School before moving on to St Gabriel's Secondary School on the Crumlin Road.

When he left school in 1971, he served his time as an apprentice asphalter. A happy go lucky lad of 6ft 1in he is remembered by all who knew him as the big fellow who was always laughing and smiling. Known by his nickname, Sid, he was good at all sports. He loved football, snooker and handball and played football for the Star of the Sea team in the Down and Connor League. He was a keen Spurs fan.

Sean was always keen to join the Republican Movement and became a member of the Fianna before joining the Army in Ardoyne at the age of 17, during a period when it was being hard hit by many arrests and imprisonments. On 18th May 1973, Sean and his comrades planned to engage British soldiers outside Toby's Hall in Butler Street. As he left a house in Fairfield, with his rifle concealed in his coat, undercover soldiers in the roof space of an empty house ambushed him.

Sean was shot in the chest and killed and a comrade was wounded but managed to escape. A woman who tried to help him was threatened by British troops who put a gun to her head and forced her away. Sean was then brutally kicked and jumped upon and tossed into a Saracen armoured car. As the troops drove off a priest who tried to get to Sean to give him the last rites was verbally abused.

Óglach Dermot Crowley

26th August 1954 - 25th June 1973

The name of Dermot Crowley is forever linked in memory with that of his life long friend Tony Ahern. They grew up together in Mayfield, Co. Cork and went to school together in the "North Mon". They had noted careers in sports and both he and Tony represented their club, Clann Eireann, and their County in juvenile and youth athletics, winning numerous trophies. Dermot was the much loved son of May and Jerry, and brother to Donal, Colm, June and twin sisters, Catherine and Rosaleen.

The uprising and terrible suffering of the Irish people in the North in the early 1970's found in Dermot a staunch defender. From early 1972 he was on active service with the 1st Battalion, East Tyrone, where for over a year, he distinguished himself through his coolness, calm approach and determination.

Dermot was heart broken when his friend and comrade Volunteer Tony Ahern, not yet turned 18, was killed in Fermanagh on the 10th May 1973 while inspecting a land-mine on the Roslea/Clogh Road. Tony is widely remembered as having the greatest respect for Dermot. This respect was mutual and they complemented each other's attributes, Tony being of big physique and kindly humour, and Dermot having mature and constructive debating skills. They made a great team.

Volunteer Dermot Ahern was killed while transporting a bomb near Omagh, on 25th June 1973, in the company of two Tyrone Volunteers, Sean Loughran and Patrick Carty, all three died.

Volunteer Dermot Crowley is buried in Rathcooney, County Cork. He was 18 years old when he died.

Óglach Sean Loughran

8th March 1936 - 25th June 1973

"The Crow" Loughran, as Sean was better known to his wide circle of friends and comrades is described as having had "a wonderful wit and sense of humour which would have enlivened any company". "The Crow" is a nickname which refers to the fact that Sean had intensely dark black hair.

Sean was born in Dungannon, County Tyrone in 1936; he was first interned because of his role during the 1950s campaign, and later in 1964, when he was captured at an Army training camp in County Waterford. Upon his release Sean decided to move to England where he got married to Pauline and had two children.

At the end of the sixties/early seventies Seán was unable to watch the events unfolding in Ireland from abroad and he decided to come home in the early part of the seventies. Sean immediately returned to active service. His comrades recall him as a "daring volunteer who played a full role in the struggle". It was with an immense sense of loss that they laid him to rest in St. Malachy's Graveyard, Edendork on Thursday 28th June 1973.

Volunteer Sean Loughran died on the 25th June 1973 as a result of an accidental explosion which occurred on the outskirts of Omagh. Killed alongside him were his comrades Volunteer Dermot Crowley, a native of County Cork and Volunteer Patrick Carty, originally from Bundoran, Co. Donegal. Sean was 37 years old when killed on active service.

Óglach Patrick Carty

13th July 1945 - 25th June 1973

Patrick was originally from Bundoran, but moved with his family to Dungannon when aged 11. He decided to join the I.R.A. after the B Specials attacked a Civil Rights demonstration he attended; two of his friends and a young girl were shot and injured. At the time of his death he held the distinction of being a wanted man on both sides of the border. In 1972 he "ghosted" his way out the main gate of the Glass House, Curragh Military Camp. At this point he was wanted in the North. He evaded capture by first avoiding cameras, as the state forces failed to find a suitable photograph for his "wanted" poster.

It was to Tyrone he returned after his escape, and returned immediately to active service. It was no surprise then that at his graveside oration he was described as a fearless young man, modest in manner and above all else dedicated to the Republican cause. His other love was Gaelic football. As a youth he played for Dungannon Clarkes and the day before his death had been in Ballybofey for the Tyrone v Donegal game.

Volunteer Patrick Carty died on June 25th 1973 when the bomb he and his two comrades, Volunteer Sean Loughran and Volunteer Dermot Crowley were transporting exploded accidentally. Counties Tyrone and Donegal united in their respect for Patrick and their grief at his death, had resolutions passed naming Dungannon and Bundoran Sinn Féin Cumainn in his memory.

Óglach Pauline Kane

22nd April 1922 - 21st July 1973

Pauline was born into a large family in the Burrenbridge area just outside Castlewellan. At the time of her death she lived at 6 Burrenreagh Park and indeed her family were close neighbours of the Rice family who would themselves lose a son on active service.

As a young girl Pauline attended school in the locality and is remembered as being a girl who was full with a zest of life. Like many young people of her generation she was deeply affected by the campaign for civil rights and the brutal response by the British Army to that campaign with the massacre of Bloody Sunday. Like so many young women of her generation Pauline decided that the best way to combat the injustices in our country was in the ranks of the Cumann na mBan.

Despite being only 21 years of age at the time of her death, Pauline was already highly regarded by her comrades in the locality. She tragically lost her life on active service in Newcastle through an accidental explosion when the car in which she and two comrades were travelling was blown up. Her comrade and boyfriend Alphonsus Cunningham was killed alongside her that day while another comrade Mick Doran suffered severe injuries. She was the seventh and thus far last Republican from the South Down locality to have lost their life as a result of an accidental explosion.

Óglach Alphonsus Cunningham

30th November 1951 - 21st July 1973

Alphonsus Cunningham was born on the 30th November 1951 and lived all his short life at the family home at 4 Dunmore Cottages, Glassdrumman, where he attended the local Primary School before moving to St Columban's Secondary School in Kilkeel. On leaving school he went into the plumbing business and became an excellent tradesman.

His two main passions in life, outside of his love for his country and its people, were cars and his local GAA club, where he was a popular member. A gifted footballer he took part in the semi-final of the Longstone tournament the week before he died. The final, which Glassdrumman went on to win, was postponed as a mark of respect to Alphonsus.

He was a young lad of 22 who was full of life and like other lads of his generation he enjoyed socializing, whether driving around in his old Renault 10 or in his local club with his mates.

An active member of the Republican Movement in the Mournes, he brought his footballing passion and tradesman's skills to his work with the local IRA unit.

He lost his life as a result of an accidental explosion alongside his comrade Pauline Kane during an IRA operation in Newcastle on the 21st July 1973.

Óglach Gerard McGlynn

June 1955 - 10th August 1973

Volunteer Gerard McGlynn was a native of Castlederg and lived on the Castlefin Road just outside the town. He was a popular and highly committed Volunteer who often left his place of work, sometimes at a moment's notice, to play his part in the fight for Irish Freedom.

On the 10th August 1973, Gerard and his comrade Seamus Harvey were transporting a bomb and were about 200 yards from the customs post at Kilclean, on the Donegal border, when the device accidently exploded killing both volunteers instantly.

Although only 18 years old at the time of his death, Gerard was a seasoned Volunteer who had taken part in many operations against the British in the border region. Like many of the young men of his age from the Castlederg and Strabane areas he knew the risks that had to be taken and he was determined in his pursuit of his objectives.

In a statement released shortly afterwards the West Tyrone Brigade of Óglaigh na hÉireann said; "The fact that one of the young Volunteers had appeared in the Special Criminal Court in Dublin as recently as last week shows the determination, commitment and dedication of both these young men. They firmly believed in the cause for which they fought and they made the supreme sacrifice for their beliefs. We, their comrades, shall hold their names and memories dear."

Óglach Seamus Harvey

6th June 1951 - 10th August 1973

Seamus was a married man with a young family and had been living in Co Donegal for about eighteen months prior to his death. Because of his Republican activities he was forced to flee his home town and live life 'on the run' across the border.

At the young age of 22 this must have been a terrible burden for Seamus and his family but, like many others, he was not deterred by his forced exile and returned across the border many times during this period to engage the British forces based in the area. He was very active in West Tyrone and was well respected within his local brigade.

A few weeks before his death Seamus and three other young men appeared in court in Dublin charged with IRA membership and possession of weapons. The threat of a lengthy prison term did not deter him from continuing to remain active within the ranks of the IRA.

On the 10th August 1973, Seamus, along with Gerard McGlynn, were on active service and they were travelling in a car towards the Donegal border. When they were about 200 yards from the customs post at Kilclean, the bomb they were transporting accidently exploded killing both volunteers instantly.

Óglach Daniel McAnallen

18th February 1946 - 16th August 1973

Dan McAnallen was 27 years old when he died. He was survived by his mother, Hannah, three brothers, three sisters and his young wife, Bertha.

Dan died during an attack on Pomeroy R.U.C. barracks, on 16th August 1973. Shortly after 10 o'clock on that Thursday night a rocket launcher misfired during the operation. The explosion was responsible for the deaths of Volunteer Patrick Joseph Quinn and Dan. The bodies of the two volunteers were found at daylight the next morning at Best's Crossroads on the Ballygawley Road.

A British Army statement said that the two volunteers had received attention from a local priest and a doctor. Their remains were taken to Dungannon Hospital, from where they were carried to the Donaghmore Road for the Final Salute.

Daniel McAnallen was buried in Eglish with full military honours. His graveside oration was delivered by Sinn Féin Vice President, Máire Drumm, who was herself later shot by loyalists in Belfast's Mater Hospital. At the time of his death Volunteer Dan McAnallen was a member of the East Tyrone Battalion.

A statement in the local newspaper after the funeral of Daniel McAnallen reported that the British soldiers "joked and laughed, appearing to enjoy the anguish of his wife, mother and family."

"Fuair sé bas as son Saoirse na hÉireann.
Go ndeanfaidh Dia trocaire ar a anam."

Óglach Patrick Quinn

20th July 1957 - 16th August 1973

Patrick Joseph Quinn was born on 20th July 1957. The oldest son of Rose and Alfie, the family moved to Lisnahull in Dungannon in 1972, having lived in Belfast for a time. He was a quiet lad, thoughtful by nature with a talent for sport. He joined St. Anne's Boxing Club and had a job in Tyrone Crystal.

When 15, he was captured transporting a weapon. Remanded to the Crumlin Road Gaol for 3 months and then St. Patrick's Training School. Patsy escaped from St. Pat's and went to Monaghan.

On August 16th 1973 Patsy was part of an Active Service Unit which attacked Pomeroy RUC barracks. The attack lasted for almost 20 minutes, during which the barracks was raked with fire from three positions and pounded with mortars from a fourth. During the operation, a rocket launcher misfired and killed Patsy and Dan McAnallen. Due to the heavy fire from the RUC barracks, Patsy and Dan's bodies were placed in a shelter at Best's Crossroads.

Patsy was buried with full military honours, in accordance with his and his family's wishes. Girls and women carrying wreaths marched behind the coffin, which was flanked by uniformed members of Na Fianna Éireann. He rests in St. Malachy's Cemetery, Edendork.

Volunteer Patsy Quinn was aged 16 years and one month when he died on that Thursday night. It was his parent's 17th wedding anniversary. He was a much loved son, brother and friend.

Óglach Francis Hall

17th February 1944 - 30th August 1973

Francis 'Freddie' Hall, was born in the Shore Road area of Belfast, on the 17th February 1944. He was educated at St.Patrick's, Bearnageeha.

When he left school at the age of 16, Freddie joined the Merchant Navy. In 1965, when he was 21, Freddie married. Two years later, he left the Merchant Navy and took up employment as a steel erector.

Freddie joined the Republican Movement in late 1970, and his dedication gained him the respect of his comrades, and all who knew him. He was part of an experienced and active unit that operated throughout the six counties.

In August 1973, Freddie and his comrade, Volunteer Anne Marie Pettigrew, were both seriously injured in Elaine Street, off the Stranmillis Road in Belfast. It was the result of an accidental explosion.

One week after the explosion Volunteer Freddie Hall died on 30th August 1973. He left a young widow and a five-month-old son. His comrade, Cumann na mBan Volunteer, Anne Marie Pettigrew, died from her injuries two days later on September 1st.

Volunteer Freddie Hall was buried alongside his comrades in the Republican plot in Milltown Cemetery, Belfast.

Óglach Patrick Mulvenna

5th February 1954 - 31st August 1973

Patrick Mulvenna was born on 5th February 1954, the eldest of a family of six. He lived in Ardoyne, North Belfast and later moved to the West Belfast district of Ballymurphy. He attended St Kevin's Primary School before he moved on to St Thomas's Secondary School. After leaving school he worked as an apprentice joiner. He continued at this until the outbreak of the present phase of the struggle in 1969.

He then joined Na Fianna Éireann where he helped to form the first Fianna slua in the Ballymurphy area. Following the introduction of Internment in August 1971, Patrick was to spend the rest of his life on the run.

On 31st August 1973, he was ambushed in Ballymurphy along with several of his comrades by British troops who were stationed in a secret observation post above the shops in the Bullring. Paddy died instantly. Two other Volunteers, including Jim Bryson, were seriously wounded in the attack. Jim Bryson died from the wounds he received in this ambush on 22nd September.

Both Paddy and Jim died as a direct result of trouble then going on with the armed wing of the so-called Workers Party. Members of the Workers Party openly gloated at the deaths of the Volunteers. They were disappointed that they had not killed them.

Óglach Anne Marie Pettigrew

9th February 1954 - 1st September 1973

Anne Marie Pettigrew was born on 9th February 1954 in the Oldpark area of North Belfast. She went to school locally at the Sacred Heart Primary School until the family moved to West Belfast.

She continued her education at St Kevin's Primary School in the Falls Road area and then at St Rose's Secondary School in Beechmount until she was 15. She then went to work as a trainee hairdresser. She left this employment and became a trainee dressmaker in Beltex Mills off the Crumlin Road, however because of sectarian attacks in the area she was forced to leave her job.

Anne Marie joined Cumann na mBan in early 1971. A cheerful outgoing person she became a dedicated volunteer. She specialised in explosives and became part of a unit which planted incendiary bombs all over the North. Her background was Republican, her great-uncle Samuel was a Volunteer during the Twenties who escaped from jail in the Free State and took refuge in the Wicklow hills.

In August 1973, alongside her comrade Volunteer Francis Hall, incendiary devices they were using exploded and both Volunteers were very badly burned.

Anne Marie died from her injuries in hospital a week later on 1st September 1973. Francis Hall had died two days previous.

Óglach Francis Dodds

8th October 1941 - 9th September 1973

Francis Dodds of 73 Locan Street, Belfast was born on 8th October 1941. Frankie, as he was better known was arrested on September 20th 1972 when a car he had hired was found to contain a quantity of explosives. Charged with possession of explosives Frankie was remanded to Long Kesh. He arrived at the Cage barefoot after his interrogators confiscated the shoes he had been wearing.

Later that night there was some trouble in the prison camp between the POWs and the prison administration. The British Army was sent into the cages to 'pacify' the POW's and Frankie suffered a severe beating. His injuries were so bad that when his wife visited him in hospital the next day his arms were heavily bandaged and he was unable to walk without the aid of crutches.

After a long spell on remand, Frankie was released on bail and it was then that he discovered he had contracted varicose disease of the legs.

When eventually his trial was heard in Belfast's High Court, Frankie was sentenced to 4 years imprisonment, which he began on 17th March 1973. His leg began increasingly to disturb him but when he told the prison doctor he was given only aspirin to ease the pain. On September 9th 1973, the Republican POWs in Long Kesh were stunned and saddened when they heard that Frankie had collapsed and died while playing table tennis in the canteen hut. According to comrades his death could have been avoided if proper attention to and care for the POWs had been forthcoming.

Instead the complete lack of any useful medical provisions within the camp resulted in this young Volunteer's death.

Óglach James Bryson

29th April 1948 - 22nd September 1973

James Emerson Bryson, from Ballymurphy, was born on 29th April 1948. On leaving St Thomas's Secondary School, Whiterock Road, he found work as an apprentice bricklayer. Marrying in August 1969, Jim and his wife had one son, also named Jim.

Shortly after internment was introduced, Jim joined the ranks of Óglaigh na hÉireann. He was arrested on 29th December 1971 and interned on the 'Maidstone' but with six comrades he escaped to freedom only 19 days later, on 17th January 1972. Living a life on the run, yet constantly engaging in actions against the British, Jim remained free until September 1972, when he was arrested, charged with possession of a handgun and remanded to Long Kesh. However, within six months of his capture he had devised an escape plan.

On 20th February 1973, whilst himself and a fellow POW were being taken along the tunnel which links Crumlin Road Jail with the courthouse, they overpowered their prison warders and stripped them of their uniforms. The plan was to coolly walk through the court building and escape by commandeering a car on the Crumlin Road. Only Jim was successful. Once out of the building he disposed of the borrowed uniform and headed for the Shankill Road, where he stopped a car and asked for a lift to the Royal Victoria Hospital saying his wife had been taken there. The occupants of the car obliged, dropping him off at Divis Street, from where he walked to a safe house. After the news of his second escape hit the headlines, it was revealed that the two occupants of the car had been armed UDR men.

Free again, Jim was soon active as an IRA volunteer. Jim and three comrades were travelling in a car in their native Ballymurphy on 31st August when British soldiers in a secret observation post opened fire on them. Vol. Paddy Mulvenna died instantly and Jim and another Volunteer were badly wounded. Jim died of his wounds on 22nd September 1973.

Óglach Michael McVerry

1st December 1949 - 15th November 1973

Michael McVerry was born on 1st December 1949, the first son of Michael and Claire McVerry. His only sister Carmel was two years older. He attended Cullyhanna Primary School, and from an early age was fascinated by Irish history. He attended Bessbrook Technical College, and then started work on various building sites around the Six Counties.

After Harry Thornton was shot dead by the British Army, Michael joined Óglaigh na hÉireann, quickly establishing himself as an example to other Volunteers by always leading from the front. Imprisoned in the Curragh Camp, he endured a hunger and thirst strike before escaping and immediately returning to the struggle.

Shortly after his escape he lost his hand on active service. However, despite his injuries he would not give up the fight. Michael was also a man before his time, and would often talk about how the armed struggle would ultimately lead to the negotiating table, predicting that talking would be harder than fighting.

Michael's tactical brain and raw courage were witnessed during many daring and successful operations throughout the South Armagh countryside where he became a local legend. In an operation where Michael typically led from the front, he was tragically killed during an attack on Keady Barracks on 15th November 1973.

The large turnout for his funeral and indeed for the unveiling of a monument in his honour, a year after his death, are testimony of the respect he earned and the esteem in which he was held by the people in his beloved South Armagh.

Fiann Michael Marley

6th August 1956 - 24th November 1973

Michael Joseph Marley was born on 6th August 1956 at 21 Sultan Street and reared at 10 Dunville Street. He was educated at St Peter's Primary School, Raglan Street and St Peter's Secondary School, Britton's Parade.

After leaving school Michael found work as an apprentice bricklayer with Farrans building contractors. His hobbies included football and, like most teenagers, he enjoyed going to dances with his mates.

It was his fondness for Irish culture and language that led him to enrol in classes to learn to speak in his native tongue. This love of his country and being a witness to the obvious oppression and discrimination that existed within his community, led him into the ranks of the Republican Movement.

Michael became a member of Na Fianna Éireann in September 1973 and just a few months later he was shot dead by the British Army while on active service in the Divis Flats area of the Lower Falls.

He was 17 years old at the time.

Óglach Desmond Morgan

4th February 1953 - 26th November 1973

Dessie was born in Brackaville on the 4th February 1953. The only son of Maureen and Jim "Dixie" Morgan. He had three sisters. He loved all sports and played for his local team, Owen Roes G.F.C. He also enjoyed soccer, and is remembered for his "brilliant left foot". He was also a frequent visitor to the old cinema at Lineside. Dessie was a happy-go-lucky lad who made friends easy. Upon leaving school he got an apprenticeship as a plumber. When Dessie was murdered the loss to the family was immeasurable. His father, Jim died of cancer in 1969 and Dessie was the man of the house. He was a great son and brother.

Parades to commemorate the 50th anniversary of the Easter Rising were banned but undeterred, the people of Coalisland assembled to remember the events of 1916 and as they passed Patterson's Corner, 13 year old Desmond Morgan joined in. Two years later on Saturday the 24th August 1968, he was one of 3,000 people who marched for four miles from Coalisland to Dungannon, demanding their Civil Rights. Five years later, Dessie was shot by the R.U.C. on that same Dungannon Road. It was the 26th November 1973 and he died aged 19.

Coalisland was described by R.U.C. as, "a hostile, unfriendly and highly dangerous town." This was after the events of the July 1970. From early afternoon, the police blocked all roads into the town to enable the Orangemen from Newmills to march through the area. Given that local people were continually denied their right to assemble, this operation for the benefit of people not from Coalisland enraged local people. When they attempted to enter the Town Square that evening rioting broke out. In the thick of it was Dessie. That night when the C.S. gas cleared and the B men stopped firing Dessie Morgan headed home, and on his head, was a bowler hat. Shortly after that Dessie joined the I.R.A.

Volunteer Dessie Morgan is buried in the Republican Plot in St. Mary and St. Joseph's Cemetery overlooking Coalisland.

Óglach Joe Walker

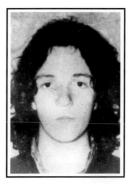

26th May 1955 – 3rd December 1973

Joe Walker, the son of Lily and Patsy, was the oldest in a family of ten children. He had two brothers and seven sisters. Being the oldest Joe assisted his parents in caring for the younger members of the family.

In his younger days Joe had a keen interest in racing pigeons. Unfortunately, his in-depth knowledge of the sport betrayed him when he mistakenly identified the wrong sex of two of his best pigeons for over a one-year period!

As the conflict deepened, Joe endured a particularly hard time during his detention for a three day period in the infamous Ballykelly Interrogation Centre. Joe was an apprentice butcher in his final year with a well-known firm in Derry. Shortly before his untimely death, Joe was awarded compensation for a hand injury he received during his time with the firm.

Ironically, despite receiving a substantial amount of compensation for his personal injury, Joe never got to enjoy his money as he was killed in action less than a week after receiving it. But then, money was never a motivating factor for Joe.

Joe was shot and killed during a shooting incident in the Creggan Estate on Monday 3rd December 1973. Along with other comrades, Joe engaged British forces in the Rath area of Creggan. Unfortunately, a British foot patrol was hidden in the Central Drive area and opened fire on the hijacked taxi from which Joe had earlier fired over fifteen shots at the enemy. Despite dying at the relatively young age of eighteen, Joe had participated in quite a few attacks upon British forces in the Creggan.

Óglach Jim McGinn

2nd October 1953 - 15th December 1973

Jim McGinn was born in Strabane and was twenty years old at the time of his death on 15th December 1973. With an outgoing character and friendly nature he was renowned for his sense of humour that endeared him to young and old alike.

He had a great love for his native culture and this was reflected in his involvement with An Comhaltas Ceolteoiri Éireann. He was an active participant in the struggle for Civil Rights and was an avid reader, who was influenced by the writings of James Connolly. It is said that Connolly's writings left a deep impression on him and instilled in him the desire to struggle for social and economic justice and to actively challenge British rule in his country.

A full-time active service volunteer with the West Tyrone Brigade of Óglaigh na hÉireann, Jim and three other volunteers from his unit were preparing an attack on British forces in the Clady bridge area when the bomb they were transporting exploded. Volunteer Jim McGinn was killed instantly and his three comrades were injured, one seriously.

As news of his death spread throughout his native Strabane, black flags were flown from homes throughout the town in a spontaneous gesture that showed the respect in which he was held from within the wider West Tyrone community.

Óglach Brendan Quinn

10th June 1955 - 24th December 1973

Brendan Quinn was born in Daisy Hill Hospital, Newry on 10th June 1955. His parents Tommy and Eileen were from South Armagh and he was the third oldest of five children. With his brother Tom and sisters Margaret, Ann, Deirdre and Teresa, Brendan was part of a tight knit family unit. Proud of its cultural tradition, it was also steeped in republican history. His grandfather James Quinn from Fountain Street, Bessbrook was a member of the Fourth Northern Division, IRA and was arrested following an attack on Camloch RIC Barracks. James's sister, Nan Quinn, was a member of Cumann na mBan. It was she who taught Brendan both history and dancing lessons.

Brendan attended St Joseph's Primary School, Cloughreagh and finished at St Paul's High School. He left school at 15 and worked at J&J Foods, Newry before moving to the meat factory for a short spell. He frequented the old Bosco in Linenhall Square and befriended Seán McKenna Snr, a well-known republican. Brendan joined the Paul Smith Sinn Féin Cumann, selling "Republican News" every week. He would continue his paper run every Sunday in Carlingford. He joined the ranks of Óglaigh na h-Éireann at 17, committed to breaking the link with England. Sincere in his republican beliefs, he proved to be a fearless soldier and a disciplinarian.

Three weeks before his death, Brendan had to go on the run. But in true family tradition, he returned with the intention of spending Christmas with them. On Christmas Eve morning, he left home in Cloughreagh, never to return alive.

On 24th December 1973, Brendan died along with his comrade Eddie Grant in an accidental explosion in Clarke's Bar (now known as the Armagh Down) in Monaghan Street. A customer was also tragically killed. Brendan is buried in the Republican Plot in Carrickcruppen beside a fellow comrade, Raymond McCreesh, who died on hunger-strike less than seven years later.

Ar dheis láimh Dé go raibh a h-anam uasal

132

Óglach Edward Grant

16th August 1956 - 24th December 1973

Charles Edward Grant, better known as Eddie, was born on the 16th August 1956 in Newry. He had six sisters and four brothers. His father Dominic and the rest of the family experienced personal grief when at the young age of 43, his wife Kitty died suddenly. This put immense pressure on the family as a whole. Eddie's sister Margie stepped into the 'mother's role'.

Eddie lived at Main Avenue, Derrybeg. He attended St Patrick's Primary School and then went on to Newry High School on the Ashgrove Road. When he left school, he went to work at the FMC meat factory on the Warrenpoint Road. This was a stopgap while waiting to join the Merchant Navy. Prior to the outbreak of the 'troubles' Eddie, like many others at that time joined the T.A. Cadets, which were based on the Downshire Road and where he gained some valuable military experience. Nicknamed 'Starchy' by his mates, he was best known in Derrybeg as a raker, always up to some devilment. He grew up with a group of friends who also took the same decision to join the ranks of Óglaigh na hEireánn. They went on to become a very effective fighting unit. He enjoyed all outdoor pursuits, especially camping. He also joined St Catherine's Band where he played the cymbals.

Eddie came from an old Republican family. His cousin Paul Smith died at Edentubber and his uncle John McEnerney was a Vice Commandant of the 4th Northern Division IRA. When he first decided to give his services to the cause, he attended a few Republican Club meetings with his friends, but he soon decided that his loyalty lay with the 'Provisionals'. No task was too great, he was always willing to Volunteer for active service.

On the 24th December 1973, Eddie and his comrade Brendan Quinn were killed in an accidental explosion at Clarke's Bar on Monaghan Street. Unfortunately a civilian also died alongside the two Volunteers. The memories he left behind are very precious to his family, friends and comrades.

Óglach Patrick McDonald

31st March 1952 - 15th March 1974

Patrick McDonald was born in Dungannon on the 31st March 1952, one of twin boys. He spent his early schooldays at the Presentation Brothers and St. Patrick's Secondary. Leaving school at 16, he was employed as a milk delivery man before going on to work in the local textile factory.

Paddy was known for his love of all things Irish. He played Gaelic and was renowned for many a verse of a good song. On Easter Sunday 1969, Paddy was in the Colour Party, the first in Dungannon to parade through the Market Square.

On the night of 15th March 1974, one remembered for its severe weather conditions, Paddy and his friend Kevin Murray were killed when the bomb they were planting exploded accidentally at the bridge near Shiel's Timber Yard, not far from their homes on the Ballygawley Road.

As the remains of the two neighbours were brought home from the local hospital, black flags hung from almost every home along the way.

Paddy was buried in the family plot in Edendork the following Monday morning. His comrade and neighbour Volunteer Kevin Murray having been laid to rest the previous day in the same cemetery. Over 70 wreaths were placed on each grave.

Among the mourners was Paddy's fiancée. They had been due to be married in August.

A dedicated soldier, Volunteer Paddy McDonald is missed by his family, his friends and his comrades.

Óglach Kevin Murray

9th March 1945 - 15th March 1974

Volunteer Kevin Murray was 29 when he was killed in an explosion in Dungannon, along with Volunteer Patrick McDonald, on Friday 15th March 1974. He was buried on St. Patrick's morning in St. Malachy's Cemetery, Edendork.

His family write,
"Volunteer Kevin Murray died on Active Service, 15th March '74. A loving father to us, his children, Helen, Colm, Edel and Kevin, he paid the supreme sacrifice, giving his life for his country. Our mother, Margaret, during her life, told us many nights, whilst we sat together, that our father was totally committed and courageous in his beliefs for a United Ireland. She explained to us the pride he had for his comrade, Paddy, who died with him.

Although very young, we all remember that fateful night. We would love to have had a father see us grow up, see his grandchildren, to know how much we love and miss him. We have listened to his old comrades talk about his Active Service days in East Tyrone and it fills us with admiration and sheer pride. After our father was buried, we slowly came to understand who he was and what he and his comrades were setting out to achieve. It took years, but we firmly believe he gave his life for a just cause.

We listened to both our mother and grandmother tell of how he worked hard for his family and gave us as much time as was possible. What memories we have are precious for that gallant soldier, husband, father."

Óglach Daniel Burke

13th April 1923 - 9th April 1974

Danny Burke was born on the 13th April 1923 in Ross Street, Belfast. His parents Billy and Lizzie had six children, Danny was their fourth. He attended Raglan Street Primary School, which he left at 14 to serve his time as a barber, the occupation of his father. He also found employment as a bookies' clerk and for some years worked in a factory in Castlereagh.

Throughout his life Danny was a keen GAA enthusiast and played both hurling and football for St. John's GAA club. He married Annie and together they had six children, Catherine, Liam, Donal, Brian, Michael and Eilis.

Danny followed his father's footsteps again in joining the Republican Movement and remained true to his Republican politics for the rest of his life. He became the first manager of the P.D. club in Andersonstown and it was while working here that he was shot dead by the British Army.

On the 9th April 1974, in an entirely unprovoked attack, the British Army opened indiscriminate fire on what they regarded as a Republican Club; a bullet went through the thin wooden walls and hit Danny in the heart.

Jim Murphy Sinn Féin

1932 - 20th April 1974

Jim Murphy came from Corraveigha, Derrylin. He was a 42 year old unmarried man who had his own garage business. He lived with his aunt. A quiet and reserved man, he was well-known and respected all over Co. Fermanagh. In 1969 he joined in the Civil Rights campaign and when Internment without trial was introduced in 1971 he helped form the Civil Resistance Movement in Co. Fermanagh.

He raised funds for the dependents of internees and political prisoners, organising many successful social functions in his native Derrylin. A passionate believer in justice and fair play for all he was respected throughout the whole community.

He was also involved in the local newspaper ConcERNEd, the official organ of the Fermanagh disobedience committee, an independent journal that was prepared to challenge the injustices of the State by highlighting the plight of the prisoners and other victims of British oppression.

A victim of constant harassment by the British army and the R.U.C., Jim Murphy was shot dead in the forecourt of his own garage.

He was found shot dead in the forecourt of his garage on the 20th April 1974. He had been shot four times with a .45 revolver suffering fatal wounds to his lungs and heart, the victim of a pro-British death squad.

Óglach Teddy Campbell

1917 - 3rd May 1974

Teddy Campbell was a life-long Republican who was born in 1917 at 53 Lagan Street in the Markets area. His Republican activities resulted in his receiving a two and a half year sentence in 1940. When this sentence was completed, he was interned until 1945 along with his brother Gerry.

On his release, he threw himself once again into the struggle for his country's freedom. He was again imprisoned in the Fifties. His brothers Gerry and Phil were also incarcerated at this time. He was released in 1960.

Remaining an active Republican during the Sixties, he was responsible for the organisation and staffing of the Lower Falls barricades in 1969. He directed operations for the defence of the area during some of the most dangerous periods of sectarian loyalist pogroms.

Teddy took care of weapons and supplies at a time when not too many people were keen to do so. In September 1972 he was arrested for possession of weapons. Although he had ample warning, he refused to abandon the weapons in his care. He accepted full responsibility for the dump and was sentenced to eight years imprisonment.

In Long Kesh he was subjected to severe beatings and medical neglect. He was among the most savagely beaten on 22nd September 1972 when the British army attacked Cage 6 in the Kesh. He required 60 stitches in the head.

He was dying when the British transferred him out of Long Kesh and he died at the age of 57 in Musgrave Park Hospital. There can be no doubt that the mistreatment he received in jail resulted in his death on 3rd May 1974.

Óglach Frederick Leonard

6th June 1954 - 7th May 1974

Frederick Leonard, or 'Big Freddie', as he was better known to his friends, was born on 6th June 1954 in Anderson Street in the Short Strand area of East Belfast. He was born the fifth in a family of six children. He received his education at St Matthew's Primary, Seaforde Street then Lagan Village, Ravenhill Road before moving on to St Augustine's Secondary School on the Ravenhill Road.

Of a quiet nature, Freddie's favourite pastimes, like so many young men, were playing snooker and having a pint of lager in one of the local clubs. In 1970 he entered the plumbing trade, gaining employment in Crowe's on Great Patrick Street. He joined the Auxiliary IRA in late 1971 and later enlisted as a Volunteer in Óglaigh na hÉireann in the latter half of 1972. He died from wounds received when members of a pro-British death squad opened fire on himself and fellow workmen as they sat having a tea-break in a hut on a building site in Ballyduff on the Shore Road on 7th May 1974.

In accordance with his mother's wishes, he was not given a military funeral nor buried in the Republican Plot at Milltown Cemetery. However, three years later, again at his mother's request, his name was rightfully included on the Republican Roll of Honour.

Óglach Eugene Martin

2nd February 1956 - 13th May 1974

Eugene Owen James Martin was from the townland of Dunavally and was an apprentice draughtsman. He had found employment quickly after leaving St. Patrick's Intermediate in Dungannon, where he had been a quiet and diligent student and school prefect.

A steady and mature lad for his 18 years, Eugene saw the daily activities of the state forces, the harassment of the people and the disrespect they showed for our ways and he joined the East Tyrone Brigade.

Volunteer Eugene Martin died instantly on the 13th May 1974 when the bomb he and his comrade, Volunteer Sean McKearney were transporting exploded. It was around 11 o'clock that night, only two miles from his home that Eugene lost his life.

At the funerals of the two Volunteers Loyalists jeered and taunted the mourners. As a Final Salute, a volley of four shots was fired over the two coffins by a lone Volunteer, who had emerged from the crowd before the cortège continued down the Benburb Road to the Church.

Volunteer Eugene Martin is buried in The Moy Cemetery. His friend and comrade, Volunteer Sean McKearney is buried nearby.

Óglach Sean McKearney

18th January 1956 - 13th May 1974

When Sean McKearney left school he went to work as a butcher's assistant in the family shop. The family had a long and honourable history of soldiering, on both his mother and father's side. Then in later years his brother Padraig was killed at Loughgall. Five years after that the family butchers, where Sean had worked in his youth, was attacked by loyalists and another brother Kevin and his uncle John were murdered. His brother Tommy also served a lengthy sentence for defence of his country.

Volunteer Sean McKearney was killed on the 13th May 1974 on the forecourt of the filling station at Doneydale, two miles from Dungannon when the bomb, he and his comrade, Volunteer Eugene Martin were transporting accidentally exploded. They died instantly. At the inquest it was believed that Sean was carrying the bomb.

Sean had been the subject of intense harassment by the state forces. Earlier that year he had been arrested, fingerprinted and questioned, before being released without charge.

Volunteer Sean McKearney aged 19, was buried in The Moy close by his friend and comrade 18 year old Volunteer Eugene Martin.

Óglach Michael Gaughan

5th October 1949 - 3rd June 1974

Michael Gaughan was born on 5 October 1949, in Co Mayo. He was reared in Ballina, Co Mayo. He was the eldest of six children. Michael was one of the earliest IRA Volunteers to be imprisoned in England in this phase of the struggle. He was sentenced to seven years at the Old Bailey in London, in December 1971, for his part in a bank raid.

Michael spent the first two years of his sentence in Wormwood Scrubs in London and then was moved to the Isle of Wight's top security prisons, first Albany, and then in 1974 to Parkhurst. He went on Hunger Strike on 31 March 1974, with other republicans who were in English jails at the time. Michael was force fed from 22 April. He refused medical treatment and died from pneumonia. The force feeding tube had pierced his lung. He died on 3 June 1974 at the age of 24.

From the Isle of Wight, to Ballina, Michael's funeral brought thousands on to the streets. On Friday the 7th June and Saturday 8th June, thousands of people lined the streets of Kilburn in London and marched behind his coffin, which was flanked by an IRA guard of honour. On Saturday, his remains were met by thousands more in Dublin, and flanked by IRA volunteers again; his remains were brought to the Franciscan church on Merchant's Quay. On Sunday he was buried with full military honours.

Óglach Gerard Craig

15th April 1957 - 24th June 1974

Gerard Craig was the youngest of seven children, five boys and two girls. The family was devastated with the sudden death of their mother Elizabeth in 1968 aged 52. Gerard himself was only eleven years old. His father John was left to bring up the children on his own.

At seventeen, Gerard Craig was a confident, lively young man. An ardent Manchester United supporter, he spent most of his free time as a child proudly wearing his United top. A fine footballer, many observers were convinced that Gerard could have made a career from it.

Then came the day when Gerard was shot at close range with a rubber bullet on his way to mass. This put an immediate end to his footballing dreams, as he was going blind in one eye. Despite severe headaches, Gerard tried his best to get on with his life, socialising with friends, listening to the music of Thin Lizzy and Slade.

Gerard joined Maydown Training Centre with his friend David Russell and became an apprentice painter as he could not work around machinery.

Gerard joined Óglaigh na hÉireann because he was tired of the harassment and brutality meted out to local youngsters by both the RUC and the British Army.

Gerard and his friend David Russell died when the bomb they were carrying exploded accidentally outside a supermarket in Greenhaw Road on 24th June 1974.

Óglach David McKinley Russell

15th May 1957 - 24th June 1974

Davy Russell came from a Protestant background. He was a laid-back, easy-going sort of man, whom nothing could rile. I remember him swinging in his hammock in his back garden, at ease with the whole world. We used to stroll in the countryside, laze about on the river bank on sunny days, and go to the occasional dance. He served his apprenticeship in Maydown and Springtown Training Centres as an engineer.

We used to just walk about at night, and in the early Seventies, you couldn't go ten yards without being stopped by a British Army foot patrol. In those days our general attire was wrangler coats and jeans and when the Brits stopped us they'd say we were wearing IRA clothes. When Davy would point out that he was a Protestant, they'd accuse him of being in the UVF. At the end of the day, Davy got fed up with this never-ending harassment and decided to join the Republican Movement like the rest of his friends.

Davy always stuck out like a sore thumb with his big head of hair, the love beads on his wrists and around his neck, his wide legged wranglers and his cherry red Doc Martin boots. You could have spotted him a mile away!

David was killed on the 24th June 1974 alongside Gerard Craig when a bomb they were carrying exploded accidentally in Shantallow.

Óglach Patrick Teer

31st March 1954 - 2nd July 1974

Patrick Teer was born on March 31st 1954 in Beechmount, Belfast. He attended St. Thomas' School locally and later worked as a window cleaner. He was a keen sportsman, with a particular love for Gaelic games.

He joined Fianna Éireann in early 1972, having a keen interest in anything pertaining to the Republican Movement. For his Republican activities, he was arrested and interned on the prison ship Maidstone. After spending five weeks there, he was released.

After joining the IRA, he was active for quite a while before he was captured and interned in Easter 1974 in Long Kesh. There, he became an occupant of Hut 23, Cage 3.

In the middle of June, British soldiers entered Cage 3 and began physically assaulting the internees. Patrick suffered head injuries during the assault. On June 29th, Patrick collapsed during an exercise period. Patrick lay for two days without medical treatment before he was rushed to the Royal Victoria Hospital the following Monday.

On Tuesday, 2nd July 1974, Patrick Teer died of meningitis, most probably as a result of injuries received at the hands of British troops.

Óglach Martin Skillen

25th March 1952 - 3rd August 1974

Martin Patrick Skillen was born on 25th March 1952 and lived at 53 Norglen Gardens, Turf Lodge. He was educated at St. Anthony's and on leaving school he found employment as a bricklayer.

In 1972 he was taken to Palace Barracks, Hollywood, where he received a severe beating. He was the interned in the prison ship Maidstone and later in the cages of Long Kesh.

In the summer of 1974 there was trouble between the Republican Movement and the armed wing of the Workers Party, the so-called 'Official IRA'. Martin was about to take up a firing position at the corner of Sevastopol Street and the Falls Road when he was spied by an undercover unit of the Crown Forces hiding in the derelict Clonard Picture House.

They opened fire and Martin was mortally wounded. However, he scrambled back up Sevastopol Street allowing his comrades to retrieve the Armalite rifle he had been carrying. Martin, aged 22, died shortly afterwards.

Óglach Paul Magorrian

27th September 1952 - 14th August 1974

Paul Magorrian was born into a highly respected family in Castlewellan and as a young boy attended the local schools before going on to work in the family business in the town. A highly motivated and respected member of the South Down Brigade of Óglaigh na hÉireann, he was 22 years of age when he was shot dead by the British Army near his home at St Malachy's Estate, Castlewellan, on the 14th August 1974.

On one occasion during an operation an armoured RUC car was in pursuit of the IRA volunteers when Paul managed to shoot their tyres out thus avoiding certain capture. On another occasion when he was examining weapons in a safe house and a knock came to the door, sensing it was enemy forces, he quickly hid the weapons under the settee and lifted the young baby of the house in his arms. He calmly sat there feeding the child as the British raiding party searched the house. Once again his quick thinking saved the day.

Great controversy surrounded his death, as it was obvious he was intentionally left to die from his wounds. The RUC failed to get medical help despite the fact that a local doctor lived nearby and they also refused assistance from a local nurse and a civilian ambulance crew. Even the local priest was held back from administering the Last Rites.

Paul was buried on the 16th of August 1974, with full Republican honours, after a funeral attended by thousands of people.

Óglach Patrick McKeown

12th April 1945 - 27th August 1974

Patrick Coleman McKeown was born on 12th April 1945 in his grandmother's house in Castle Street, Newry. His parents were Thomas and Ellen and he had four brothers and two sisters, Michael, Edward, Thomas, Francis, Sarah and Nuala. Patrick was educated at the Abbey Primary and later at the Abbey grammar. He did well academically and went on to train as a mental health nurse at Muckamore Abbey, Co. Antrim, and later at Daisy Hill Hospital. Prior to this, he was employed for a time at the Northern Waterproof Company, presently the site of the Council offices.

Patsy, as he was known, loved all types of dancing. His nickname was "Buddy" because of his likeness to Buddy Holly. While working at Muckamore Abbey, Patsy met his wife-to-be, Margaret. They got married shortly afterwards and had four children, Patrick, David, Siobhan and Carmel. They lived at Violet Hill Avenue on the Armagh road and except for brief periods of nurse training, he always lived at home. He decided to leave the nursing and took up employment at Bessbrook Products, better known as the Pye factory, presently the site of Newry's Norbrook Laboratories.

Patsy was acutely aware of the political situation and was deeply affected by events such as attacks on the nationalist people by the B-Specials, internment and Bloody Sunday. In response to these events he took the decision to join Óglaigh na hÉireann. He did his best to keep his life as an active volunteer from his family, although his father may have had some inclination because he indicated some years after Patsy's death that he was aware of his involvement.

On 27th August 1974, a blast occurred at a house in the staunchly Republican Barcroft Park estate. Patsy took the full force of an accidental explosion which completely demolished the house. His death came as a compete surprise to his mother, family and all his friends and workmates. He always will be remembered with pride by his family, friends and comrades.

Ar dheis laimh De go raibh a h-anam

Óglach Michael Hughes

28th June 1958 - 18th October 1974

Michael Hughes was born in Banbridge Co Down on 28th June 1958. He was the oldest of seven children born to Patrick and Teresa. He had one brother called John and five sisters, Kate, Elizabeth, Angela, Lorraine and Patricia. Michael began his academic career at St. Peter's Primary School Bessbrook. He did well at school and moved on to the Abbey CBS Newry and then to St. Joseph's. His teenage years were thrown into turmoil when he had to come to terms with the death of his father Patsy, who was killed in an accidental explosion on the Dublin Road. His father's death had a big impact on the teenage Michael.

From an early age Michael was active on the streets against the British forces and he then decided to follow in his father's footsteps and join the ranks of Óglaigh na h-Éireann. He became heavily involved with republican activity in the Derrybeg area and his leadership qualities soon impressed all those around him. He was a close friend and comrade of Eddie Grant who also died in action as a result of an accidental explosion on Christmas Eve 1973.

Apart from his active involvement in the IRA, Michael also enjoyed his social life. Nicknamed "Sticky" by his friends, he liked nothing better in his free time than frequenting the local Community Centre. With his ginger hair, he was instantly recognisable to everyone. He enjoyed football and reading books about Irish history. Realising the hardships faced by large families, Michael decided to look for a full time job to help alleviate his mother's difficulties. He secured employment at the Nylon factory on the Armagh Road but alas had only completed two weeks work when he was killed.

On Friday 18th October 1974, Michael was on active service when he was shot dead on an Ulsterbus by the British Army. He was only 16 years of age. On the day of his burial, his comrades marched along Main Avenue, Derrybeg in military formation in a fitting tribute to a fellow soldier. Michael will always be remembered with pride by his family and friends.

Óglach Michael Meenan

24th August 1958 - 30th October 1974

Michael Meenan was the third eldest son of Bridie and Barney and lived at Ardnamoyle Park, Shantallow when he joined Na Fianna Éireann and then Óglaigh na hÉireann, 3rd Battalion in Shantallow.

Although youthful, 'Ben' as he was known to his friends and comrades, soon proved himself a very dedicated and very capable volunteer and it was not long before he became an explosives engineer. Ben took part in many successful operations in the city area against the British occupying forces and contributed immensely to the overall war effort in Derry.

At about 8.30pm on Wednesday 30th October 1974 Ben, accompanied by another Volunteer set off in a blue cortina car that had been secured earlier that day. Their objective was to go to the Strand Road and place a bomb in the Maxol filling station. While the other Volunteer checked the area out for British military presence, the bomb exploded accidentally in the car and Ben died instantly. No one else was injured and Ben's comrade was able to return to base.

Ben was afforded a military funeral by his comrades in the 3rd Batt and a unit of Cumann na mBan provided the honour guard. He was laid to rest in the Republican Plot at the City Cemetery.

Óglach Hugh Gerard Coney

25th March 1950 - 6th November 1974

Hugh Gerard Coney was born on the 25th March 1950 at Clonoe, Coalisland. He was the fourth of five children born to James and Kitty. Educated at St. Patrick's Primary School, Annaghmore. As a skilled footballer and snooker player his interest lay mainly in sport. On leaving school he started work in Kelly's pipe-making factory in Coalisland. Gerard had red, unruly hair, which earned him the sometime title of "Red Hugh", but he was best known as "Cowardly." If ever a name didn't fit, this was it, as even as a child he had nerves of steel and was game for anything much to the amusement of his friends and the consternation of his parents. It had been his refusal as a four year old to go through a field with a bull in it that earned him this wholly inapplicable tag.

In 1968 Gerard went to England to play in a snooker tournament and stayed on to work there. On his return the Civil Rights movement was in full swing and he immediately got involved, later joining the I.R.A. His brother Frank (R.I.P.) suffered from Muscular Dystrophy and drove a three wheel invalid car, nicknamed "the Claudia", like her namesake, it frequently carried a "cargo."

Gerard was arrested in 1970, and charged with possession of a mine. In custody he received a severe beating. Released in 1971 he resumed activities and in 1973, when his friend Vol. Kevin Kilpatrick was killed on Active Service, his resolve intensified. He was interned in Long Kesh in 1973 and helped in the digging of a tunnel in Cage 5. As he emerged from the tunnel to make good his escape, he was shot dead by the British Army.

Hundreds of workers in Tyrone spontaneously came out in sympathy with the family expressing their anger at the slaying. His funeral was huge, and people from all over Ireland paid their respects to a brave soldier. Volunteer Gerard Coney is buried in the Republican plot, in Clonoe Graveyard.

Óglach Gerard Fennell

10th August 1946 - 8th November 1974

Volunteer Gerry Fennell was born on August 10th 1946 in Belfast, and was educated at Millfield Primary School, St.John's and St. Thomas's Secondary School. He enjoyed boxing and was a member of the Immaculata boxing club. He gave up what could have been a promising career as a boxer, following the death of his trainer, Jack McCusker.

Shortly after his marriage in 1966, Gerry and his wife moved to London, but when they returned to Belfast for a short holiday in 1972, they decided to stay. Gerry found work as an apprentice engineer at Whiterock Industrial Estate, where he was working up until the time of his death.

The Fennells had two children, Sharon, and Geraldine, who was born five months after her father's death.

Volunteer Gerry Fennell was an active and dedicated republican respected by his comrades and friends. He was shot dead by British occupation forces, while on active service in his home area of Twinbrook, on November 8th 1974.

Óglach James McDade

24th July 1946 - 14th November 1974

James McDade was born in 17 Oakfield Street in the Ardoyne area of North Belfast, in July 1946. He had four brothers and two sisters and one of his brothers Gerard was also a Republican Volunteer, who was shot dead by the British Army a few days before Christmas in 1971.

James was educated at Holy Cross Primary School and St Gabriel's Secondary School where he was known as a talented footballer. Born into a very musical family, he was also an accomplished singer.

When James left school he went to England in search of work and while there he got married and had two sons, Gerald and Anthony.

From a Republican background, James joined Óglaigh na hÉireann in England in 1972 and played an active part in bringing the war to Britain's doorstep. Although a young man himself, James was a highly respected Volunteer who was greatly admired by his younger comrades. He was diligent and thoughtful.

On 14th November 1974 he was on Active Service near the telephone exchange in Coventry when the bomb he was planting exploded accidentally.

His remains were brought home to his native Belfast and he was buried after a funeral service in St Paul's Church, Falls Road.

Óglach John Rooney

2nd June 1955 - 15th November 1974

John 'Roon' Rooney was born on the 2nd June 1955, in the predominately Loyalist Creggagh estate, where he spent the first 16 years of his life with friends of all religions. A keen Liverpool fan, John also loved hurling and he played hurling each summer for Toomebridge, where the family holidayed. A keen hunter, he would often disappear for the day with his ferrets and lurchers.

The Rooney family was intimidated out of Creggagh in 1971 by Loyalists and moved to Twinbrook, where they suffered sustained harassment from the British Army. The family home was repeatedly raided, once on Christmas Eve when soldiers opened the children's presents.

After leaving school John joined his local IRA unit along with his close friend Volunteer Bobby Sands. At the same time John's attempts to find work were frustrated by repeated death threats from Loyalists, and he was to see many of his friends, both Catholic and Protestant, murdered by loyalists.

Volunteer John Rooney died after being knocked down by a car in Twinbrook on 15th November 1974, aged 19.

Óglach John McDaid

6th April 1958 - 7th December 1974

John McDaid joined Na Fianna Éireann around 1973 when he was about 15 years old. He had been a student at St. Columb's College, and at the time of death he was attending the Strand Tech doing an OND Business Studies course, but he sometimes worked in his father's bakery at Meenan Square.

John's family were well known in republican circles and it was no surprise to his friends that he joined Na Fianna. He was outgoing, intelligent and full of life. His companions in the Fianna were Brian Coyle and Eddie McSheffrey and with John's undoubted ability, it was only a matter of time until they joined the IRA. This happened in 1974 although all of them were underage.

John expressed an interest in engineering and quickly became the leading engineer in the Bogside area. At that time the city centre and particularly the area inside the Derry Walls, was guarded 24 hours a day with everyone entering being frisked to prevent bombings.   Perhaps for this reason republicans regarded it as a coup to breach this security. Bomb materials would be smuggled inside the walls and assembled there. John was in the process of taking a bomb outside a building in Bridge Street when it exploded accidentally, killing him and injuring his comrade Tommy Gallagher, who was arrested near the scene.

John's body lay in the house for a long time because the British army engineers would not enter the house. A photo of him lying dead appeared in a British tabloid within days.

Óglach Ethel Lynch

16th November 1952 - 7th December 1974

Ethel Lynch was born in November 1952 at 64, Fox's Corner. Educated at Rosemount Girls P.S. and St. Mary's Secondary School in Creggan, Ethel left school and worked in several shirt factories before finally settling in the Essex factory in Bligh's Lane.

She was a frequent visitor to Long Kesh where her brother Jimmy was interned and she also wrote lots of letters to other internees. The death of a close family friend, Eamonn Lafferty, coupled with Bloody Sunday and numerous raids on her home, saw Ethel joining Óglaigh na hÉireann. During one of the frequent raids on their house, Ethel complained to the officer in charge of racial discrimination. One of the British soldiers found a black doll which belonged to one of Ethel's sisters. They immediately rounded on one of their own fellow soldiers who happened to be black, and said that the doll was his sister. Ethel would stand for none of it and said she wouldn't let anyone be insulted in her house.

On the 3rd December 1974, around 3.00pm, a priest called to the family home to inform them that Ethel had been involved in an explosion at Crawford Square. A local doctor was quickly on the scene and administered first aid until the ambulance arrived. Despite being severely injured, Ethel gave a false name and address. A priest from the nearby cathedral travelled to the hospital in the ambulance with her and she told him her real name. He heard her last confession and after that Ethel lapsed into unconsciousness.

During her three days in intensive care, she was guarded twenty-four hours a day by the RUC Special Branch, who constantly harassed her family as they arrived to visit her. Ethel died at 2.20a.m. on Saturday 7th December. She was buried with full military honours.

Óglach Brian Fox

25th October 1947 - 21st December 1974

Brian Fox was born on 25th October 1947 in Belfast. He started school at St.Theresa'a Primary school on the Glen Road, and then at Harding Street CBS. After his 'O' Levels, Brian moved to St.Patrick's Bearnageeha where he took his 'A' Levels. When he left school he went to work for Eastwoods.

He always had a keen interest in Irish culture and history, and was a fluent Irish speaker by the time he was 18.

An active Republican from his early teens, Brian was involved in all forms of resistance to oppression. His fervent dedication was born of the firm belief that Ireland's destiny lay in the hands of its people.

From the commencement of this campaign, Brian was active as an organiser and trainer. He played a leading role in the struggle and was involved in every facet, taking every opportunity to engage the enemy.

After his marriage, Brian and his wife emigrated to Canada where he was involved in organising the Irish-Canadian community to help the struggle at home. During a holiday home, Brian decided that due to the deteriorating situation, it was time for him to return to Ireland.

Brian Fox gave himself wholeheartedly to the struggle once again, with a fervour and zeal admired and emulated by his comrades. It was while on active service in England, that Volunteer Brian Fox died as a result of an accidental shooting on 21st December 1974. His remains were brought home to Belfast where he was buried with his comrades in Milltown Cemetery.

Óglach John Francis Green

18th December 1946 - 10th January 1975

John Francis Green was born in Lurgan, Co. Armagh on 18th December 1946; he was the third child of Edward and Kathleen Green. A married man, he and his wife Ann had three children, Ursula, Gerard and Frances.

A member of the North Armagh Brigade of Óglaigh na hÉireann he was arrested in December 1972 and Interned on the prison ship Maidstone and later in Long Kesh until his escape in September 1973, dressed as a priest. His younger brother Leo, was also imprisoned and took part in the hunger strike in 1980.

Forced to live on the run he stayed in the Monaghan and Castleblaney areas where he remained active with the IRA, returning periodically to his native Lurgan.

On the evening of 10th January 1975 he left Castleblaney and drove to a farmhouse at Mullyash, where he had been staying. He spoke to the farmer and indicated that he was going to have a shave while the farmer went to attend a neighbour's cattle. When the farmer returned he found John Francis lying at the bottom of the stairs having been shot a number of times. His killers, believed to be a combination of British Army, UDR and Loyalist paramilitaries, had left a number of live bullets on top of his body

Thousands of people attended John Francis' funeral which had an IRA Guard of Honour. He was laid to rest in the Republican plot in St. Colman's Cemetery, Lurgan.

Óglach James Moyne

6th April 1947 - 13th January 1975

Vol. James Brendan Moyne was born on 6th April 1947. Known by his family and comrades as either Jim or "Mossey", he was raised in Cable Street in the Bogside. Jim was a kind, generous and fun loving person who enjoyed a laugh and a joke. From an early age Jim had a love for drawing, and also enjoyed playing soccer and followed Gaelic football. After his time at the Christian Brothers' School in Derry he went on to work as a qualified Dental Technician in the town.

Jim became involved in the Republican movement in 1970, as he realised the injustices of the state on the working classes in the north of Ireland, injustices that he was later to be the victim of. Jim spent some time "on the run" before he was interned on 22nd April 1973. He had bronchitis and in July 1973 was transported to the Royal Victoria Hospital in Belfast where he spent two days in an oxygen tent before being taken straight back to Long Kesh.

He was still there in October 1974 when the camp was burned down and after that riot he, like his comrades, spent weeks huddled on the mud under makeshift shelters, which contributed to the deterioration of his health. In the early morning of the 13th January 1975 Jim suffered an asthmatic attack, prison warders failed to respond to the alarm bell and this combined with persistent medical neglect Jim died and was in effect killed by the state.

Jim was brought home to Derry and buried with full military honours.

Óglach Kevin Coen

20th January 1975

Kevin Coen was a native of Rusheen near Riverstown in County Sligo. A man with no airs or graces, he was a great lover of Irish culture and a highly respected member of the Southern Command of Óglaigh na hÉireann.

His natural leadership qualities were apparent to all who came into contact with him and his total dedication to the struggle for national independence was an inspiration to many. He was the type of person who would never ask anyone to do something if he wasn't prepared to do it himself, and it was this attitude that earned him the greatest of respect from his comrades.

He was one of the many ordinary people, who, faced with extraordinary situations, remained resolute and strong in the face of great adversity.

On the 20th January 1975, Kevin was on active service at Cassidy's Cross, near Swanlinbar on the Fermanagh-Cavan border when he was shot dead during a gun-battle between the local IRA unit and the British Army.

Leitrim Republican, John Joe McGirl, gave his funeral oration. He is buried at Sooey Cemetery.

Óglach John Kelly

16th July 1948 - 21st January 1975

John 'Bap' Kelly was born in Mofat Street on 16th July 1948. He was educated at Bearnageeha School on the Antrim Road, and on leaving school he worked as a van driver.

During the Lower Falls curfew in July 1970, Bap was arrested and sentenced to five years imprisonment on arms charges, serving his time in Long Kesh. Bap, a born entertainer, soon set to work organising concerts for his fellow POW's, and he will always be remembered by them for the way in which he helped to keep their morale high with his wit and banter.

Released in 1974, after serving three and a half years of his sentence, he immediately reported back for active service with his local IRA unit. Simultaneously, Bap, a married man and father of four small children, decided to exploit his talents as an entertainer and he became an overnight hit as a cabaret artist on the local club circuit. He wrote and recorded his now famous 'Say Hello to the Provos', which was such a resounding success that he was invited to the USA where he made an LP record of the same name.

Returning home to Belfast on 22nd December, just in time for Christmas, he was killed within one month in an accidental explosion, while transporting a bomb with his comrade Óglach John Stone. Both Volunteers died instantly. It was 21st January 1975.

Óglach John Stone

19th June 1952 - 21st January 1975

John Stone, from Ballymurphy, was the fourth child in a family of five. A car sprayer by occupation, John joined Óglaigh na hÉireann in 1970.

He was an active Volunteer in Ballymurphy and was popular with his comrades. He was arrested in 1974 and interned in Long Kesh, which he used to obtain a better understanding of Irish history and the conflict he had committed himself to.

Not long after his release he was forced to go on the run. He evaded capture on several occasions and was always active within his unit.

Christmas 1974 was the first Christmas Day he had been able to spend with his family for four years. Tragically it was the last time they were to see him. John was killed on active service on January 21st 1975, when a bomb he and John (Bap) Kelly were transporting, exploded accidentally.

Óglach Sean Boyle

16th June 1953 - 1st February 1975

Sean Boyle was the first child of John and Rose Boyle. Born on June 16th 1953 he spent his early years in Tullywinney, Drumherriff before moving to Belleek in 1956. He attended the local Primary School and then St Paul's Secondary School in Bessbrook. From an early age Sean would help out on his uncle's farm and from this he developed a love for outdoor activities.

His family had a strong sporting tradition and Sean was an excellent Gaelic footballer, playing initially for Loughgilly underage team and Belleek senior team with his father when he was only 16. He was later to play for Whitecross and St. Patrick's, Cullyhanna. As a child Sean took part in many feisanna around south Armagh, on one occasion taking first prize for reading the poem "The Ballad of William Bloat".

Upon leaving school Sean got an apprenticeship with McParland brothers where he served his time as a bricklayer.

Sean's comrades remember him as a extremely eager soldier who would participate fully in all aspects of volunteer life and was always willing to assist others in any way that he could. He was also described as "always having a way of making you laugh, with a carefree manner and a ready smile".

Sean met his partner Angela Murphy and they married in St Patrick's Church, Cullyhanna on August 14th 1974. The couple settled in Dundalk where Sean managed 'The Emerald Bar'. Sadly only a few months later, on the 1st February 1975, Sean died in a car accident near the Ballymascanlon Hotel, County Louth.

Óglach Bridie Dolan Cumann na mBan

15th August 1911 - 9th February 1975

Bridie Dolan was born on 15th August 1911, into a strongly Republican family. Her uncle, James McQuillan, was one of the few Irishmen to join Major John MacBride in the Boer war. Her cousin James was forced to flee Ireland in the 1920's due to his republican activities.

Bridie joined Cumann na mBan with her sisters, and they had their first brush with the authorities when they refused to remove their Easter lilies returning from a 1916 commemorative Mass in St. Patrick's Chapel. The group was sentenced to Armagh Jail for terms ranging from two weeks to one month. (In the 1970's, Bridie's nieces, Dolores and Marion Price were imprisoned in Armagh following a lengthy hunger strike and forced feeding ordeal in England).

An accidental explosion in the 1940's left Bridie with severe injuries to her eyes, and she lost both her hands. Despite her injuries Bridie continued to dedicate her life to the Republican Movement, lovingly cared for by her sister Maureen. Her support was absolute through the 1940's, 50's and 60's. She had no hesitation in giving her support to the republican movement in the 1970's.

At every protest and rally in the early 1970's, Bridie was to be seen, until her health deteriorated. Volunteer Bridie Dolan died on 9th February 1975.

Óglach Tom Smith

22nd March 1948 - 17th March 1975

Tom Smith was born on 22nd March 1948. His parents were James and Kathleen, he had five brothers, Sean, Paul, Nick, Michael and Patrick, and one sister, Phyllis. He lived originally in Donore Avenue, but then moved to Mount Pleasant Buildings in Harold's Cross. He worked in Jacobs Biscuit Factory until his arrest in 1973.

He became an active member of the IRA in the late 1960s. He was sentenced to life imprisonment in 1973 for armed robbery.

On St Patrick's Night in 1975, Tom was shot dead by Free State Soldiers and a number of others were wounded during an attempted escape from Portlaoise Prison.

The Minister for Justice failed to notify the family of Tom's death for at least 12 hours. He misled them about the whereabouts of his body, and he ordered a post mortem at which a representative of the deceased was not present. In an attempt to deliberately disrupt the family's funeral arrangements, on the orders of Mr Cooney, Tom's body was secretly transferred from Portlaoise to the Dublin City morgue. Orders were given to harass mourners in scenes not seen since the blackest days of the Civil War. Tom was buried with full military honours.

Every St Patrick's Day since then, a commemoration is held in honour of his memory at the Republican Plot in Glasnevin where he is interred.

Fiann Robert Alsopp

23rd August 1959 - 25th March 1975

Robert Alsopp from the New Lodge area of North Belfast was born on the 23rd August 1959. He attended St Malachy's Primary School before moving to St Patrick's Secondary on the Antrim Road. It was during his schooldays that he earned the nickname 'Swab'.

Like most of the people of his generation, he liked going to dances and was a keen footballer. A member of the Artillery Youth Club, he had travelled to Holland with a number of friends from the club and they had a memorable holiday.

He was a young lad who enjoyed life and was always smiling, even the British Army in the area referred to him as 'Smiler'. Quick-witted - he was once stopped by a British Army foot patrol who queried him about an IRA badge he was wearing when he responded by saying it means "I'm Robert Alsopp"!

He was a person who was greatly concerned about his friends and neighbours and liked to help people and make sure they were okay. It was no surprise therefore that, having witnessed at first hand the Loyalist pogroms that were unleashed on nationalists in the Six Counties, he made the decision in 1969 to join Na Fianna Éireann.

Robert died after an accidental shooting during an arms lecture on the 25th March 1975. He was fifteen and a half years old at the time.

Óglach Neil Lafferty

8th January 1923 - 26th April 1975

In 1943 Neil was interned by the then Stormont Government after an attack known as the 'Clady ambush', when two RUC men were killed. He was active again in the 50s campaign and when the present phase of the struggle resumed in the late 60s - early 70s, he did not hesitate to report back for active service with the local battalion of Óglaigh na hÉireann in his native Clady.

He was interned twice in the 1970s and his health was a cause for concern to his family and friends. However when he died suddenly in Altnagelvin Hospital, seven months after his release from Internment, there was a tangible shock within the local community.

Neil had been a great ambassador for the Republican cause and inspired many of the younger generation with his determination and resolve to see his country free.
His friend and comrade Liam McElhinney delivered the graveside oration and spoke of the respect that Neil commanded both from inside and outside the Movement.

As his funeral procession crossed the border en route to Donneyloop, hundreds of Free State forces closed in on the mourners in a blatant attempt of intimidation. Despite this, the cortege continued to the graveyard where Neil's remains were laid to rest in the family plot.

Neil Lafferty was a sterling republican soldier, but was also a proud and loving husband and father, leaving behind his wife Bridie and seven children, four of whom were imprisoned for their Republican beliefs.

Óglach Francis Rice

2nd December 1957 - 18th May 1975

Frankie was born on the 2nd December 1957 and was the eldest of a large family from the Burrenbridge area, outside Castlewellan. As a young boy Frankie played football for Bryansford and worked part-time in the Oak Grill in Castlewellan until he left school. Then he went to work as a book-keeper for Kelly's paint and wallpaper shop in Ballynahinch.

Growing up in the nationalist town of Castlewellan, Frankie witnessed at first hand the daily harassment and intimidation of his friends and family by the British Army and UDR and made a conscious decision to fight this oppression of his people. He joined the local unit of Óglaigh na hÉireann and helped form a branch of Fianna Éireann, the youth wing of the Republican Movement in the Burrenbridge/Burrenreagh area.

Frankie was abducted by a Loyalist 'death squad' and despite being tortured refused to tell his captors anything. This was evidenced by the fact that after his death his loyalist killers claimed he was a member of the Official IRA.

Frankie's death so soon after the tragic death of Paul Magorrian was a severe blow to the Republican Movement in the Castlewellan area but the bravery he showed in facing his death proved to be an inspiration to young Republicans throughout the South Down area.

Óglach Francis Jordan

1st November 1954 - 4th June 1975

Francis Jordan was born on the 1st November 1954 in Jonesborough, Co.Armagh. He was the eldest child, and only son of Kevin and Christine Jordan. He had five sisters, Sheila, Imelda, Caroline, Majella and Paula. He attended school in Jonesborough, and formed many friendships that were to last the whole of his relatively short life. When he left school Francis worked on the family farm at Edenappa, Jonesborough, and as a barman in The Old Border Inn, Carrickarnon.

The early 1970's were a difficult time for young people, who had to endure constant harassment by the Crown Forces, particularly in South Armagh. The introduction of internment, Bloody Sunday, and the continuing suppression of the rights of nationalist people, led Francis to join the 3rd Battalion, I.R.A South Armagh. In an effort to increase surveillance in the Killeen area, the British installed a multi-million pound computerised spy tower at the Cloughogue checkpoint. Under Francis' command, a bomb destroyed the tower shortly after its installation.

In another celebrated operation, Francis organised the hi-jacking of a light aeroplane from an airfield south of Dundalk. It was flown to Faughil mountain where bombs were dropped on British troops who were dug in on the mountain. On 4th June 1975, Francis, with other members of his unit, was on a bombing mission in Bessbrook when they were confronted by British soldiers who opened fire. Francis was wounded, and even though this was obvious to the soldiers, they left him lying on the roadside without assistance, which resulted in his death.

Francis was buried with full military honours in his native Jonesborough, his funeral being one of the largest ever seen in the area. His death was a tragic blow to his family and a great loss to the Republican Movement.

Óglach Séan McKenna

23rd July 1932 - 5th June 1975

Séan McKenna was 42 when he died near Dundalk on Thursday 5th June 1975. Séan, a father of 8, looked much older than his years because of the torture inflicted upon him while imprisoned.

Séan's health began to deteriorate when he was arrested on 9th August 1974. He was held, hooded and tortured for 9 days in Ballykinlar Army Base, torture which he withstood but which left him a physical wreck. Yet, this did not deter him from playing a full and significant role in the struggle after his release.

Séan's comrades in the Republican Movement and from the prisons remember him as a kindly man who showed unfailing courtesy towards others. He was a dedicated Republican who was not afraid to speak his mind in defence of the struggle.

On Saturday the 7th of June as Séan's remains were brought from Newry, Co. Down to County Monaghan, thousands of people came out to pay their respects along the way, especially in the towns of Castleblaney and Monaghan. Séan McKenna is buried at Clara, near Emyvale. Even on the day of his funeral there were attempts to intimidate and harass his family and mourners. At one point mourners were forced to repel the Gardaí from the graveyard.

Séan was survived by his eight children and loving wife. Sinn Féin vice-president Máire Drumm giving the oration said "Séan was a brave and gallant soldier who has made a place not only in the history of Ireland, but of mankind."

Fiann James Templeton

28th January 1960 - 29th August 1975

Jim lived in Peveril Street on the Lower Ormeau Road, beside the railway tracks where Scoil an Droichead now stands. Part of a loving family; consisting of his father, Jim, mother Margaret, and two sisters, he attended the local primary school and St. Augustine's Secondary School, on the Ravenhill Rd. He was a tall, slim lad with light, well-cropped, fair hair and bright blue eyes set in a round baby face. He was at times thoughtful, generous, moody, playful, a totally unpredictable youth; always great fun to be with and a good friend.

He loved to be well turned out in the fashion of the time; short coloured trousers, black socks and well polished DM's. He especially liked the 'ould wrangler suit.' Discos! He would travel the town to try them out. He was no different in many respects to young teenagers, he hungered for fun and his future. He got his first job in a bag factory in Talbot Street.

Jim joined Na Fianna Éireann in the Ormeau Road area in 1973, attending many lectures and meetings to prepare him for the time when he would join the IRA. The reality was however, that any teenager, eager to join in the fight did so whenever the chance arose, and Jim was no exception. There are many who will recall his eagerness in that respect.

On the night of 29th August 1975, Jim and a friend were talking to a doorman at the Rose and Crown public house when a car pulled up and a loyalist gunman opened fire hitting Jim twice in the body. Jim's mother arrived at the hospital as he was being wheeled into the theatre. They were able to speak for a few emotional and heart breaking moments, during which time he expressed his wish to live. He died a short time later.

Fiann Jim Templeton was 15 years old.

Óglach Seamus McCusker

16th March 1935 - 31st October 1975

Seamus McCusker was born in Ballinagh, County Cavan, on 16th March 1935. He moved to Belfast fourteen years later and settled in St Matthew's parish. After training as an electrician, he worked for various companies, and even worked in the shipyard for a while. He met and married Betty when he was 26 years old. They had three children, Gregory, Miles and Felicity. After living in the Tullymore area for a while the family moved to the Bawnmore/Whitehall area.

Seamus was a quiet man who was inclined to give credit to others when credit was more rightly due to himself. During the turbulent days of August 1969 Seamus was already speaking of the need for the IRA to go on the offensive against the British army and their local militias. When this offensive came, Seamus took full part in it. His record as a Volunteer was second to none.

In October 1971 Seamus was captured and imprisoned in Crumlin Road Jail. When he arrived in 'C' Wing with the rest of the internees every inch of his body was a mass of bruises. Characteristically, Seamus played down the brutal beating he had taken, asking instead how the morale was among the rest of the prisoners. Seamus was released from internment in mid-1974 and soon assumed the responsibility for staffing the Sinn Féin incident centre in the New Lodge. Before long he had endeared himself with the local people with his ability to listen sympathetically and his efforts to help.

On 31st October 1975, Seamus McCusker was murdered by members of the Workers Party at the foot of the New Lodge Road. At the time he was on his way to deal with a local person's problem.

Fiann Kevin McCauley

25th April 1962 - 6th November 1975

Fiann Kevin McCauley was born on 25th April 1962, and lived with his parents, Winifred and Leo, his younger brother Patrick and sister Jackie, on Belfast's Grosvernor Road until 1969. The family then moved to the Ladybrook estate in Andersonstown. He attended St Mary's Primary School, Divis Street and La Salle Secondary School, Andersonstown. His school friends still remember Kevin as a quiet-natured, good student who loved to play soccer.

From an early age Kevin was aware of the Republican resistance struggle, and his country's history. His grandfather, James McCauley from Swanlinbar, County Cavan, was an IRA Volunteer during the Tan war, and spent a period interned in the Curragh Camp, County Kildare.

In the early 1970's, Kevin's aunt, Marie McCauley, served a four-year sentence in Armagh Women's Prison. It was not surprising that with such a strong Republican background, that Kevin joined Fianna Éireann.

On the evening of November 6th 1975, Kevin and some friends left St. Michael's youth club, and were carrying on with an unattended dumper on the site of Ballyowen old peoples home on the Andersonstown Road.

The dumper ran out of control, careered down the road and crushed Kevin against another piece of machinery. Fiann Kevin McCauley was thirteen and a half years old when he died. His flag draped coffin passed the spot where he died. He is buried in a family plot, just inside the main gates of Belfast's Milltown Cemetery.

Óglach Paul Fox

20th April 1955 - 1st December 1975

Paul Fox was born on the 20th April 1955 and lived at 11 Iveagh Parade, Belfast.

Having gone to school locally, he left to serve an apprenticeship as a welder. He was forced to leave this job because of sectarian threats against him. The firm's manager had to escort him home for his own safety.

A very religious boy, he would have liked to have joined an order, but chose to wait until the national struggle was brought to a successful conclusion.

He joined the Republican Movement in 1970 and was on the run since he was 16. He was interned in Long Kesh from November 30th 1972 until February 14th 1975.

Along with Laura Crawford, he gave his life for Ireland when a bomb they were transporting exploded accidentally in a car park in King Street, Belfast, on 1st December 1975.

Óglach Laura Crawford Cumann na mBan

20th November 1950 - 1st December 1975

Cumann na mBan Volunteer Laura Crawford was born on 20th November 1950, in Belfast's lower Falls. She had two brothers and seven sisters. Laura attended St. Peter's Primary School and St. Louise's College. When she left school at 17, she went to work as a shorthand typist for Nurse & Jones solicitors. She was full of life, loved dancing and was a keen folk fan. Laura joined Cumann na mBan late in 1973. She was a very active Volunteer, and despite her confessed fear of explosives, she put this to one side when called upon, participating in a number of successful attacks on the Crown forces.

On one occasion, when she and another volunteer were transporting explosives into the lower Falls for an operation the next day, the car was stopped by a British army patrol. Calmly rolling down the window, she began chatting to the British soldier who, so surprised that someone in a staunch republican area was willing to speak to him, gave the car interior a cursory inspection and waved it through the checkpoint. The following day's operation which could have been jeopardised, was successful. Security was always predominant in Laura's thoughts and actions, keeping a distinct line between her role as a soldier of Cumann na mBan, and her private life.

On the night of 1st December 1975, Laura and IRA Volunteer Paul Fox drove into the car park in Castle Street. As they were parking the car the bomb they were carrying exploded, killing both young Volunteers. At the time of her death, Laura's sister, Geraldine, was serving a sentence in Armagh Women's Prison, herself having been shot during an engagement with Crown forces.

Volunteer Laura Crawford was buried with full military honours in Milltown Cemetery, Belfast.

Óglach Terry Brady

20th June 1921 - 5th December 1975

Terry was a life long republican and from 1940 until 1945 was interned in Derry Jail, Crumlin Road Jail and on the prison ship Al Rawdah. He was an ardent Gael and became fluent in the Irish language.

In the early 50's he helped organise the Volunteers in the Lurgan area and was active in protecting Catholic areas from Loyalist attacks during those times.

During the present campaign he was an active Volunteer right up until the moment of his death which was sudden and due to heart seizure. Terry's death occurred while he was on his way to welcome home the last internees from Lurgan.

Terry, who spent the early 1940's interned and who worked hard on behalf of internees in the early 1970's, died on 5th December 1975 on the last day of Internment.

Óglach Sean Campbell

11th May 1955 - 6th December 1975

Sean Campbell grew up in Faughart, County Louth in a house straddling the border - a constant reminder from an early age of the division of his country. Sean was the third eldest of six sons, some of who were imprisoned for their Republican activities.

On leaving school he worked as a tiler and was a popular young man with great energy and a love for life. He played Gaelic football for Roche Emmets in Co. Louth. One of his great interests was his motorbike and he was regularly seen riding around the local roads. It was an interest that also proved useful in his work as an IRA Volunteer.

Sean was part of one of the first sniper teams in South Armagh where his coolness under pressure was valued. An extremely active and highly respected Volunteer he was killed alongside his comrade Jim Lochrie while on active service on 6th December 1975.

When they died the South Armagh Brigade of Óglaigh na hÉireann lost two of their most dedicated volunteers.

Members of the Gardai clad in riot gear surrounded the graveyard as he was being buried but this did not prevent his comrades paying their final salute as a volley of shots had already been fired over Sean's coffin the night before.

Sean is buried in Kilcurry Cemetery, North Louth and his death was a tragic loss to his family and the entire Republican Movement.

Óglach Jim Lochrie

15th April 1956 - 6th December 1975

Volunteer Jim Lochrie was born on the 15th of April 1956. He lived with his family in Dromintee, a small rural community in South Armagh. He was educated at Dromintee Primary School and the Abbey Grammar School in Newry, where he completed his O' Levels before cutting short his education to become a full time active service member with the 1st Battalion, South Armagh Brigade of the IRA.

Jim, who was affectionately known as Finn, was a warm and fun-loving individual who was well liked and respected by all who knew him. He had a love for Irish culture and sport and he played for his local club in Dromintee and was also selected for the Armagh minor panel.

He had a vision of unifying his country and understood the risks that needed to be taken in the fight for national liberation. He clearly understood the concepts of strategy and tactics and was a forward thinker - a rare quality during one of the most active periods of military activity.

He died close to his family home, along with his comrade Sean Campbell, while on active service on the 6th December 1975. His death was a tragic loss, not only to his family and friends but to the entire community of South Armagh.

ROLL OF HONOUR

1969
Gerard McAuley
Liam McParland

1970
Henry McIlhone
Thomas Carlin
Joseph Coyle
Thomas McCool
Jimmy Steele
Michael Kane
Peter Blake
Tom McGoldrick

1971
James Saunders
Charles Hughes
Tony Henderson
Billy Reid
Patrick McAdorey
Seamus Simpson
Eamonn Lafferty
James O'Hagan
Terry McDermott
Dorothy Maguire
Maura Meehan
Martin Forsythe
Michael Crossey
Tony Nolan
Charles Agnew
Martin Lee
John Bateson
James Sheridan
Gerard McDade
Jack McCabe

1972
Danny O'Neill
Michael Sloan
Eamonn McCormick
Peter McNulty

Gerry Donaghy
Phelim Grant
Charles McCann
Joseph Cunningham
David McAuley
Gerard Bell
Gerard Steele
Robert Dorrian
Joseph Magee
Albert Kavanagh
Gerard Crossan
Tony Lewis
Sean Johnston
Tom McCann
Colm Keenan
Eugene McGillan
Sean O'Riordan
Patrick Campbell
Samuel Hughes
Charles McCrystal
John McErlean
John Starrs
Michael Magee
Edward McDonnell
Jackie McIlhone
Joseph Fitzsimons
Martin Engelen
Joseph Campbell
Tony Jordan
John Finucane
Dennis Quinn
Julie Dougan
John Dougal
Louis Scullion
James Reid
Tobias Molloy
Joseph Downey
Seamus Cassidy
Seamus Bradley
Robert McCrudden
Colm Murtagh

Michael Clarke
Anne Parker
Patrick Hughes
Oliver Rowntree
Noel Madden
James Carlin
Martin Curran
Michael Quigley
Joseph McComiskey
Jimmy Quigley
Daniel McAreavey
Patrick Maguire
John Donaghy
Joseph McKinney
Hugh Heron
John Patrick Mullan
Stan Carberry
John Brady
James Carr
Bernard Fox
Sean Hughes
Louis Leonard
Eugene Devlin
James McDaid

179

1973
Francis Liggett
James Sloan
James McCann
Tony Campbell
Vivien Fitzsimmons
Leo O'Hanlon
Patrick McCabe
Edward O'Rawe
Brian Smyth
Tony Ahern
Kevin Kilpatrick
Joseph McKenna
Thomas O'Donnell
Sean McKee
Dermott Crowley
Sean Loughran
Patrick Carty
Pauline Kane
Alphonsus Cunningham
Gerard McGlynn
Seamus Harvey
Daniel McAnallen
Patrick Quinn
Francis Hall
Patrick Mulvenna
AnneMarie Pettigrew
Francis Dodds
James Bryson
Michael McVerry
Michael Marley
Desmond Morgan
Joe Walker
Jim McGinn
Brendan Quinn
Edward Grant

1974
Patrick McDonald
Kevin Murray
Daniel Burke
Jim Murphy
Teddy Campbell

Frederick Leonard
Eugene Martin
Sean McKearney
Michael Gaughan
Gerard Craig
David Russell
Patrick Teer
Martin Skillen
Paul Magorrian
Patrick McKeown
Michael Hughes
Michael Meenan
Hugh Coney
Gerard Fennell
James McDade
John Rooney
John McDade
Ethel Lynch
Brian Fox

1975
John Francis Green
James Moyne
Kevin Coen
John Kelly
John Stone
Sean Boyle
Bridie Dolan
Tom Smith
Robert Alsopp
Neil Lafferty
Francis Rice
Francis Jordan
Sean McKenna
James Templeton
Seamus McCusker
Kevin McCauley
Paul Fox
Laura Crawford
Terry Brady
Sean Campbell
James Lochrie
David Kennedy

1976
Martin McDonagh
Rosemary Blakely
Francis Stagg
James O'Neill
Sean Bailey
James McGrillen
Paul Best
Sean McDermott
Peter Cleary
Jim Gallagher
Colm Mulgrew
Brian Coyle
Thomas Kane
Derek Highsted
Peter McElchar
Patrick Cannon
Danny Lennon
Noel Jenkinson
Paul Marlowe
Frank Fitzsimons
Joseph Surgenor
Máire Drumm

1977
Seamus Harvey
Trevor McKibben
Brendan O'Callaghan
Tommy Tolan
Paul McWilliams
Sean O'Conaill

1978
Jackie McMahon
Paul Duffy
Henry Heaney
Dennis Heaney
Jackie Mailey
Denis Brown
Jim Mulvenna
Pat Harkin
Patrick Duffy

1979
Lawrence Montgomery
Frankie Donnelly
Billy Carson
Peadar McElvanna
Martin McKenna

1980
Kevin Delaney
Robert Carr
Terence O'Neill

1981
Peadar Mohan
Liam Hannaway
James Burns
Bobby Sands
Francis Hughes
Raymond McCreesh
Patsy O'Hara
George McBrearty
Charles Maguire
Joe McDonnell
John Dempsey
Martin Hurson
Kevin Lynch
Kieran Doherty
Thomas McElwee
Mickey Devine

1982
Danny McMullan
Eamonn Bradley
Peter Corrigan
Jeff McKenna
Sean Burns
Gervase McKerr
Eugene Toman
Phil O'Donnell

1983
Colm Daltun
Eddie Dynes
Dan Turley
Brian Campbell
Colm McGirr
Henry Hogan

1984
Declan Martin
Richard Quigley
William Price
Brendan Watters
Paddy Brady
Ciaran Fleming
Antoine MacGiolla
Bhrighde
Danny Doherty
Willie Fleming
Sean McIlvenna

1985
Mick Timothy
Charlie Breslin
David Devine
Michael Devine
Tony Campbell
Charles English
Réamonn MacLochlainn

1986
Tony Gough
Tom Magill
Seamus McElwain
Philip McFadden
Brian Dempsey
Patrick O'Hagan
Jim McKernan

1987
Gerard Logue
Laurence Marley
Finbarr McKenna
Declan Arthurs
Seamus Donnelly
Tony Gormley
Eugene Kelly
Paddy Kelly
Jim Lynagh
Pádraig McKearney
Gerard O'Callaghan
Margaret McArdle
Paddy Deery
Eddie McSheffrey
Peter Rodden

1988
Brendan Burns
Brendan Moley
Mairead Farrell
Dan McCann
Sean Savage
Kevin McCracken
Caoimhín MacBradaigh
Hugh Hehir
Seamus Woods
Brendan Davison
Brian Mullen
Gerard Harte
Martin Harte

1989
James Joseph Connolly
John Davey
Gerard Casey
Seamus Twomey
Liam Ryan

1990
Sam Marshall
Sean Bateson
Dessie Grew
Martin McCaughey
Tommy Casey
Fergal Caraher

1991
Patrick Sheehy
Noel Wilkinson
John Quinn
Malcolm Nugent
Dwayne O'Donnell
Colum Marks
John O'Rawe
Eddie Fullerton
Tony Doris
Lawrence McNally
Peter Ryan
Danny McCauley
Pádraig O'Seanacháin
Tommy Donaghy
Bernard O'Hagan
Patricia Black
Frankie Ryan
Damien Brolly

1992
Proinsias MacAirt
Pat McBride
Paddy Loughran
Joseph McManus
Sean O'Farrell
Kevin Barry O'Donnell
Patrick Vincent
Peter Clancy
Brendan Seery
Danny Cassidy
Christy Harford
Sheena Campbell
Pearse Jordan
Malachy Carey

1993
Peter Gallagher
James Kelly
Alan Lundy
Michael Motley
Thomas Begley

1994
Martin Doherty
Pól Kinsella

1996
Edward O'Brien
Eugene Martin
Jimmy Roe
Malachy Watters
Diarmuid O'Neill
Pat McGeown

1997
Patrick Kelly

1999
Harry Burns

Óglach David Kennedy

23rd April 1920 - 10th December 1975

David Kennedy, or Davey as he was more commonly known, was born in Armagh in 1920 into a family of four and was raised in Hagan's Row. As a young man he worked in the local laundry, where he met Maude, his future wife and together they had twelve children. He was a man with strong family values and he loved his children dearly. He had a great sense of humour and his main sporting interest was in the local sport 'bullets' - or road bowls.

Born into a generation that was directly influenced by the sacrifice of the men and women of 1916, he was an active member of Óglaigh na hÉireann from the 1950s and took part in the Operation Harvest campaign. When the campaign for Irish Independence resumed in the late 1960s - early 1970s Davey got re-involved.

His experiences had taught him that the struggle needed to be fought on many fronts and in this regard no role was ever too great or too small for Davey. While holding a position on the Brigade Staff he still found time to help out with collections for POWs and sold An Phoblacht, the Movement's weekly newspaper.

He was an active member of the Republican Movement in North Armagh right up until the time of his death on the 10th December 1975. A man with strong political and family values, he earned the respect and admiration of all who met him.

Óglach Martin McDonagh

3rd March 1952 - 13th January 1976

Martin Gerard McDonagh, who was better known to his friends as 'Bugsie', was born on 3rd March 1952 and lived in North Belfast. He was educated at St Mary's Grammar School on the Glen Road, West Belfast. After leaving school he went on to become a housing manager with the Housing Executive.

A quiet and dedicated Republican, he joined Óglaigh na hÉireann, quickly earning a reputation as an efficient and reliable operator. Security was always uppermost in his mind and, though he was a tireless worker for the Republican cause, he never gave his family and friends any reason to suspect his involvement in the Movement.

On 13th January 1976 Martin and his comrade, Cumann na mBan Volunteer Rosemary Blakely, died in an accidental explosion while on a commercial bombing operation in North Street Arcade inside the Belfast city centre 'security zone'.

Óglach Rosemary Blakely Cumann na mBan

17th January 1957 - 13th January 1976

Rosemary Blakely, from the Newington area of North Belfast, was born on 17th January 1957. Having three sisters and one brother, Rosemary was the second eldest of the family and received her education at the Holy Family Primary School and the Dominican College, Fortwilliam.

On leaving school, Rosemary joined the Civil Service, working as a clerical officer by day and studying for her 'A' Levels by night. On the morning of her death, Rosemary received her entrance papers to St Mary's College. Joining Cumann na mBan in 1973, Rosemary impressed her comrades with her liveliness and her great sense of humour. Whilst maintaining a high level of activity in operations against the British forces, she kept a low profile of her involvement, eluding their notice. Rosemary was often heard complaining that she was not being called out on active service enough. A superstitious person, Rosemary was heard to remark "It's January 13th - touch wood" on the morning of her last, fatal operation, on 13th January 1976.

Rosemary died, along with her comrade Óglach Martin McDonagh, in an accidental explosion while planting a bomb in a shop in North Street Arcade inside what was referred to at the time as the 'Belfast city centre security zone'. She was just four days off her 19th birthday.

The huge turnout at her funeral was testimony to her popularity inside and outside the Republican Movement. Shortly afterwards, the London Daily Mail carried a large feature on Rosemary, ending with the naive question, "How could such a respectable, intelligent, gentle girl join the IRA?"

It was exactly these qualities which motivated Rosemary to join the Republican Movement to fight the injustices of the British occupation.

Óglach Francis Stagg

4th October 1942 - 12th February 1976

Frank Stagg was born on 4th October 1942, the seventh child of a family of 13 near the village of Hollymount in County Mayo. He attended Newbrooke primary school and later the CBS school in Ballinrobe. On leaving school he worked as an assistant gamekeeper with his uncle before emigrating to England.

In England, he secured employment as a bus conductor and later as a bus driver. In 1970 he married a Mayo woman, Bridie Armstrong from Carnicon. He joined Sinn Féin in Luton in 1972 and shortly afterwards joined the IRA. Frank was arrested in April 1973, and charged with conspiring to commit arson. At his trial the following October with six others, he was sentenced to ten years imprisonment. Refusing to do prison work, insisting that he be treated as a political prisoner, Frank spent most of his time in jail in Albany Prison, Isle-of-Wight and later in Parkhurst, Long Lartin and Wakefield prisons in solitary confinement. Frank went on his fourth hunger strike in two years on December 14th, 1975, in Wakefield prison Yorkshire. Michael Gaughan had died on hunger strike the previous year.

On 12 February 1976 Frank Stagg died having fasted for 62 days. His remains were diverted by the Irish Government to Shannon Airport, and Special Branch seized the coffin and locked it in the airport mortuary refusing relatives access. His body was taken to Ballina by Special Branchmen to a grave 70 yards from where he had asked to be buried in the Republican plot. Six feet of cement was placed on top of the coffin to prevent his transfer. On the Sunday, the Republican Movement held its ceremonies at the Republican Plot, despite the presence of a massive force of Gardaí. A volley of shots was fired, and following an oration by Joe Cahill, a pledge was made that Frank Stagg's body would be moved to the Republican plot in accordance with his wishes.

Frank's wishes were fulfilled six months later, on 6th November; his remains were removed by IRA Volunteers, and reinterred beside Gaughan in the Republican plot.

Fiann James O'Neill

21st December 1958 - 12th February 1976

James 'Pavlo' O'Neill, born 21st December 1958, came from the New Lodge Road area of North Belfast where he was the oldest of four children, two brothers and one sister. James attended the Christian Brothers' School, where he was given the nickname of 'Pavlo.' Later he attended Harding Street Secondary School. James had all the interests of an average young boy and upon leaving school took work as an apprentice joiner.

Pavlo came from a Republican background. His Uncle, Volunteer Michael Kane, was killed on the New Forge Lane while on active service during an accidental explosion on 4th September 1972. James was only eleven years of age at the time of his Uncle's death. It therefore came as no surprise to Pavlo's family and friends when he, like so many others of the time, joined na Fianna Éireann.

The death in England of Volunteer Frank Stagg on hunger strike, caused much rioting back home. On 12th February, 1972, at the age of seventeen, during the ensuing riots on the Antrim Road, young James lost his life. His family remember him as a son to be proud of in many ways, but most of all for the strength of character and courage he showed during the volatile time of his death. It is with great sorrow he is sorely missed and will always be remembered by his family.

Óglach Sean Bailey

16th April 1955 - 13th February 1976

Born on 16th April 1955, Sean was the first born of a family of seven. His parents, James and Mary Bailey, lived at 6 Malcomson Street, Springfield Road with Mary's parents, John and Maggie McVeigh and Sean's great granny Kate. As a baby in the fifties, his granny, Maggie, would put Sean in his pram on top of the Republican paper, the War News, to be distributed to supporters in the area. 6 Malcomson Street was always an open door to Republicans in the forties, Tom Williams and Seamus 'Rocky' Burns being frequent visitors. Granny Maggie McVeigh died age 62 when Sean was 3 years old and was given a Republican funeral. In August 1969 Sean, then age 14, and his father helped defend the Clonard area from Loyalist mobs. It was at this time a friend, Fiann Gerard McAuley, was shot dead and Sean joined Na Fianna Éireann in the Pool area.

Sean, better known to his friends as 'Stu' left the Fianna at sixteen and joined 'C' Company, Óglaigh na hÉireann, in the Clonard area, before moving to 'A' Company in the Beechmount area. His comrades remember Stu as a quiet, dedicated and loyal young man. Sean met local girl Geraldine McGranahan and they were married in early March 1973, making a home for themselves in Earlscourt Street, and had a baby daughter, Seaneen. Sean worked for Hughes' 'Peter Pan' Bakery and then at the Silk and Rayon factory. He also played football for a local team but put the Republican Movement before everything else. Asked by his mother, not to leave the Movement but to slow down, he told her he hadn't joined the Army to take a back seat.

Despite being injured during the 1975 feud, Sean, still on crutches, carried on his work for the Republican Movement. On Thursday night, 12th February 1976, on Active Service at Nansen Street, Sean was critically injured in an accidental explosion. At 3:40am on Friday morning, 'Stu' lost his fight for life and Ireland lost a true son.

Óglach James McGrillen

21st April 1951 - 15th February 1976

James McGrillen was born in the Markets area on 21st April 1951. Later the family moved to Ballymurphy where Jim attended St. Kevin's Primary School and later St. Thomas' Secondary School on the Whiterock Road.

Jim worked for short while at Belfast Docks after leaving school in 1967 and then became a self-employed lorry driver. Jim, or 'Grizzle' as his friends knew him, married in 1970 and he and his wife had three children: Karen, Marie and Jean.

A second cousin of Bobby Sands (his father had been reared with Bobby's mother), Grizzle had a better than average understanding of the republican struggle. Both his parents came from staunch republican families, and he was well aware of the danger and hardship he would encounter when he volunteered for active service with Óglaigh na hÉireann.

A courageous, dedicated young republican soldier, he lost his life on active service in 1976.

Paul Best Sinn Féin

11th June 1956 - 18th February 1976

Paul Best was born on the 11th June 1956, and lived with his family at Divis Drive, adjacent to Turf Lodge, the area to which he dedicated himself. He was educated at Holy Child Primary School, St Theresa's and St Gabriel's.

He trained as a chef, and later worked in a variety of occupations throughout Ireland. Paul joined Sinn Féin in 1973, and quickly became an active force within the Martin Forsythe Cumann. He was editor of the Cumann's newspaper "An Troid", and having developed an oratorial ability which he used whenever possible, he became Cumann PRO, and Sinn Féin organiser for Andersonstown.

When the Cumann set up an incident centre in Norglen Road in 1975, Paul moved out of his home to ensure that the centre was always open to the local people. Paul was often the victim of attacks by local 'Sticks', in the incident centre, and on one occasion they burned his motorcycle. In November 1975, during fierce fighting between the Republican Movement and the Sticks, Paul, without regard for his personal safety, went to help a pensioner whose home had been damaged in an explosion. He was abducted by the Sticks, and shot twice in the back.

One bullet was removed in Belfast's Royal Victoria Hospital, but one was left as it was embedded so deeply. Confined to a wheelchair, Paul's father brought him back to the people he loved, in Turf Lodge, shortly before returning to hospital for more surgery. On February 18th 1976, Paul died from his injuries while undergoing surgery to have the remaining bullet removed.

His Sinn Féin comrades escorted Paul Best's remains to the family plot in Milltown Cemetery, Belfast.

Óglach Sean McDermott

20th April 1955 - 5th April 1976

Sean McDermott was born in Derry City on April 20th 1955. Shortly afterwards the family moved to Liverpool, returning to Belfast in 1961. Sean attended St. Theresa's Primary School and St. Mary's Grammar school in Andersonstown. He had a keen interest in Gaelic football and the Irish language, and had gained his Fáinne at the age of 13.

In May 1972 Sean was shot by British soldiers at Derrin Pass, in Andersonstown. When he had recovered from his injuries he was arrested and interned in Long Kesh. At 17 he was one of the youngest internees. When he was released from Long Kesh, in March 1975, he immediately reported back to the IRA for active service, while devoting some time to furthering his studies. He was offered places at St Joseph's teacher training college, and on a journalism course at the College of Business Studies. Sean's commitment to the republican movement was total and for him there was no choice, his duty to the movement came first.

Following a commercial bomb attack on the Conway Hotel in Dunmurry, on 5th April 1976, Sean's unit was prevented from using their pre-planned escape route. Sean entered a local house, intending to take the occupant's car to escape. The householder was an RUC reservist, and under the pretext of getting his keys, lured Sean upstairs, where he shot him at point blank range in the stomach. Sean's comrades on that fateful operation included Volunteer Kieran Doherty, who later died on Hunger strike in Long Kesh in 1981, and Volunteer Mairead Farrell, one of three women POWs who went on hunger strike in Armagh Women's Prison in December 1980, and who was executed by British undercover forces in Gibraltar in March 1988.

Volunteer Sean McDermott was buried with full military honours in Milltown Cemetery, Belfast.

Óglach Peter Cleary

18th September 1950 - 15th April 1976

Peter Cleary was born on 18th September 1950, the second eldest of thirteen children, the eldest son of Mary and the late Hugh. His mother recalls that Peter was like a father figure to the other children.

He was in his late teens when many people in the Six Counties, both Catholic and Protestant, took to the streets to demand Civil Rights. Like others of his era he witnessed the brutal reaction to this peaceful campaign by the British Government and their Unionist allies at Stormont.

Peter's knowledge of Irish history and the experience of seeing his people being oppressed by a foreign State paved the way for his active involvement in the 1st Battalion of the South Armagh Brigade of Óglaigh na hÉireann. The many successful attacks against the British crown forces is testimony to the time and energy Peter invested in the Irish Republican Army in South Armagh before his untimely death.

In April 1976, British undercover forces took Peter from a house in Forkhill. After beating him unconscious, they summarily executed him as he lay on the ground. However, Peter's death did not deter his comrades nor future generations, rather it has inspired all who continue to work for justice, equality and freedom.

But, sadly, in the words of his brother, "Ireland has lost a great son".

Óglach Jim Gallagher

22nd May 1955 - 17th May 1976

"We were in Cage D of Magilligan Prison at the time of Jim Gallagher's release, and the news of his tragic death only six days later came as a great shock to everyone.

Jim had been busy in the woodwork hut shortly before his release, busying himself with some craft work making gifts for family and friends.

Jim had a big beaming smile, a friendly nature and a mass of long dark hair. Like all prisoners, Jim took some slagging and gave out an equal amount. He could fight his corner, and fight it well.

He was highly intelligent and well read on socio-economic matters, had excellent debating skills and confidence in his arguments. He had all the makings of a great socialist worker and activist.

I used to delight in listening to Jim challenge, and demolish, the dubious political credentials of his debating opponents. Had he lived, I have no doubt that he would have been a great ambassador for the Republican struggle.

Jim was travelling on a bus which was passing the Fort George army base when a British soldier opened fire, killing him and wounding several others."

A Friend

Colm Mulgrew Sinn Féin

8th January 1950 - 5th June 1976

Colm Mulgrew was born on 8th January 1950 in Cookstown, County Tyrone. He went to school at St Patrick's Primary School in Dungannon. The family moved to Belfast where he attended St Malachy's College.

Colm worked as a laboratory technician, dealing with water pollution and other matters. At the time of his death he was doing an Open University Science Degree. In 1971 he married Chris Treanor and they lived in Camberwell Terrace, Newington.

After joining Sinn Féin in 1973, Colm's hard work and dedication soon ensured that he was appointed organizer of North Belfast Comhairle Ceantair.

On Saturday, 5th June 1976 at 7.55pm, Colm was shot dead by Loyalist gunmen when he answered a knock on his door.

Óglach Brian Coyle

3rd April 1959 - 30th June 1976

Brian Coyle was born into a family of three girls and two boys. He was born and raised in St. Columb's Wells and attended the local Long Tower Primary School. Brian experienced the bad housing, the discrimination, the rioting and the RUC's excesses during the Civil Rights period. These, and life in the Free Derry area, had a profound effect on him.

Brian joined Na Fianna Éireann when he was fourteen and became good friends with Eddie McSheffrey. Both teenagers were the driving force of the Fianna in the Bogside and Brandywell areas.

Brian was dissatisfied with what he felt was a limited role for the Fianna and was constantly lobbying the Army for more responsibility. To everyone's surprise, Brian was arrested and charged with possession of explosive substances. Brian had discovered that fireworks contained a black powder, which could be used in greater quantities to make small explosive charges. His interest in science at school had more to do with the presence of acids rather than things academic.

On his release from St. Pat's he immediately joined the IRA. On the afternoon of June 30th 1976, the British army came into the Bogside in large numbers to raid the shopping units at Meenan Square. Brian was preparing an attack on the raiding party when a grenade exploded accidentally. Brian was rushed to Altnagelvin Hospital but was dead on arrival.

He was buried with full military honours. Just hours before his funeral, Volunteers from the Bogside Company of which he was a member launched a sniper attack on British soldiers at Butcher Gate, killing one British soldier.

Óglach Thomas Kane

5th August 1947 - 6th July 1976

Thomas 'Tucker' Kane from the lower Falls area of Belfast, was born on 5th August 1947, the second eldest of six children. He attended St. Finian's School, Falls Road, and he left when he was 15 to work for the NSPCA in May Street. Later he spent time working for some of Belfast's best-known scrap merchants. 'Tucker' and Kathleen Dowling married on December 5th 1966 and set up home in the Riverdale area. They had two children, David and Maria.

Local Volunteers in the Riverdale area had received a lot of help from Tucker prior to him joining the IRA in mid-1971. He proved to be a fearless fighter, never known to be foolhardy or careless on operations, and insisting that everyone carried out their orders according to plan. His friends remember him as the kind of person who, once he had become your friend, he remained a true friend in the truest sense of the word.

Tucker was arrested and interned on the Maidstone Prison ship, but his incarceration was to be short-lived. In January 1972, he and six other Republicans escaped from the ship by climbing through a porthole, and braving the cold water, swam to the shore. They commandeered a bus to the Markets area from where they were safely taken across the border. It wasn't long before Tucker was back in action again. On one occasion, crown forces ambushed him and a couple of other Volunteers. In the gunfight that followed Tucker was grazed by a couple of bullets. The friendly doctor who tended to his wounds removed a splinter of copper from his temple and gave it to him as a keepsake.

In July 1976, Tucker was driving along the Glen Road when he was involved in a traffic accident. He survived only for a few days on a life support machine, but died from his injuries on 6th July 1976. He was buried in a family plot in Milltown Cemetery, where a black marble Celtic cross was later erected over his grave.

Derek Highsted Sinn Féin

9th January 1940 - 16th July 1976

Derek joined the Republican Movement when he was fifteen. He was interned just before his seventeenth birthday, making him the youngest internee at the time.

On his release from prison he completed his training as a plumber. Like many young Irishmen, he left Ireland to go to England to find employment. This however did not stop Derek from continuing his Republican work and he was soon active organising in London. He took part in and spoke at many rallies in Hyde Park and other venues throughout England.

He took a particular interest in Irish prisoners imprisoned in English jails. He spent a lot of time with Michael Gaughan and Frank Stagg when they were on Hunger Strike. He campaigned tirelessly for them and organised many rallies and events in London and beyond. These rallies helped highlight the campaign for the repatriation of Irish prisoners.

When both Volunteers died on Hunger Strike he organised the removal of the remains back home to Ireland for burial. He was the driving force for the fund raising activities for Prisoners and Sinn Féin. He was married to a native of Donegal and they had a family of one son and one daughter.

On 16th July 1976, he was working in Wales when he met his death in tragic and suspicious circumstances. Many of his friends and comrades believe that there was Crown Forces involvement in his death. At the time of his death he was the leader of Sinn Féin in London.

Óglach Peter McElchar

26th August 1956 - 17th July 1976

Peter McElchar was from Knock, Ballybofey, Co. Donegal. Although from the Twenty Six counties he quite clearly knew that the struggle for Irish independence didn't stop at the border. Though only a volunteer with Óglaigh na hÉireann for a short period prior to his death he was an active and committed member of his local unit.

On July 17th 1976 at 2.15pm, Peter who was 20 years old, and his comrade Patrick Cannon, were killed when the bomb they were transporting to a commercial target in nearby Castlederg exploded.

The fact that Peter and his comrade were both from the 26 counties seemed to anger the British and their unionist allies who condemned the young Volunteers and attempted to insult their memories. They failed to understand the selfless motivation of young men like Peter, underlining the ignorance of those within the British and unionist establishment to deal with the reality that their enforced presence in Ireland will forever be opposed by people from throughout the 32 counties.

Since partition and the emergence of the 'Orange State', many men and women from the 26 counties have continued to play a full role in the struggle for Irish freedom and have been an inspiration to the Volunteers in the six counties.

Peter was one such comrade and his comrades in the Donegal/West Tyrone areas fondly remember him.

Óglach Patrick Cannon

28th November 1955 - 17th July 1976

Patrick Cannon was from Edenmore, Co Dublin and like his comrade Peter McElchar from Co Donegal, he was acutely aware of the struggle for Irish Independence that was being waged in the occupied six counties of his country. He was not one to stand idly by and travelled hundreds of miles from his own native Dublin to engage the British forces of occupation.

He made the conscious decision to join the Republican struggle and was to pay the ultimate sacrifice for his convictions on 17th July 1976.

Patrick was seriously injured in the explosion that killed his comrade Peter McElchar as they were travelling towards Castlederg in Co Tyrone. He was taken to the Tyrone County Hospital in Omagh but because of the seriousness of his injuries he was being moved to a hospital in Belfast when he died en route.

Patrick had seen through the propaganda of those who attempted to portray the liberation struggle as a sectarian battle. He was a freethinker who was not fooled by the lies and deceit of the British and their propagandists and his bravery inspired many from his native Dublin to join the ranks of the IRA.

Every year Dublin Republicans gather to pay tribute to Vol. Patrick Cannon, the young man who refused to let distance deter him from participating in the struggle for Ireland's freedom.

Óglach Danny Lennon

11th November 1953 - 10th August 1976

Danny Lennon was born in Belfast on 11th November 1953. His family were no strangers to the republican cause, as his mother Eileen had been a member of the Belfast Brigade, Cumann na mBan during the 1940's and 50's. Joining the IRA in 1970, Danny quickly became one of the most active and dedicated members of 'B' Coy, 1st Battalion, regarded at one stage by British intelligence as Andersonstown's 'most wanted man'. In 1971 his brother Sean (Ginty), was interned in Long Kesh. Danny was arrested in October 1972 after an IRA operation in Carryduff. He was captured with three comrades and sentenced to six years. Those who were imprisoned with him remember him as a constant source of inspiration to fellow POW's.

When he was released from prison in early 1976, Danny was immediately back on active service with the reorganised 'B' company. It was while on active service on August 10th 1976 that Danny and his comrade were pursued by a mobile British army patrol. Over sixty shots were fired at the car, causing men, women and children to run for cover. At Finaghy Road North, one bullet hit Danny who was driving the car, killing him instantly. The car, out of control, struck a young family on the footpath, killing three young children and seriously injuring their mother. Danny's comrade was injured, and the gun they were carrying was found to be dismantled and unusable.

The deaths gave rise to the 'Peace People', which was backed by the British propaganda machine. While the peace movement was soon exposed and discredited, the self-sacrifice of young Volunteers like Danny Lennon will remain an inspiration to future generations.

Volunteer Danny Lennon was buried with his comrades in the Republican plot in Milltown Cemetery, Belfast.

Noel Jenkinson Sinn Féin

1929 - 9th October 1976

Noel was born in County Dublin in 1929 from a Protestant background. His father was a gardener and they moved around the country a lot. They moved from Loughrea to Dublin, living near Monkstown Castle and then on to the lodge off Monkstown Avenue. They then moved to Sallynoggin. While here, Noel spent 3 years in a hospital with TB.

He was described as a fun loving person who enjoyed being out in the pubs. He sometimes would buy a bottle of champagne on a Friday. When someone would ask him what he was celebrating he would tell them "Friday". He emigrated to England and worked as a bus conductor. He became a shop steward and secretary of the Highgate Branch of the Transport and General Workers Union. He was a member of the Communist party but was expelled in 1964 for his support for the Cuban Revolution. He was a supporter of the Maoist pro-Albanian group CPGML and visited Albania.

He was arrested for the 1972 Aldershot bombing. At his trial the judge, Sebag Shaw took part in the cross-examination and questioned him on his support for communism and his position on capitalism. He was sentenced to a 30-year recommended sentence. While imprisoned he joined the Republican Movement.

Noel was found dead in his cell in 9th October 1976. Another prisoner said that Noel was complaining of pains and that the screws gave him either tablets or powder. There was an official inquest into his death but no independent autopsy. But it was stated that the prison medical staff had not given Noel any medication.

Noel was the father of four children one of whom died.

Óglach Paul Marlowe

1945 - 16th October 1976

Paul Marlowe was an active member of the Republican Movement from 1970 up until his death on 16th October 1976.

He was born in Ardoyne and moved to England for a period. He returned home to help right the wrongs that he knew were happening in the North.

A former British soldier, Paul gave the benefit of his experience to the Army, one of his main interests being the training of young Volunteers. He was active in the Ardoyne Unit and then moved to the 1st Battalion. He was interned in Long Kesh for a short time. On his release he immediately reported back for active service.

Paul Marlowe died on active service on October 16th 1976 at the age of 31. His death was the result of an accidental explosion in which Joseph Surgenor and Frank Fitzsimons also died.

Óglach Frank Fitzsimons

29th January 1947 - 16th October 1976

Francie Fitzsimons, from Short Strand, was born on 29th January 1947, the fourth in a family of seven children, three of whom died while babies. He attended St Matthew's School, Seaforde Street, and later the Belfast Technical College. Francie had been a member of St Matthew's boxing club from the age of 12. He won many prizes in the sport, including the County Antrim light-welterweight, the Ulster junior light-welterweight and was a finalist in the Ulster senior championship. He represented Ireland at international level on one occasion. On finishing school he started work in Purity Brand meat plant on the Castlereagh Road, but later decided to take up an apprenticeship as a bricklayer. He married Ann Lyttle, a local girl, in 1968 and they had two sons Harry and Martin.

His family background was steeped in Republicanism. A cousin Volunteer Joey Fitzsimons and a brother in law Volunteer Joe Magee were both killed in action in 1972. His uncle Felix 'Yank' Kelly had been interned on the Al Rawdah and was picked up in the first internment swoops of 1971. Another uncle, Dickie Glenholmes Senior, was interned on the Argenta and his son Dickie, Francie's cousin, spent several years interned in the Seventies. Both of Francie's brothers, Harry and Paddy, were interned in the Seventies.

Francie was on the barricades in August 1969 and was a member of the CDL – the local civil defence committee - before deciding to join Óglaigh na hÉireann in 1973. Within a few months he was arrested at a British army checkpoint when the magazine of a gun was found in the back of his car. He was sentenced to three years imprisonment and was released in 1975 and immediately reported back for active service.

Francie was killed on active service on 16th October 1976 along with his close friend Joey Surgenor and Vol. Paul Marlowe, a comrade from West Belfast. They were killed in an accidental explosion while transporting a bomb for use against the occupation forces.

Óglach Joseph Surgenor

10th April 1952 - 16th October 1976

Joey Surgenor from Sheriff Street, Short Strand, was born on 10th April 1952. He and his twin sister, Geraldine, were the youngest in a family of six children. His father, a Protestant, died in 1972 whilst Joey was a POW in Belfast's Crumlin Road Jail.

Educated at St Matthew's Primary School, Seaforde Street, and St Augustine's Secondary School, Ravenhill Road, Joey left school in 1969 to work at a variety of jobs, which included being an errand boy for Solomon and Peres Record Wholesalers, as an orderly in the Royal Victoria Hospital and as a building labourer. Always carefree, with a vibrant sense of humour, Joey's main pastimes were football and reading novels. His paramount interest, however, was the Republican struggle and after a short spell manning barricades defending the nationalist Short Strand enclave in 1969, Joey eagerly joined the new IRA unit which was being organised.

A dedicated and fearless fighter, he took part in the gun-battle around St Matthew's Chapel on 27th June 1970, and when arrested in October 1971 he was already a veteran of Republican engagements against the enemy forces. Sentenced to eight years for causing an explosion at the Buffs Club, Albertbridge Road, Joey, or 'Budgie' as he was affectionately nicknamed by his comrades, used his time in captivity to educate and re-dedicate himself to the Republican ideal, impatiently awaiting the day of his release to involve himself once again in the continuing war against the British. That day came on 10th June 1976, and Joey, by now a fluent Gaelic speaker, walked free from Long Kesh and immediately reported back for active service with Óglaigh na hÉireann.

He died as a result of an accidental explosion only five short months later, on the evening of Saturday 16th October 1976, when he and two comrades, Francie Fitzsimons and Paul Marlowe, were en route to bomb a British army observation post situated beside Belfast City Gasworks in the Markets area.

Máire Drumm Sinn Féin

22nd October 1919 - 28th October 1976

Máire Drumm was born in the townland of Killeen in South Armagh on 22nd October 1919. She grew up in the tradition of militant republicanism which was so strong in the area. After completing school in Armagh, Máire moved to Belfast to find employment. It was while making regular visits to the republican prisoners in Crumlin Road Jail from her own area, that Máire met Belfast IRA Volunteer Jimmy Drumm. They were married in 1946 after Jimmy's release, and eventually settled in Andersonstown in West Belfast. The Drumms had five children, Seamus, Margaret,Sean,Catherine and Máire Óg.

It was from the pogroms of 1969 that Máire emerged as a gifted leader and organiser, her home became an open house for refugees from beleaguered areas of the city. Máire was among the first to warn that the 'peace-keeping' British troops were an occupation force. When the lower Falls was curfewed in July 1970 it was Máire who led the 'pram invasion' of women pushing prams laden with supplies into the besieged area, in defiance of the Brits. Máire's leadership qualities were recognised and when Sinn Féin was reorganised she was elected as vice-president of the party. Refusing to be silenced in spite of constant harassment, Máire was to serve several periods of imprisonment in Armagh and Mountjoy. Refused a visa to travel to the USA for eye treatment, Máire underwent surgery in Belfast's Mater hospital. It was while recovering from her operation that Máire was murdered on October 28th 1976. Loyalist gunmen, dressed as doctors, entered the ward and killed Máire, wounding another patient in the attack. At the time of her assassination, Máire's youngest daughter was serving a sentence in Armagh Women's prison.

"We must not take any steps backward, our steps must be onward; for if we don't the martyrs who died for you, for me, for this country, will haunt us for eternity."

Máire Drumm, Ard Comhairle Sinn Féin was buried with full honours in the family plot in Milltown Cemetery, Belfast, close to the Republican plot.

Óglach Seamus Harvey

10th October 1956 - 16th January 1977

On the 10th October 1956, Seamus Harvey was born to the parents of Patrick and Margaret Harvey. He was their third son of a family of three boys and one girl. Seamus spent his childhood playing in the fields around his family home in the town land of Drummuckavall.

On the 29th May 1963 he began his schooling in the newly built Shelagh School where his older brother Sean was given the honour of reading the Proclamation from the steps of the school before the pupils entered on the first day of opening. Seamus finished National School in the summer of 1970 and in September of that year he attended De Le Salle Secondary in Dundalk.

Seamus liked all sorts of sport, particularly Gaelic football and he became a very skillful player. He joined the Malachi Football Club and then moved to play for Crossmaglen Rangers.

After leaving school he went to work with a local building contractor, and in the autumn of 1973 he and some local youths formed the Shelagh Youth Club in the old school.

Seamus loved life and lived it to the full, and wherever he was, there was sure to be a bit of craic. He joined the Irish Republican Army in 1973 and took a keen interest in local community affairs. His cunning intellect, courage and dedication made Seamus stand out among his comrades and he was involved in virtually every operation carried out in his area.

The whole community joined in grief with his family as they laid him to rest in Crossmaglen Church Yard.

Óglach Trevor McKibbin

26th September 1957 - 17th April 1977

Trevor McKibbin was born on 26th September 1957 and lived at 27 Etna Drive in the North Belfast district of Ardoyne. He attended Holy Cross Primary School on Butler Street and St Gabriel's Secondary School on the Crumlin Road in Ardoyne. It was while at school that he developed a great interest in sports, especially football. He was also very interested in woodwork and he excelled at Art. On leaving school in 1973, he worked at labouring and bricklaying before starting work for Enterprise Ulster.

Both before and after he joined Óglaigh na hÉireann, he was subject to constant harassment, being arrested and questioned on numerous occasions by the Crown Forces.

On 17th April 1977 Trevor was shot in the back by British troops on waste ground at Flax Street in his native Ardoyne. The British soldiers alleged that he had been carrying a rifle - they also claimed to have challenged him to halt five times before shooting him down. Trevor, however, was unarmed at the time of his shooting.

At his funeral, on 20th April 1977, a pro-British death squad were responsible for a car-bomb which killed two young mourners. Sean Campbell was killed instantly and Sean McBride died later from his injuries.

Óglach Brendan O'Callaghan

5th July 1955 - 23rd April 1977

Brendan O'Callaghan was born on July 5th 1955 and was educated at St.Peter's Secondary school, Whiterock Road. On leaving school he joined his father working as a lorry driver.

Married on February 19th 1972, to Amelia, the young couple set up home at Carrigart Avenue in the Lenadoon estate in West Belfast. They had two children.

In 1975 Brendan was arrested on arms charges, and was held on remand in Crumlin Road Jail for several months, before the charges against him were eventually dropped in 1976.

After his release from prison, Brendan joined Óglaigh na hÉireann, and was a dedicated and respected Volunteer.

It was while he was on active service on April 23rd 1977 that Brendan was shot dead by undercover British forces at the Hunting Lodge Lounge Bar on the Stewartstown Road, not far from his home.

Volunteer Brendan O'Callaghan, 1st Battalion, Belfast Brigade Óglaigh na hÉireann, was buried with full military honours in the republican plot in Milltown Cemetery.

Óglach Tommy Tolan

19th June 1946 - 27th July 1977

Thomas 'Todler' Tolan from Ballymurphy was born on 19th June 1946. He joined the IRA in September 1971, at the same time as his close friend and comrade Jim Bryson. Interned in January 1972 and held aboard the Maidstone, Todler along with Bryson and five others escaped by climbing through a porthole and swimming ashore, where they commandeered a bus and drove to safety. Todler had been interned for just 11 days.

Re-arrested in September, Todler was charged with 'unlawfully escaping Her Majesty's custody', but when the case came up it was held that there was no case to answer. On his way out of court, Todler was arrested once again and interned in Long Kesh, where he immediately set to work planning another escape. This one was foiled, however, and he ended up with the POWs in the sentenced cages for 18 months. This sentence completed he was transferred back to the Internment cages.

Cathleen McCartland, a 12-year-old niece of Todler's, was tragically killed in a roof top accident on August 12th 1973. She was a member of Cumann na gCaillini.

Eventually under growing international pressure the British government was forced to abandon Internment Without Trial as a policy. Todler was one of the last Republican POWs to walk free in December 1975. He immediately reported back for active service.

Todler got married on July 9th 1977. He had only returned from his honeymoon when he was cold bloodedly ambushed and murdered by Official IRA gunmen as he walked home through his native Ballymurphy on July 27th. It was indeed tragic that Todler and his lifelong friend Jim Bryson, who had built such a reputation for themselves as daring and courageous Freedom Fighters, with their fierce and relentless attacks on British occupation forces, were to die at the hands of renegade Irishmen.

Óglach Paul McWilliams

27th May 1962 - 9th August 1977

Paul McWilliams, from the Whiterock area, was born on 27th May 1962. He attended St. Thomas' Secondary School.

Brought up in a republican family, in an area that witnessed much oppression from the British Army and the RUC, he made a conscious decision at a young age to join the Republican Movement - he joined Fianna Eireann. Like many of his peers he had personal experiences of harassment and a number of his family members were imprisoned for their Republican beliefs.

For the last few weeks of his short life, Paul had lived in an atmosphere of increasing repression by the British occupation forces in a working class Nationalist ghetto which had suffered much at the hands of the biased and bigoted sectarian political system.

On 9th August 1977, the sixth anniversary of the introduction of Internment, Paul was taking a short-cut through 'the bungalows' to the post office on a message for his mother, when he was shot in the back by a British soldier from the wall of Corry's timber yard.

Séan O'Conaill Sinn Féin

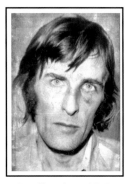

1st October 1977

Séan O'Conaill was a native of County Clare, and spent most of his early life in the county. When he left school he worked locally for a time before like many young people of his generation he left his family to find employment in England. Séan was always known for his interest in history and politics and his organisational skills. He involved himself in trade union activity and in improving working conditions.

In 1969 when the Civil Rights and civil disobedience campaigns commenced in the North, Séan was to the fore in many of the solidarity groups that were formed in many parts of England.

As more and more republicans and nationalists found themselves imprisoned, he was working along with the various prisoners' welfare and campaign groups. It was as a result of this type of work that he came to the attention of the Special Branch, so much so that he was charged under the conspiracy laws. The charge was false but it was designed to remove a dedicated political activist from the streets.

Séan was popular with the Irish POWs in the different prisons he was with them. Like them he was constantly seeking ways to improve conditions for all prisoners. Séan joined Sinn Féin in prison.

While in Parkhurst he fell in to ill health. The prison medical provision was inadequate and his condition deteriorated. Finally he was moved to Moorglen Hospital in Southampton, but he never recovered his good health and he died on 1st October 1977.

Séan was buried in Milltown Cemetery, Belfast.

Óglach Jackie McMahon

24th May 1959 - 10th May 1978

John 'Jake' McMahon from Short Strand was born on 24th May 1959, the only son in the family of five children. He attended St Matthew's Primary School, Seaforde Street, and then St Augustine's Secondary School, Ravenhill Road, leaving in 1975 to work as a packer in Glennan's in Hill Street.

Jake spent a year on remand in Crumlin Road Jail after being arrested in 1976 by the British occupation forces in a 'petrol-bomb factory' in Unity Flats. However, charges against him were eventually dropped when it could not be proven that he in fact was responsible for the petrol-bombs or indeed had any knowledge of their existence prior to his arrest.

Released in 1977, Jake experienced only a short period of freedom. He was arrested by an RUC patrol on the evening of 18th January 1978, while returning home after a social evening with friends in Belfast's city centre. He was not seen alive again. Two companions who were with him at the time and witnessed the incident, which took place close to Musgrave Street RUC Barracks, told relatives that they were sure he had been taken into the barracks.

Four months later, on 10th May 1978, just two weeks before his nineteenth birthday, his badly decomposed body was found floating in the River Lagan, just yards from where he had been stopped.

It has never been discovered who murdered Jake McMahon. At first the RUC at Musgrave Street Barracks denied all knowledge of the arrest on 18th January. But under pressure from relatives and in the light of the evidence of Jake's two companions, they conceded that they had taken Jake into custody 'for a few hours before releasing him'.

Óglach Paul Duffy

29th June 1957 - 26th February 1978

Paul Duffy was 21 years old when he was murdered by British undercover forces on 26th February 1978.

A statement issued by the I.R.A. at the time of his death said,
"When he and a companion left the hay barn they were called upon to halt by soldiers who had the area staked out for some time and who were in a position to arrest Volunteer Paul Duffy, who was unarmed. He raised his hands in the air to show that he was giving himself up but was shot in the forehead from a short distance. At this, his comrade made off and was seriously wounded by the gunfire.

The wounded man drove to Mullinahoe Parochial House but when the local priest reached the scene of the shooting intending to administer the Last Rites, he was told by the British army that there was no one there. Later that evening he was called by Coagh R.U.C. to the scene and shown the body."

Paul Duffy was a well known and liked young man. Members of Ardboe and Mountjoy G.F.C. formed a guard of honour at his funeral in the Church of the Most Blessed Sacrament, Mullinahoe.

Volunteer Paul Duffy is buried in Ardboe.

Óglach Henry Heaney

12th October 1912 - 4th June 1978

Henry Heaney was a dedicated Republican from his early youth and was imprisoned during the 30s campaign. In February 1975 he, along with his son was sentenced to 15 years and was moved from Crumlin Road jail to the cages of Long Kesh where he shared a hut with his good friend Bik McFarlane. He quickly became a father figure to many of the younger prisoners.

A man of great religious faith he said a daily rosary and even while in prison he was always up early and dressed in his best suit for Mass on Sundays. He had a sweet tooth and his particular favourite was brandy balls and he always managed to acquire chocolate for his family when they visited.

Despite his age and failing health, he never wanted to be treated any differently from the rest of his comrades. Henry succumbed to ill health and died on the 4th June 1978 in Musgrave Park Hospital's Military Wing, still in custody and under armed guard.

He now lies buried in the Republican plot in Lurgan in a grave which he had previously help dig for his good friend and comrade Thomas Harte.

To many people Henry was a dedicated Republican from his early youth. To his family he was a loving husband, father and grandfather whom they sadly miss.

Óglach Dennis Michael Heaney

1st November 1956 - 10th June 1978

Dennis was the youngest of four boys, in a family of thirteen children born to Eilis and Dennis Heaney. To his family, Dennis was a loving, caring son and brother. He enjoyed his music, was a big fan of Jethro Tull and Horslips and played traditional music on the fiddle. He had a droll sense of humour and was lively and full of craic. Dennis had a natural warmth about him and was good with people. At the time of his death he was reading 'Catch 22'.

On Saturday, 10th June 1978, Dennis, aged 21 years, was assassinated by British undercover forces at the junction of Harvey Street and Chamberlain Street, in the Bogside area. The soldiers' claim that they shot Dennis in the stomach and chest while he was armed and facing them was exposed by the findings of the inquest. The autopsy clearly demonstrated that all the bullets that struck Dennis had entered from behind. The first bullet to the leg brought him down and a soldier then stood over him and fired three bullets into his back, killing him.

Less than four weeks before he was killed, Dennis was arrested and held for three days by the RUC. He was released following a public outcry over allegations of torture, later confirmed by a local doctor. Before he was released, members of Special Branch told Dennis that they would pick their time and place and kill him.

Volunteer Dennis Heaney was buried with full military honours, on Tuesday, 13th June 1978. Thousands of mourners lined the route to the local cemetery. The cortege was led by a lone piper playing laments, with a guard of honour of Na Fianna Éireann, Cumann na mBan and Cumann na gCailini. At the gates of the cemetery, three volleys from rifles were fired in a last farewell to a young Volunteer of 1st Battalion, Derry Brigade, Óglaigh na hÉireann.

Óglach Jackie Mailey

19th September 1947 - 21st June 1978

Jackie Mailey, better known as 'Jake', was born on 19th September 1947 in the Ardoyne area of North Belfast. He started school in 1952 at the Holy Cross Boys School, Butler Street, and went on to St Gabriel's Secondary School were he remained until he was 15 years old.

Upon leaving school, he became apprenticed as a tiler. He joined the Republican Movement and was a dedicated worker. He was an excellent snooker player but his dedication to his political work kept him from taking part in competitions.

He married in 1971 and they had three children, all boys: Sean, Seamus and Niall, who was only one year old when his father died.

Along with two comrades, Volunteers Denis Brown and Jim Mulvenna, Jackie Mailey was murdered by undercover British soldiers on Wednesday morning, 21st June 1978. The three of them were on active service but unarmed, trying to plant a bomb at Ballysillan Post Office Telecommunications Depot in Belfast. A number of British undercover soldiers were waiting in ambush for them and surrounded them as they arrived. They then opened fire on the defenceless Volunteers, mercilessly cutting them down. Two civilians who happened to be passing were also shot. The British Army admitted to firing 200 hundred rounds in the slaughter.

Óglach Denis Brown

13th May 1950 - 21st June 1978

Denis Brown, better known, as 'Dinny', was born on 13th May 1950 in the Ardoyne area of North Belfast. He was educated at Holy Cross Boys Primary School in Butler Street. At the age of 11, he began his secondary education at St Gabriel's on the Crumlin Road until at the age of 15, he went on to become a barman.

He joined the Republican Movement and was very active, shirking no task. He married in 1970 and three children - two boys and a girl - were born to the Browns. The children were named Mark, Damien and Bronagh.

At Ballysillan Post Office Telecommunications Depot, Vol Dinny Brown was brutally slaughtered by undercover British soldiers while on active service. Two friends and comrades, Volunteers Jackie Mailey and Jim Mulvenna, were also callously murdered, along with two passers-by. The Volunteers had planned to bomb the depot and had proceeded to the target without any weapons. They were, however, surrounded by a number of undercover British soldiers who cut them down. The British army later admitted firing 200 shots at the three men.

Denis Brown and his two comrades were killed on active service on 21st June 1978.

Óglach Jim Mulvenna

26th January 1950 - 21st June 1978

James Gerard Mulvenna was born on 26th January 1950. His family lived at the time in Raglan Street and he was baptised in St Peter's Church. The family moved to Ardoyne shortly after and Jim started his school days in Holy Cross Primary School. He went to secondary school at St Gabriel's, Crumlin Road, which he left when he was 15. His first job was on a building site, following which he started as a trainee in Mackies, which he left to take up employment as a rent-collector in the Ardoyne area.

When the campaign began in 1969, he quit his job and joined the IRA, to which he devoted all his energy. While engaged on active service on 13th February 1972, he was shot and seriously wounded - he was hit nine times. For a long time he recuperated in Musgrave Park hospital. Having recovered, he was sentenced to four years in Long Kesh. After the judge had passed sentence, Jim, who had refused to recognise the court, said: 'Irishmen and Irishwomen have struggled to free this country. Now that the struggle is nearly ended I am proud to have been part of it'.

Released in 1976, he met Kathleen Magee, the girl who would later become his wife. They married and moved to live in Ballycastle Street. It was here that their daughter Ciara was born in January 1978. Jim had many varied interests. He was an avid reader of Irish and European history and Geography. He also enjoyed restoring old furniture and he loved arts and crafts.

Jim was a cousin of Vol. Patrick Mulvenna who was killed in action in August 1973. The last time Jim left home was on 20th June 1978. He and two comrades, Vols Denis Brown and Jackie Mailey, planned to bomb Ballysillan Post Office Telecommunication Depot but they were ambushed by Crown Forces who killed the three unarmed Volunteers in an orgy of gunfire which also claimed the lives of two passers-by.

Óglach Pat Harkin

12th February 1945 - 2nd October 1978

Pat Harkin came from a family of twin sisters, three other girls, and seven brothers from the Brandywell area of Derry. Big Pat was one of Derry's real characters. A greyhound lover and like his brothers, Pat was well known in 'doggie' circles around the North West. An easy-going, witty man, he was deadly serious when the occasion demanded.

Before coming a Volunteer Pat worked hard at his trade as a steel erector travelling all around the North erecting electric pylons for the Electricity Board.

After witnessing events on the streets of Derry and Belfast, Pat was one of the first to take up arms to defend the areas. He was an active Volunteer during the Free Derry No-Go era.

While on the run in Buncrana Pat's exploits became legendary. On one occasion Pat skinned and cured a deer that had just been shot on a hunting expedition in the wilds of Donegal. While eating the deer one of his comrades almost choked to death on Pat's well aimed bullet.

He had a great interest in the welfare of his fellow volunteers, and often went out of his way to ensure that they did not go hungry and had at least one good meal a day.

Pat liked his football and it was while playing a charity match that he took a heart attack and died. The 'Pat Harkin Cup' named in his honour, is the only summer cup competition left in Derry, proof of the esteem with in which Pat is still held in his community.

Óglach Patsy Duffy

14th March 1928 - 24th November 1978

In one of the earliest examples of the British "Shoot to kill" tactic, unarmed Volunteer Patsy Duffy was shot dead by the British Army in Maureen Avenue in November 1978.

Although Patsy was a well known republican in the Brandywell most people did not know that he was one of the IRA's most valuable members in the area. He controlled a network of helpers and dumps in the district and played a vital role in the armed struggle in Derry at that time.

Patsy was a life long republican and an honest and hard working family man. He was a skilled mechanic and fitter but because of the discrimination in the job market against the nationalist people he had to move away from his home on several occasions to find work.

Patsy was actively supported in his role as a republican activist by his devoted family, his wife Moira and children Patrick, Mary, Marguerita, Martina, Raymond and Bridín. Indeed on the night he was killed, he had just left his sixteen year old daughter in his car along with his grandchild, Mary's son Martin, while he entered a nearby house to check one of his arms dumps.

Unknown to Patsy, British undercover soldiers were lying in wait and opened fire without warning. They fired a total of 38 rounds, hitting Patsy fourteen times, killing him instantly.

He was buried with military honours.

Óglach Laurence Montgomery

12th June 1954 - 5th January 1979

Laurence Montgomery was born and reared in the North Belfast district of Ardoyne. When what many refer to as 'the Troubles' began in 1969, Laurence witnessed at first-hand the blatant repression of, firstly, the RUC and then later the British army.

Shortly after this, he joined the Republican Movement. He was extremely security-conscious. Although he was virtually unknown in Republican circles because he preferred the cloak of anonymity to pursue his Republican beliefs, he was deeply involved in the liberation struggle for many years.

His secrecy kept him out of the clutches of the occupation forces, and while internment depleted the ranks of the Belfast Brigade, it was young people like Laurence who were left to carry on the struggle.

Towards the end of his life, he expressed deep concern for his comrades in the H-Blocks of Long Kesh who by now were into their third year on the 'blanket' protest. Like other Republicans, he found his own convictions greatly reinforced by their courage and strength.

On 5th January 1979, alongside his comrade Volunteer Frankie Donnelly, he was killed in an accidental explosion not far from his North Belfast home in Ardoyne. He left behind his wife Maureen and their two young children, Laura and Kieran.

Óglach Frankie Donnelly

26th August 1954 - 5th January 1979

Francis 'Frankie' Donnelly was born on the 26th August 1954 in the Ardoyne area of North Belfast, an area that had suffered greatly under Unionist rule. The son of Francis and Mary, he was also known as Fungus.

Educated in North Belfast, Frankie first joined the Auxilary IRA, before becoming active with Óglaigh na hÉireann. Frankie was interned twice in the 1970s, following in the footsteps of his father, who had been interned in the 1940s.

Frankie was a quiet person who kept his counsel but who always had time for others. If he could help he would and he was a natural listener, being interested in people. He also enjoyed attending football matches, the odd bet and a game of snooker or pool.

Frankie married his wife Rosemary on his birthday in 1978 and was an expectant father when he lost his life.

Frankie died with his comrade Volunteer Laurence Montgomery in an accidental explosion on 5th January 1979 in his native Ardoyne.

He is buried in Milltown Cemetery alongside his comrades.

Óglach Billy Carson

19th February 1947 - 25th April 1979

Billy Carson, from the Cliftonville Road area, was born on 19th February 1947. Originally from the Lower Falls, Billy, the third child and eldest son in a family of 11 children, was educated at St Peter's Primary School, Raglan Street. He played hurling and Gaelic football for the school team and was a swimming enthusiast. He always retained his love for playing hurley and even after leaving school in 1962, when he went to work as a dock labourer, he still found time to turn out regularly to play for the Sarsfields hurling team.

In 1967 he married and moved to live in the Cliftonville area. Both of Billy's parents, Margaret and Samuel were staunch Republicans, Samuel being interned between 1942 and 1945 in Crumlin Road and Derry Jail. Billy himself joined the Republican Movement in late 1970 while the IRA were re-organising in the aftermath of 'the Split'.

Although living in the North of the city, Billy spent a great amount of his time in the Lower Falls, where he was active in 'D' Company, 2nd Battalion. A courageous fighter, Billy was also scrupulously security conscious, and whilst continually remaining highly active he was one of the very few who evaded internment or even arrest on suspicion of being an IRA Volunteer right up until the time of his death.

Billy died in the early hours of Wednesday, 25th April 1979, only hours after being shot by loyalist gunmen as he entered his house in Rosevale Street off the Cliftonville Road. Two assassins had called at his house earlier that evening but when his children, Stephanie and Jim, explained that their parents had gone out, they left. One hour later, they returned and sat with the children in the house until, at 11:30pm, Billy and his wife Annie returned home. The gunmen met him at the door and shot him several times before disappearing into a nearby loyalist stronghold.

Óglach Peadar McElvanna

29th December 1955 - 9th June 1979

Born on 29th December 1955, Peadar was the tenth of fourteen children. He attended Armagh Catholic Boys School, and being a keen footballer he joined the local Harps GFC.

At the age of fifteen, while returning home from a football training session, Peadar fell victim to a random attack by the RUC. He was struck by an RUC Landrover, mercilessly beaten and left for dead. This attack left him with permanent deafness in one ear. In 1972, at the age of sixteen, Peadar was interned in Long Kesh. His refusal to recognize the Long Kesh Commissions meant that he was not released from Internment until 1974.

Upon his release he returned to Armagh CBS, completed his A-Levels, and secured a place at Queens University in Belfast. He was, however, never to attend University as in the summer of 1975 he was rearrested on arms charges, and after a successful bail application went on the run, living at various locations in Armagh, Monaghan and Dublin.

While on the run he endeavoured to continue his academic career, embarking on a course in accountancy through a college in South Dublin in 1978. He also secured a position as a trainee accountant with a city centre firm. This was again short-lived as he was arrested once more and held on remand in Portlaoise on a charge of attempted murder. At the subsequent trial Peadar was acquitted of all charges and for the third and final time in his short life he shook the hand of freedom.

On 9th June 1979 Peadar was mortally wounded in a confrontation with undercover British soldiers at Lagan, outside Keady in Co. Armagh.

Óglach Martin McKenna

1955 - 23rd October 1979

Martin McKenna, from Greencastle, North Belfast, was born in 1955 and educated at Harding Street Christian Brothers School. After school he became a motor mechanic and could often be seen driving around in a variety of old 'bangers'.

He joined the Republican Movement in 1971 and became an active Volunteer. He was nicknamed 'Wild Bill' because he had a long beard and wore a cowboy jacket. Martin was a young man who, like most his age, enjoyed a few jars and was a good man for the 'craic'.

Martin was interned in 1973 and released in mid-1975. Charged with possession of explosives in the Summer of 1976, he became one of the first blanketmen in the H-Blocks of Long Kesh when he was sentenced to 14 years imprisonment. However, he was only to serve 17 months in jail because his appeal was successful.

Martin was the first of the blanketmen to be released and immediately began to campaign ceaselessly on behalf of his comrades who were still imprisoned. He addressed countless protests and public meetings all over the thirty-two counties as the H-Block campaign began to gain momentum.

Martin McKenna was killed in a car crash at Tinkers Hill on the main Newry/ Banbridge Road on Tuesday, 23rd October 1979. He was engaged to marry his girlfriend, Christine Polland, the following February.

Óglach Kevin Delaney

10th March 1953 - 17th January 1980

Kevin Delaney, from Ballymurphy, was born in the Lower Falls area on 10th March 1953, the eldest in a family of eleven children. He attended St Joseph's Primary School, Colinward Street, after the family moved to live in Ballymurphy in 1959. Kevin, or 'Dee' as he was affectionately nicknamed, was a keen boy scout and was a member of St Peter's Boy Scouts for two years. He also began attending the 43 Club in Divis Street and it was there that he first developed his interest in the Irish language. At the age of 13 Dee joined a slua of na Fianna Eireann in the Kashmir area.

When 'the Split' came in 1969 'Dee' took the correct course and, with his comrades in the Ballymurphy area, helped organise and build the Republican base in that area. Arrested in late 1971 he was sentenced to ten years imprisonment which he served in the Cages of Long Kesh. In the Cages, he spent much of his time studying the Irish language, reading up on the Irish struggle and familiarising himself with the writings of many of the world's revolutionary writers.

On his release he reported back immediately for active service. At the same time, he busied himself organising and planning ways in which the social problems in his home area, probably one of the most socially-deprived in the Six Counties, could be relieved. The war against Britain was his most immediate concern however, and within three years of his release from jail Kevin was killed on active service on 17th January 1980, in an accidental explosion while he was transporting a bomb on a train between Dunmurray and Belfast. Two civilians also died in the explosion.

Kevin was survived by his young wife Edie, whom he had married only several months previously, and by their son Sean Paul and their daughter Ceire, who was born after her father's death.

Óglach Robert Carr

7th April 1959 - 1st April 1980

Robert Manus Carr, commonly known as Bob to his friends, was born on 7th April 1959 in Quay Street, Newry. His parents, Noel and Josie, lived in the O'Neill Avenue area and they had one other child, Mary. Educated at the Abbey Primary he moved on to complete his schooling at St Joseph's. There he formed a close bond with a schoolmate and they were to remain close friends, almost inseparable, up until Bob's untimely death. On leaving school, Bob started an apprenticeship in bricklaying. He went to the Training Centre and from there to a steady job in the building trade. Such was the quality of his work that a number of builders were after his services.

He had a great love for fishing and was often seen at the Albert Basin showing off his expertise. He bought an aquarium, which he proudly displayed in the family living room. In swimming he won two medals and could often be seen perfecting his skills at the 'Blue Motion', a disused quarry full of water. He was a strong young man both physically and in his republican beliefs. He saw injustice all around him and experienced at first hand the harassment of the British Army who constantly stopped and searched him. In the mid 70s he joined a local unit of the IRA determined to fight for his country's freedom. During this period he was arrested and interrogated for three days. Bob met a local girl, Maureen McManus, and they got married in 1978. A daughter Rachel was born to them in May the following year. He was now living in Fathom Park.

In March 1980, Bob was critically injured in an accidental explosion at the Customs Post on the Dublin Road. He received terrible burns to his body from which he never recovered. He died on 1st April, six days before his 21st birthday. News of his death came as a great shock to his family and friends. His family treasure his memories and his comrades remember him with pride.

Óglach Terence O'Neill

23rd October 1958 - 1st July 1980

Terence O'Neill was born in the Ormeau Road area of Belfast in 1958 and Teddy, as everybody knew him, joined na Fianna Éireann in 1971, at the age of 14. A short time later, his family moved to the Turf Lodge area.

It was when he lived in Turf Lodge that he joined the ranks of Óglaigh na hÉireann. His Republican activities made him a target for constant harassment from the Crown forces. Despite this, Teddy's commitment to the Republican struggle never wavered. He met and married his wife Mary, who bravely bore the hardship which flows from having a spouse in the IRA and the constant worry and loneliness of having a loved one on the run. They had one child, Sinead.

On 1st July 1980, near the Ballymurphy Tenants Association on the Whiterock Road, Óglach Teddy O'Neill made the ultimate sacrifice for the country he loved. After carrying out a punishment shooting, he and his comrade, both wearing hoods, were spotted by an RUC mobile patrol. Teddy had concealed his pistol and his comrade was unarmed. Heavily-armed RUC men leapt from their vehicles and opened fire without warning on the two Volunteers. Teddy was hit and fell seriously wounded. His comrade escaped the indiscriminate fusillade of bullets.

As Teddy lay on the ground, bleeding profusely, an RUC man ran up to him and fired several rifle-shots into his body. He was then dragged along the ground for about 30 yards and thrown into the back of an RUC landrover.

After the shooting, British troops and RUC who flooded the area looking for Teddy's comrade were fiercely resisted by local people. The spirit which had driven Teddy O'Neill to such sacrifice was alive and well among the people he had loved and given his all for.

Óglach Peadar Mohan

31st August 1952 - 1st February 1981

Peadar Mohan was born on the 31st August 1952. His parents, Peter and Brigit, had 5 children, Margaret, Peadar, Patsy Philip and Frank.

The family home in Kilcrow, Clontibret, Co Monaghan was approximately 2 miles from the Armagh border. Peadar attended the local primary school St Mary's and then the 'Tech' in Monaghan town. He got a job in a local furniture factory as a polisher and played the pipes in the local O'Neill Pipe Band. He played football for the local GAA club Clontibret O'Neills.

The close proximity to the border, Internment, Bloody Sunday, brutal repression by the forces of the British State impacted on Peadar and many others in Monaghan at that time. He joined Óglaigh na hÉireann. He quickly assumed a leadership role and played a full and active part in IRA activities in the area bordering Armagh and Monaghan.

Arrested in 1973, he was in Mountjoy during the famous helicopter escape. He was then moved to Portlaoise with the rest of his comrades. On his release he immediately returned to active service. Within a year he was back in Portlaoise convicted of IRA membership.

On release he again returned to active service and in 1977 was arrested and did time in the Crumlin Road on remand and then in the H-Blocks.

Released in June 1979 he died on active service on 1st February 1981.

His courage, determination and leadership at a crucial and difficult period helped create the political landscape in which we find ourselves today.

Óglach Liam Hannaway

29th January 1916 - 2nd February 1981

Liam Hannaway was born in 1916, into a family with a strong republican family dating back to the Fenians, and as a youth Liam joined Na Fianna Éireann, and then Óglaigh Na hÉireann, a connection he was to maintain throughout his 65 years.

During his lifetime he was to suffer imprisonment when in 1940 he was arrested after an operation at Leopold Street barracks charged with possession, he was sentenced to 7 years penal servitude. Over 30 years later, in 1972, he was again arrested and interned in the prison ship, the Maidstone and then held in Long Kesh. During this spell of imprisonment Liam participated in a Hunger Strike for political status. He was released on the grounds of ill health in 1974. Each time he was released Liam reported back to Óglaigh Na hÉireann.

Liam was involved in many aspects of the republican struggle. In 1969 he was actively involved in the organisation of defence during the Loyalist pogroms in the Clonard and Kashmir areas of Belfast. Along with his comrades, Jimmy Perry, Gerry Adams senior and Tom Magill, he was a founding member of the Felons Club. His sons clearly recall the stories of how the first meeting was held in Jimmy Perry's house in Cupar Street. During the blanket protests and Hunger Strikes Liam was very active, organising support throughout the country.

Liam's interest in Irish history led him to become involved in the Henry Joy Association. A fluent gaelic speaker, Liam devoted a great deal of his time to teaching and working for the language that he loved. Much of his time was spent promoting Gaelic games and pastimes. As an active member of Sinn Féin he promoted the organisation by speaking on its behalf in the Gaeltacht. Liam died on 2nd February 1981, still an active Volunteer in Óglaigh Na hÉireann.

Óglach James Burns

12th June 1947 - 23rd February 1981

James 'Skipper' Burns was born on June 12th 1947. He came from a family of six brothers and six sisters. His father James had been interned in the Forties and was in Crumlin Road Jail with Tom Williams. When he was 16 years old, James joined Fianna Eireánn. A quiet, thoughtful person, when 'the Troubles' began in 1969, at the outset of the present campaign, James was quick to act in defence of the Lower Falls area. By this stage 'Skipper' who was married and had one young daughter, devoted a lot of his time to recruiting and training Volunteers in Óglaigh na hÉireann.

When Internment was introduced, Skipper evaded arrest until October 2nd 1971. He was taken to Palace Barracks where he was brutally beaten and interrogated for three days before he was moved to Crumlin Road Jail. After a period he was transferred to Long Kesh where he was interned for three years. He was later awarded £1,300 in compensation for his savage beating in Palace Barracks.

He spent his time in prison planning ways to escape. He was selected for the escape committee and was instrumental in planning the escape, from Cage 4, of Billy Kelly, the only person to escape from Long Kesh by getting over the wire. For a time he took part in making 'homebrew'. His comrades in Hut 31 will remember him for his disastrous efforts in this area. The whole hut was violently ill for three days after sampling Skipper's concoction!

After being released from Internment Skipper rejoined the struggle on the outside. This involved months on the run, separated from his wife and three young daughters. It was a tragic blow to the family when his wife died on February 23rd 1980.

Exactly one year later, on February 23rd 1981, Skipper Burns met his death at the hands of Loyalist gunmen who broke into his house through a back door and shot him as he lay sleeping.

Óglach Bobby Sands

9th March 1954 - 5th May 1981

Bobby Sands was born on 9th March 1954 in the predominantly Loyalist Rathcoole area. In June 1972 the family were intimidated out of their home and moved into the Twinbrook estate on the outskirts of West Belfast.

Bobby joined Óglaigh na hÉireann when he was 18. In October 1972 he was arrested and charged with possession of weapons, and would spend the next three years in the cages at Long Kesh, where he had Political Status. Released in 1976, Bobby returned to Twinbrook and reported back to the IRA. Within six months he was arrested again following a bomb attack in Dunmurry. Bobby and three other men were arrested and a further two men wounded in a gun-battle. In September 1977, Bobby and his comrades received 14 years each for possession of one revolver. Back in Long Kesh again, Bobby began his sentence this time without political status.

Under the pen name 'Marcella', he was a regular contributor to 'An Phoblacht'. The H Blocks and Armagh Jail became a battlefield between the POWs and the British government. Bobby became OC of the POWs during the 1980 hunger strike, and volunteered to lead the second hunger strike, which he began on March 1st 1981.

In April 1981, Bobby was elected as MP for Fermanagh/South Tyrone.

At 1.17am on Tuesday 5th May 1981, after 65 days on hunger strike, Bobby Sands died in the prison hospital. The first of ten republican POWs to die, Bobby had dedicated his life to his people, and to the republican cause, eventually offering up his own life, in a conscious effort to further that cause and the cause of those with whom he had shared almost eight years of his adult life.

Óglach Francis Hughes

28th February 1950 - 12th May 1981

Francis Hughes was the youngest of four brothers in a family of ten who lived in a farming community just outside the rural village of Bellaghy, County Derry. He joined the I.R.A. at an early age and in a short time saw active service and eventually went on the run. Francis is the most celebrated Republican Freedom Fighter to come out of the recent struggle. The stories of his exploits go some way to characterise the man and the level of his involvement. On countless occasions Francis was surrounded by British crown forces, sometimes alone and sometimes with comrades, but he calmly slipped through their nets with what has been described as utter cheek and nerves of steel.

The circumstances of his capture once again displayed the unselfish and courageous nature of Francis Hughes. He and a fellow Volunteer were walking through the Glenshane Pass to a safe house when they walked into a British Army undercover post. A gun battle ensued with Francis hitting two of the British soldiers, one fatally. Francis was seriously injured and was arrested the next day, 17th March. He was taken to Musgrave Park Hospital where he remained for 12 months. He was eventually charged and sentenced to life imprisonment. Francis joined the Hunger Strike and died 59 days later on 12th May 1981. He was the second Hunger Striker to die; his cousin Thomas McElwee was the ninth Hunger Striker to die.

Francis wrote to the people of South Derry when he started his Hunger Strike, one paragraph read...
"I have no prouder boast than to say I am Irish and have been privileged to fight for the Irish people and for Ireland. If I have a duty, I will perform it to the full in the unshakeable belief that we are a noble race and that chains and bonds have no part in us."

Óglach Raymond McCreesh

25th February 1957 – 21st May 1981

Volunteer Raymond McCreesh was born on 25th February 1957. He was an ordinary, hard-working and well-liked young member of his community. Although a young man, Raymond had no doubts that the future for all the people of Ireland lay in a united 32 County Republic. He took his own step on this journey towards the Republic when as a young man of 17 he joined the IRA.

In 1976 Raymond was sentenced to 14 years imprisonment following his capture on active service near his home village in Camlough in South Armagh. In the H-Blocks he immediately joined the blanket protest demanding political status for himself and his comrades. So strong was Raymond's commitment that for almost 4 years he took no visits, until informing his family in February 1981 of his intention of going on hunger strike.

Raymond died on 21st May after 61 days on hunger strike. His own lifetime's journey ended with his death in a prison hospital cell, but he remains an inspiration for others to see the journey completed.

He was buried with full military honours.

Ar dheis Dé go raibh a anam

Óglach Patsy O'Hara INLA

11th July 1957 - 21st May 1981

Patsy O' Hara was born in Bishop Street, Derry City, on the 11th July 1958. His parents had three other children. Patsy joined Na Fianna Éireann in 1970 and his brother Sean was interned in 1971 in Long Kesh.

Shortly before Bloody Sunday Patsy was wounded by British soldiers. He was unable to attend the march but watched it go by him in the Brandywell. The events that day had a lasting effect on him.

In October 1974 Patsy was interned in Long Kesh. After his release in April 1975 Patsy joined the newly emerged IRSP and INLA. In June 1975 he was arrested in Derry and held on remand for 6 months. In September 1976 he was arrested yet again and once more was held on remand for 4 months.

Patsy went to live in Dublin for a number of months and was an active member of the IRSP Ard Comhairle. He returned to Derry in January 1979 and was active in the INLA. On May 14th 1979 he was arrested and charged with possession of a grenade. He was sentenced in January 1980 to eight years. He went on the blanket in H5, where his brother Tony was already on protest.

He became OC of the INLA prisoners at the beginning of the first Hunger Strike. He went on Hunger Strike on the 22nd March 1981. On Thursday May 21st at 11.29pm he died after 61 days on Hunger Strike.

He was twenty three years of age.

Óglach George McBrearty

8th November 1956 - 28th May 1981

George was born on 8th November 1956. His mother and father lived in Rathowen Park, Creggan, where he was brought up with his brothers and sisters, Danny, Thomas, Joe, Marie, Betty, Catherine, Veronica, Donna, Loretta and the late Pat.

A footballer in his teens, he played for his school team and his local side, Creggan Celtic. He liked a game of snooker and a wee flutter at the bookies. He joined Na Fianna Éireann in 1972 aged fifteen and progressed to the Army a year later. When he left school, George worked for a period in Lipton's Supermarket, a job that didn't last long as he had to go on the run when he was just seventeen.

He was active in the Creggan company and was interned in 1974. On his release he returned to active service and was to the fore of much IRA activity in his local area.

He married Rosemary, and they had three children, Orla, Kelly and Thomas. Thomas was christened the Sunday before George died.

George had an outgoing, fun-loving personality coupled with a devil-may-care attitude that exhibited itself in his many engagements with the enemy. George was shot dead on active service by undercover British soldiers along with his friend and comrade Charles 'Pop' Maguire on 28th May 1981.

He was buried with full military honours.

Óglach Charles Maguire

25th January 1961 - 28th May 1981

Charles 'Pop' Maguire was born on the 25th January 1961, the sixth child in the family and the first boy. He was much loved and spoilt by his adoring parents and his five older sisters. In his turn he became a big brother who spoilt his younger siblings. He was also a loving husband and father to Donna and Clare.

At the age of 11 Charles went to St. Columb's College but had an unhappy time there, partly because of his beliefs and his family background. He left school and followed in his father's footsteps, learning the trade of bricklaying. He grew up loving music and I can still remember his shock and disbelief on hearing the news of John Lennon's murder.

As a child of the sixties he saw the worst excesses of British rule in Ireland - Bloody Sunday, two sisters jailed as Republican activists one of them shot and seriously injured. Coming from a republican family he was harassed from an early age and was constantly stopped and searched by the British Army and the RUC. Within days of his sixteenth birthday he was arrested for the first of many times. Having made the decision to join the IRA he became one of its more active and competent volunteers. During his service he made a considerable contribution to the war against British rule in Ireland.

Pop was shot and fatally wounded alongside his friend and comrade George McBrearty by undercover British soldiers at the bottom of Southway on the 28th May 1981. Another volunteer was wounded and a fourth ferried his wounded and dead comrades away from the scene.

He was buried with full military honours.

Óglach Joe McDonnell

14th September 1951 - 8th July 1981

Joe McDonnell was born on 14th September 1951, the fifth of eight children, in Slate Street in Belfast's lower Falls. He married Goretti Healy in 1970, and eventually set up home in the Lenadoon estate.

A well-known and popular figure, Joe was regarded by his comrades as a cool and efficient Volunteer. He was arrested in 1972 and interned, first on the prison ship Maidstone, and later in Long Kesh. On his release, Joe joined the IRA in Andersonstown, but, by 1973 he was again interned. The McDonnell home became a regular target for the British army.

Joe resumed his trade as an upholsterer when he was released from prison, but his family life was constantly interrupted by British army raids and arrests. Always security conscious, Joe guarded his involvement in the republican movement, never flaunting his activities. He was arrested in October 1976 following a bomb attack on the Balmoral Furnishing Company near Twinbrook. From the day he was sentenced Joe refused to take a visit as it meant wearing the prison uniform, he would not be criminalised. Contact with his wife and family was by means of the smuggled 'comms'.

Joe didn't volunteer for the 1980 hunger strike, but the sense of bitter determination within the H-Blocks and Armagh due to British attempts to criminalise the republican struggle, led him to put his name forward in 1981. He joined the hunger strike on Sunday May 9th 1981. In June he narrowly missed election as a TD for Sligo/Leitrim.

At 5.15am on July 8th 1981, after 61 days of agonising hunger strike, IRA Volunteer Joe McDonnell died. He was buried with full Military honours in the Republican plot in Milltown Cemetery. The British army launched an attack on his funeral as it made its way through Andersonstown.

Fiann John Dempsey

18th December 1964 - 8th July 1981

As news of the death of Volunteer Joe McDonnell reached his native West Belfast, people had taken to the streets to express their anger. Within three hours the British occupation forces had claimed another young patriot's life, that of Fiann John Dempsey from Turf Lodge.

John Dempsey was only sixteen years old when his life was cruelly ended. The shooting occurred shortly after 7.30am when a group of youths in a commandeered Ford Transit van loaded with petrol bombs, attempted to enter the Falls Road Bus Depot by the side entrance in Divis Drive.

Before entering the yard, one of the youths spotted three British soldiers who had taken up an observation post inside the depot, and shouted a warning. As the youths made off on foot, a single shot was fired, wounding John Dempsey. He was dead on arrival at the Royal Victoria Hospital. Contrary to British Army claims that they had come under attack from petrol bombs, none of the bombs had in fact been lit, or thrown.

Fiann John Dempsey was buried with full honours in Milltown Cemetery, Belfast.

Óglach Martin Hurson

13th September 1956 - 13th July 1981

Martin Hurson was born on 13th September 1956, the second youngest in a family of nine. His parents, Johnnie and Mary Ann Hurson raised the family on a small farm on the outskirts of Cappagh. He went to Crosscavanagh P.S in Galbally and then onto St. Patrick's. His mother Mary Ann died suddenly in 1970 when Martin was 14.

When Martin left school he got work as an apprentice fitter in TJ McKennas, a local firm. Before going to England for a few months coming home in 1973. As Martin started to socialise more, the crown forces constantly harassed him. He received beatings in Pomeroy where his girlfriend Bernadette lived. Like many other young lads from the area he grew to resent foreign forces in Ireland and joined the I.R.A. Martin was an ordinary young man trying to wage war. He was very discreet, and his family were never aware of his involvement. He was always ready to do what was needed and was involved in many operations

In 1976 he was arrested and charged with conspiracy to kill and membership of the I.R.A. He was sentenced to 20 years and immediately joined the blanket protest in Long Kesh. In December 1980 he joined the first Hunger Strike, which was to end before Christmas. On 29th May he joined the Hunger Strike of 1981. During his 46 days his favourite phrase was "No Problem". As he grew weaker his family and supporters attended protests all over the country. He was very determined not to give in and made his family promise not to let him down. On Monday 13th July 1981 at 4a.m. Martin died in Long Kesh with Fr. Murphy and his brother Brendan at his bedside. His father was at the prison gate with Bernadette, the prison authorities refusing her entry and mocking her request to see him.

Martin went to his death knowing that he had given his life that others may have a better life and one day a free and peaceful land. Volunteer Martin Hurson is buried in Galbally, at home again among friends.

Óglach Kevin Lynch

25th May 1956 - 1st August 1981

Kevin Martin Lynch was born on the 25th May 1956, the youngest of eight children born to Paddy and Bridie Lynch, both natives of Park in Co. Derry. Kevin excelled at both football and hurling. Following in the footsteps of his older brother Frank he was also a promising amateur boxer. His greatest passion was hurling. In 1971 he was a member of the Dungiven team which won the Feile na nGael final in Thurles. Kevin, who had his appendix removed ten days before this, played four games in two days. His mother allowed him to go on the understanding that he would be strictly a spectator. His greatest moment of glory, which he reminisced with his father just a few days before he died, was when he captained the Derry under 16 hurling team which beat Armagh in the All Ireland final in Croke Park in 1972. He won a special County Minor award in 1974.

Following this, he went to work in England for two years. The motto of the Kevin Lynch Hurling club in Dungiven is 'Misneach is dilseach', (courage and loyalty), qualities which characterised Kevin's life and death.

Shortly after his return from England, he was arrested, following a military operation in Dungiven, during which an R.U.C man was injured. Kevin took part in the first hunger strike. While on his second hunger strike he stood as a candidate in the Waterford constituency where he polled a remarkable number of first preference votes. The links formed between Waterford and Dungiven at that time remain strong today.

Kevin died on the 1st August 1981 after 71 days on hunger strike.

He is buried in St Patrick's Churchyard, Dungiven.

Óglach Kieran Doherty

16th October 1955 - August 1981

Kieran Doherty was born on October 16th 1955 in Andersonstown, the third son in a family of six children. His two elder brothers, Michael and Terence, were interned between 1972 and 1974.

Kieran attended St. Theresa's Primary School, and the CBS on the Glen Road. He loved sport, and won a GAA Antrim minor medal in 1971 for St Theresa's GAC. The Doherty brothers were also keen cyclists.

Affected like so many other of his age by the injustices around him, Kieran joined Fianna Éireann in 1971. His dedication and outstanding ability led him into the IRA very quickly. He managed to evade arrest when British soldiers came looking for him on his seventeenth birthday, but eventually in February 1973 he was arrested and interned. He remained in prison until November 1975.

In April 1976 his comrade Sean McDermott was killed, and Mairead Farrell arrested during a bombing operation. Kieran was told to lie low, but turned up for the funeral of his friend and comrade. In August of the same year Kieran himself was arrested and in January 1978 was sentenced to 18 years. Kieran joined his comrades on the protest. He joined the hunger strike on Friday May 22nd 1981, and in June was elected as TD for Cavan/Monaghan with 9,121 first preference votes.

Volunteer Kieran Doherty TD, died on August 2nd 1981, after 73 days on hunger-strike. He was buried with full military honours alongside his comrades in Milltown Cemetery, Belfast.

Óglach Thomas McElwee

30th November 1957 - 8th August 1981

The son of James and Alice McElwee, Thomas was the fifth in a family of twelve. He went to St. Mary's Primary School, Bellaghy, followed by secondary education at St. Mary's College Clady, Portglenone. Having an interest in cars he went to Magherafelt Technical College and then to Ballymena Training Centre to acquire a trade as a car mechanic. His first job was driving a digger on a job in Castledawson preparing the ground for Moyola Golf Club.

He moved on and took on a career with his much-loved cars, as a mechanic in a local garage. Thomas's hobby was stock car racing. He spent his evenings repairing old cars to take to races in Aghadowey or wherever a race was taking place. At weekends he went to dances. His favourite band was Philomena Begley and he would travel for miles to see her play. Thomas had lots of friends on both sides of the community. He was a very relaxed and friendly person. There had been raids in the McElwee home, when Thomas would be dragged out of bed in the early hours and taken to barracks in Ballykelly, Coleraine and Derry for interrogation by the Brits. This would cause a deep hatred of British injustice in Ireland.

In 1976 after a premature explosion in Fair Hill Ballymena, as a result of which Thomas lost an eye, he was taken to the Royal Victoria Hospital, Belfast. Shortly after he was taken to Musgrave Park Hospital where he was kept under armed guard, from where he was moved to Crumlin Road Jail.

After being tried and convicted in a Diplock Court, Thomas was sent to Long Kesh to serve a twenty-year sentence. He immediately joined the Blanket and No Wash protest. After four years on the protest he joined the Hunger Strike. He died after 62 days on Hunger Strike. He was 23 years of age. Thomas was the 9th Hunger Striker to die, his cousin Francis Hughes also died on the Hunger Strike.

Óglach Mickey Devine INLA

26th May 1954 - 20th August 1981

Mickey Devine was born on the 26th May 1954 in Springtown Camp in Derry. His parents had one other child. The Devine Family moved to the then newly built Creggan in 1960.

He went to the Holy Child Primary School and St Joseph's Secondary. On leaving school he got a job in Austin's in Derry's Diamond.

In July 1971 he joined the James Connolly Republican Club. This was in the immediate aftermath of the shooting dead by the British Army of Dessie Beattie and Raymond Cusack. He joined the Official IRA in August 1971.

He was on the Bloody Sunday march and the sight of the thirteen coffins in the Creggan Chapel had a lasting effect on him.

Mickey married Margaret in 1973, and had two children Michael and Louise.

In 1974 he left the Officials and joined the INLA, and he was a founding member of the IRSP in Derry.

On September 20th 1976 he was arrested with John Cassidy. On July 20th 1977 he was sentenced to 12 years and went on the blanket protest in H Block 5. He took over as OC of the INLA prisoners when Patsy O'Hara went on hunger strike.

He commenced hunger strike on June 22nd 1981, and on August 20th he died after being on hunger strike 60 days. The same day the people of Fermanagh South Tyrone went to the polls and elected Owen Carron as MP.

Michael Devine was 27 years of age.

Óglach Danny McMullan

26th August 1960 - 7th February 1982

Danny was the ninth child of twelve (seven boys and five girls) born to James and Rosanna McMullan. He was reared in the Halfgayne area of Slaughtneil, and in September 1964 Danny was the last pupil to attend Corlecky School before it closed down, transferring to St. John's Granaghan, which replaced it. St Patrick's College Maghera was the base for his secondary education and there he continued to develop a keen interest in Gaelic games. He played minor and reserve football with his local club Robert Emmets, Slaughtneil.

Leaving school at 16, he joined the building industry as a joiner, where he took up employment with his brothers, Michael and Patrick. He was a dedicated, hardworking lad with a jolly, yet caring disposition, who had many friends. From a Republican family and background, Danny was a constant target for harassment at the hands of the British Crown Forces. Frequently his home in Tirhugh was raided. His brother Francis was imprisoned after being tortured in Castlereagh. Witnessing such injustice Danny joined the South Derry Brigade of Óglaigh na hÉireann in 1977. Until his untimely death in 1982 Danny was a determined and committed member of the Army.

Danny's young life was tragically cut short by a fatal car accident on the outskirts of Rasharkin on the 7th February 1982. Ever faithful to the cause Danny died wearing the names of his Hunger Striker comrades on his belt.

His mother's rendition of 'Danny Boy' at Francis's wedding two weeks later was a very sad and poignant moment. He is still greatly missed by his family, friends and comrades and he will be remembered for the part he played in the struggle. Mary Queen of the Gael pray for him.

He is buried in St John's Graveyard, Granaghan, Swatragh.

Óglach Eamonn Bradley

1st November 1958 - 25th August 1982

"Eamonn 'Bronco' Bradley was 16 years old when I first met him. My first impression was that he commanded great respect from those whom he associated with in Na Fianna Éireann, and also those older Volunteers within Óglaigh na hÉireann.

At 16 Bronco was O/C of Na Fianna in Shantallow, and soon went on to become vice O/C of the overall town. Despite his youth he was very mature and disciplined in his role.

He liked to play pool and was a member of Pennyburn Youth Club. Unemployed, from a large family, Bronco never had very much but what little he did have he made the best of, always turning himself out well and priding himself in his appearance.

I was slightly older than Bronco and can recall his entry into Óglaigh na hÉireann. He was 17 and wanted to do everything at once. I remember one day when Bronco and his comrade secured a car and sat on an operation for almost 4 hours. When no British soldiers appeared he left his comrade off with the intention of returning his weapon to the dump. Instead Bronco kept the car and weapon and continued to "float" on his own.

On April 1st 1976 I remember calling for Bronco at his house. When his mother told me he was arrested I thought it was an "April Fool", but Bronco spent the next 5 years in Long Kesh, 4 of them on the blanket protest. On his release in 1981 he returned to active service. Sixteen months later he was shot dead in cold blood, unarmed, by two British soldiers in his native Shantallow. He was 23 years old."

Peter Corrigan Sinn Féin

19th April 1935 - 25th October 1982

Peter Corrigan was born and raised in Lower English Street in Armagh. Educated at the Christian Brothers School, Peter showed an aptitude for construction and went into the building trade after leaving school. He excelled in his chosen career and was widely known around the country for his craftsmanship in brick and stonework. He went to work in England where he met and married his wife Jean, also originally from Armagh. Always yearning for his hometown Peter and Jean moved back to Armagh and settled on Banbrook Hill and went on to raise a large family. They eventually moved to the then new housing estate of Drumbreda.

Peter joined Óglaigh Na hÉireann in 1969 and became very active. He, and two of his brothers were arrested and interned on the 9th August 1971. Release in May 1972 he continued to work within the Republican Movement until his re-arrest in 1973. He was to remain incarcerated until the end of Internment in 1975. Continuing with his studies he was awarded the Silver Trowel for theory work in building and was able to do some part time teaching at the local Technical College. When Sinn Féin entered into the political arena in the early eighties he went to work as election agent for one of the first Republican candidates, Jim McAllister.

He was continually threatened and harrassed by the Crown forces. It was when Peter was returning home on the 25th October along the Loughall Road that he was shot dead by a Loyalist murder gang. His brother and son narrowly escaped death in the attack. His son Martin was also shot dead in 1990. The Protestant Action Force, whose membership was by and large made up of members of the UDR, claimed his murder. The one person charged in connection with the murder was a full time member of the UDR.

Peter left behind a family of eleven. Another son, Barry later died from natural causes. Throughout his life the driving forces were his family and his Republicanism. The latter was to cost him his life at the hands of Loyalist killers.

Óglach Jeff McKenna

8th November 1982

Jeff McKenna was a member of Liam Mellows Cumann in the North of Dublin City. He was involved in a hit and run accident while out selling An Phoblacht/Republican News, which he did without fail every weekend. He died two days later after the life support machine he had been on was switched off.

A friend and comrade of Jeff's described him as "a source of information and encouragement", not only to his own Cumann members but to those in neighbouring Cumainn which he had helped to found. Jeff raised large amounts of money, during the H-Block hunger strikes and regularly raised funds for an Cumann Cabhrach.

Jeff although small in stature, had tremendous energy, and his dedication to Republicanism will never be forgotten.

Óglach Sean Burns

8th March 1961- 11th November 1982

Óglach Sean Burns, like his lifelong friend and comrade, Eugene Toman, was a native of Lurgan, Co Armagh. A painter by trade he managed, despite his Republican activities, to remain in steady employment and worked hard at his job.

Like most young men of his generation he enjoyed a healthy social life, when he wasn't working, and he and Eugene were virtually inseparable.

Influenced by the oppression and discrimination that existed within his community and politicised by the sacrifices of the H-Block Martyrs, Sean, after a short spell on remand in Crumlin Road jail, made the conscious decision to join the ranks of Óglaigh na hÉireann.

A dedicated Volunteer who was always on the lookout for operations.He was almost captured during an operation when the British Army and RUC surrounded the Teghnevan Estate. Forced to go on the run he could not stay away from his native Lurgan, returning home after a short spell in the Twenty Six Counties. He immediately returned to active service.

On the night of 11th November 1982, Sean and his lifelong friend and comrade Eugene Toman, both heavily disguised, were travelling in a car with another comrade Gervase McKerr. They had been under heavy surveillance by the RUC and after travelling a short distance to the Tullygally Road they were ambushed.

The car was sprayed with bullets, with over a hundred strike marks, all three Volunteers were killed. Sean Burns was 21 years old when he was killed.

Óglach Gervase McKerr

6th August 1951 - 11th November 1982

My father, Gervase McKerr was born in Lurgan in 1951. One of seven children, he had a strong Irish family background and two of his uncles were interned during the 40's and 50's campaigns. My parents, who were childhood sweethearts, were both hard workers. On leaving school my father trained to be a monumental sculptor while my mother worked as a stitcher in a local factory.

My mother, Eleanor, told how she and my father attended Civil Rights marches and how during Internment and the Hunger Strike periods, my father, a keen photographer documented the marches and rallies. We have hundreds of family photos though my father was mainly behind the camera. He liked fishing and basketball and supported the County Armagh Gaelic team. A lover of traditional music he attended a number of Fleadh Ceoileanna. He enjoyed travelling, insisting we take an annual family holiday. At one time he'd made plans to emigrate to Canada but as a 'security risk' was refused entry. We often wonder how things might have been.

On the 11th November 1982 my father was murdered in an R.U.C. ambush less than a mile from our home. I was eight years old and David was three. That night, during a raid on our home, an R.U.C. woman, who knew my father was lying dead up the road, asked me where my daddy was. The specially trained undercover unit who carried out the killing were ordered to 'shoot to kill' my father and his two passengers, Sean Burns and Eugene Toman - the car they were travelling in was hit by 108 bullets. Our mother, who never got over the loss of our father, fought hard to get justice and succeeded in taking the British Government to the European Courts of Human Rights. She was so proud of him and what he stood for. She died on 31st October 1996.

My memories of my father are of a good man who would do anything for anyone. I remember how he and my mother laughed a lot together. I hope they are doing that now.

Óglach Eugene Toman

30th March 1961 - 11th November 1982

Eugene Toman from Lurgan, Co Armagh attended the local schools before serving his apprenticeship as a plasterer. Those who knew him say he was a hard worker who would often take on jobs that had him working late into the night.

He was an ardent fan of the Furey Brothers and he would travel great distances to see them perform. His favourite song was 'Willie McBride' and he wasn't shy of giving his own rendition of the song.

As a young nationalist growing up in Lurgan, Eugene was acutely conscious of the discrimination and bigotry that existed within the State and was greatly affected by the Hunger Strikes of 1980/1981. Arrested and charged with riotous behaviour he was remanded in custody to Crumlin Road prison.

It was during his imprisonment that he decided that he could do more than take part in riots and on his release some months later, he volunteered to join the ranks of Óglaigh na hÉireann.

An extremely active Volunteer he was forced to go on the run from the British army and the RUC, staying for a period in the Twenty Six counties before returning to Lurgan.

On the night of 11th November, Eugene was travelling in a car along with his comrades Sean Burns and Gervase McKerr when an undercover unit of the RUC ambushed them.

Eugene survived the initial attack but as the car came to a halt and he tried to get out he was shot dead at close range. He was 21 years old at the time.

Óglach Phil O'Donnell

3rd June 1932 - 24th December 1982

Phil O'Donnell joined the Republican Movement in 1969, shortly after the battle of the Bogside. His ex-British army experience was soon put to good use and Phil started organising and running training camps in Donegal. During one of these training sessions Phil and several other Derrymen were arrested at a remote house in the hills at the back of Fahan in Co. Donegal by Free State forces. Several weapons were also seized. They were taken to Mountjoy prison in Dublin, and after a short time on remand were brought to trial.

Phil proclaimed in court that he and his co-defendants were 'Defenders of the Bogside'. They were declared innocent by the trial judge and released. Never one to miss an opening, Phil said: "If we are innocent can we please have our guns back". After several military operations were called off by GHQ, the IRA split and a disillusioned Phil and a few others formed a group called Saor Uladh, which was subsequently subsumed into the IRA. Phil was a strict disciplinarian, and he brought this to his work in training camps.

The morning of Internment saw Phil arrested and taken to Magilligan for questioning. He was later transferred to the Maidstone prison ship harboured in Belfast Lough before transferring to Long Kesh. Released after eight months, Phil again resumed his role in training camps, this time nationwide. Arrested once more by the Free State forces, Phil was charged with membership of the IRA and the possession of weapons. Phil spent several years in Portlaoise jail and upon his release again reported for active service.

Unfortunately Phil contracted cancer and after several months in hospital he died on Christmas Eve 1982. He was 50 years old. Phil was married to Susie.

Óglach Colm Daltun

15th January 1983

Colm Daltun was originally from Co. Cavan though he was born in Dublin. He had spent some time in Maynooth studying for the priesthood, abandoning the idea before any prospect of ordination. A fluent Irish speaker, he was a highly academic individual who was mostly self-taught.

Imprisoned in the early 1970s, he was among a group of Republicans who went on hunger-strike in Mountjoy Jail in 1972, as part of the battle to secure political status. In the aftermath of the famous helicopter escape by Republican prisoners from Mountjoy jail in 1973, the Free-State authorities moved the prisoners from Mountjoy and the Curragh to Portlaoise. The prison was seriously overcrowded and tensions were understandably high, with talk of riots. Unknown to most of the prisoners an escape plan was underway and the Camp staff feared that a riot would put these plans in jeopardy.

A camp council was formed whose job was to help deal with, and defuse, the tensions. Colm was elected to sit on the council. A few months later 19 Republican prisoners escaped from Portlaoise. Colm Daltun was a highly committed and diligent member of Óglaigh na hÉireann who had the rare ability to cause people to question themselves - which he managed to do in a friendly and unabrasive way. Just before Christmas 1974 tensions in Portlaoise were at boiling point with the prisoners being harassed on a daily basis. The outcome of these tensions was a full-scale riot where the prisoners took control of the prison for a short time. Many prisoners were savagely beaten and another hunger-strike was called. Once again Colm volunteered to take part. He was carried out of Portlaoise on a stretcher and moved to the Curragh Military Camp.

When the hunger-strike ended the doctor informed him that he had been so close to death that his body had begun the process of using up its final reserves of energy, which was the fat around the central nervous system and the brain. Many believe he never fully recovered from his time on hunger-strike and he died in Dublin a few years after his release from prison.

Óglach Eddie Dynes

13th July 1945 - 1st March 1983

Eddie Dynes was born in English Street in Armagh in 1945 and was educated at St. Patrick's Primary School, Banbrook Hill, and St. Malachy's in Chapel Lane. After leaving school he worked in Bairnswear until 1963, when, aged 17, he went to live in Canada where he gained work in a lumber camp in Alaska. He returned home four years later. He met and married Mary Cunningham and they had six children, Edward, Dominic, Mary, Patrick, Ciaran and Grainne.

Eddie was Interned during the initial swoops on 9th August 1971, spending time on the prison ship Maidstone and the cages of Long Kesh. Released in 1972, Eddie, who could turn his hand to anything, took up work as a handyman to support his young family.

A great boxing enthusiast he helped form the local boxing club in Keady where he was now living and was instrumental in bringing boxing personalities such as Henry Cooper to inspire the local youth.

Eddie Dynes was an active member of Óglaigh na hÉireann and a committed Republican right up until his untimely death in a road accident at the age of 37. He was a loving husband and father and a highly respected member of his local community.

Óglach Dan Turley

15th September 1915 - June 9th 1983

Dan Turley came from a republican family in the Clonard district, living almost within the shadows of the imposing Clonard Monastery. He was a member of the republican movement from an early age, and throughout his life remained dedicated to the cause of Irish freedom.

No stranger to prison life, like so many of his generation, Dan served his last period of imprisonment as an internee in the early 1970's. Dan Turley devoted his time to his family of seven daughters and two sons, after the untimely death of his wife, Eunice. His commitment to the republican movement went without question, and when sectarian violence erupted throughout the six counties in 1969, Dan was among the small number of active republicans who rose to the defence of the beleaguered nationalist community.

On his release from prison in the 1970's Dan had no hesitation once again offering his services to the republican movement, in spite of many health problems which had developed. Dan Turley's service to the republican movement, and to the country which he loved, ended with his death on Thursday June 9th 1983.

Volunteer Dan Turley's tricolour draped coffin was carried to his final resting place in the family plot in Belfast's Milltown Cemetery.

Óglach Brian Campbell

24th March 1964 - 4th December 1983

Brian Campbell was born on 24th March 1964, the fifth child in a family of eight, to Brendan and Kathleen Campbell. Starting school at St. Patrick's, Annaghmore, he went on to St. Joseph's in Coalisland, before going to Dungannon Technical College, for his final year. When he left school he went straight into the family garage, where his father, older brothers and uncle trained him as a mechanic.

Brian had a love for cars from a very early age. By the time he was thirteen he had his own stock car. He was also a member of Clonoe Boxing Club. He had an interest in football, but was more of a supporter than a player. Every year Brian, his family and family friends headed for Croke Park for the All Ireland Semis and Final, and he followed Tyrone wherever and however they played. As he got older he developed a great love for Irish music and the language.

Brian also knew the injustice of life. Hugh Coney had been a neighbour and Paul Duffy a cousin and by 14, Brian was experiencing harassment first hand. In June 1980, the oldest brother was sentenced to 14 years for possession, later escaping from H7 in 1983. Throughout his youth Brian became more interested in the Republican Movement. He became another statistic in the state harassment campaign, stopped frequently and arrested on several occasions, but always released without charge. On the last occasion when in Gough Barracks, they told him "that they would even up the score for Seamus' escape". The family logged this with the many other death threats they had received not realising that this one would come true within a matter of weeks.

Volunteer Brian Campbell was shot by the British undercover forces on December 4th 1983, along with him, his friend, Volunteer Colm McGirr. They were left to die without medical or spiritual attention. Volunteer Brian Campbell is buried in Clonoe Cemetery. Brian's death left a great void in a happy close-knit family. His father died on the 21st August 1987. They are greatly missed.

Óglach Colm McGirr

22nd September 1960 - 4th December 1983

Colm McGirr was born on 22nd September 1960, the youngest child of Paddy and Alice, he had three older sisters and eight big brothers. He was 23 when he died and like any young man of his age he enjoyed his social life dances, ceilidhe, fleadhs. Colm enjoyed life, and people liked him. Though his trade was as a bricklayer he was known throughout the area as a man who could and would turn his hand to anything. At 23 years old he was well respected, always willing to help and completely reliable.

He had always been that way, though it is recorded that Colm joined the Army when he turned 18, he had already saved the lives of Army Units on two separate occasions during 1974. In the first incident, Colm and his friends had been "observing" an A.S.U. on the Washingbay Road when an eagle-eyed Volunteer caught them, chastised them and chased them home. On the way home, however, Colm saw a British Army foot patrol making their way in behind the Volunteers. Colm changed course, cut through the near-by sand pits and managed to warn the Unit. Only a month later, Colm again saved local Volunteers from ambush. On his way home he discovered the British Army dug in at the rear of houses close to a dump, his vigilance undoubtedly saved lives. How Colm knew where the dump was raised many a smile, for there was an on-going joke in the country that if Colm couldn't find a dump no one could.

Arrested in November 1983, he was told in Gough Barracks that he wouldn't see 1984 alive. On the 4th December that year unarmed Volunteers Colm McGirr and Brian Campbell were murdered on the Cloghog Road in Clonoe. No warning was given, no attempt made to arrest them and, as they lay wounded, medical and spiritual attention were denied to them.

Volunteer Colm McGirr was laid to rest in Coalisland Cemetery.

Óglach Henry Hogan

16th March 1963 - 21st February 1984

Born 16th March 1963, Henry Hogan was the son of Patrick and Maureen Hogan. In his early teenage years Henry witnessed the brutal nature of Loyalism. The family were forced to leave their Ballymena home as a result of loyalist attacks. Re-housed for a short time in Ballymoney the family were then subjected to a cycle of R.U.C raids and further intimidation.

Henry became actively involved in the North Antrim Brigade in his later teenage years. He moved to Dunloy with his family in January 1984. He believed 'Dunloy' had great potential for Republicanism. Henry was also greatly inspired by Óglach Francis Hughes and likewise became steadfast in his determination to pursue freedom and independence from British rule in the six counties. He was always very positive in his role as an active volunteer and had developed clear objectives and enthusiasm. This was also enhanced by his geographical knowledge of the North Antrim area.

The brief period Henry spent living in Dunloy would most likely represent the happiest stage of his life. He made friends easily and adapted a 'carefree' lifestyle, despite the pressures of his role in Óglaigh na hÉireann.

On the evening of 21st February 1984, Henry, along with Óglach Declan Martin, was part of an active service unit in Dunloy. They became involved in a fierce gun battle with British undercover agents.

One British undercover agent was killed and at least one was injured. As the Volunteers attempted to retreat, British undercover reinforcements arrived in unmarked vehicles and Henry and his comrade were shot dead.

Henry Hogan is buried in St Joseph's Graveyard, Dunloy.

Óglach Declan Martin

13th July 1965 - 21st February 1984

Declan, born 13th July 1965, was the eldest son of Seamus and Anna Martin. He was a talented hurler and hurled for the Dunloy team. From an early age he worked with his parents either helping with younger siblings or in the work place as a 'fix it job', also in helping with his elderly grandparents, even as a companion to them.

He became aware at an early age of British oppression. On a winter night following a youth disco, himself and a companion were bundled into the back of a U.D.R jeep who claimed they were stone throwing in the area. Both these young people were nowhere near this incident as evidence proved. They had travelled for a mile, were dumped off and made to make their own way home. That night a death threat was made to them following a complaint to a local police station. They were told that there were people in that group who could carry that threat out.

This was the turning point in his life. He never ever was the same. This threat always hung over his head. The hunger strike had a profound effect on him, especially the local young men for whom he had great admiration. Later he joined the ranks of the Republican Movement. Declan, along with Volunteer Henry Hogan, was part of an active service unit that attacked a hide being used by British undercover agents in Dunloy village in 1984. One British undercover agent was killed and at least one was injured in the attack. However, the British undercover reinforcements in unmarked cars cut off the Volunteers' retreat and Declan and his comrade were shot dead.

He will always be remembered by his family and friends as a courageous, loving, helpful and friendly 'youth' struck down by a 'stranger from a foreign soil and a coward'.

Declan Martin is buried at St Joseph's Graveyard, Dunloy.

"May he sleep with the sleep of peace"

259

Óglach Richard Quigley

15th April 1964 - 21st April 1984

Vol. Richard Quigley, Richie to his friends and comrades died on Active Service on the 21st April 1984 while ambushing British soldiers in Derry City. Richard came from a family of 13 children and lived all his life in Derry's Bogside. He was a keen athlete and had competed in a number of marathons. Richard was a republican activist from his early teens. The major turning point in his young life was the Hunger Strikes of 1980/81.

At his funeral Father Jimmy Shields, a cousin of Richard's said,

"Richard had made a choice like so many young people today, whether we like it or not, a choice which reflects the reality of the times we must all live in."

Richard was employed as a fruit deliveryman and as part of his job he met and was well liked by many people throughout the city. The large attendance at his funeral was testament to his friendly and outgoing personality.

Richard was an ordinary young man who made a choice to stand up for what he believed in and fought for his community and country. As a republican soldier he typified the dedication and selfless sacrifice of many of his generation including his very close friend and comrade Vol. Charles English who died while on active service just over a year later.

Óglach William Price

11th June 1956 - 13th July 1984

William Price, from Stewartstown was the second youngest of nine children. He was highly security conscious, to the extent that many of his friends and closest associates were shocked to learn of his involvement in the Republican Movement.

He was described by a comrade as,

"an intelligent, alert and extremely eager volunteer who always knew exactly what he was doing. He was painstakingly meticulous in both the pre-planning and execution of operations and always conscious of the need to avoid either republican or civilian casualties."

Motivated by the political situation, Willie resolved to play a full part in the struggle for Irish Freedom and he subsequently joined the I.R.A. in 1979.

He was killed at Ardboe on the Lough shore on July 13th 1984 and is buried in Brocagh Cemetery a few miles from Coalisland.

The funeral of Volunteer William Price is widely remembered and acknowledged as having been the first attacked in what was to become the British policy of preventing military honours being accorded to members of Óglaigh na hÉireann. The British Army and R.U.C. brutally attacked mourners in an attempt to remove the Tricolour from the coffin. Harassment to and from funerals was common place as was verbal abuse but on this occasion mourners were beaten the full length of the funeral route in an unsuccessful attempt to prevent the funeral taking place. This policy was later seen repeated at the funeral of other Volunteers such as Lawrence Marley in Belfast.

Óglach Brendan Watters

8th May 1960 - 8th August 1984

Kevin Brendan Watters was born in Daisy Hill Hospital Newry, on 8th May 1960. His parents Edward and Elizabeth (Lily) moved into the new Derrybeg Estate in the early 60s and had another two children, Mary and Michael, both younger than Brendan. Known as 'Cindy' to his friends, Brendan attended St Patrick's Primary School in the Meadow and finished his schooling days at St Joseph's Secondary School on the Armagh Road. He was employed at the Nylon Factory. From an early age, he was very aware of the unjust society Nationalists were forced to endure in the six county statelet. He understood the reasons why physical force republicanism had to confront the root cause of the conflict he experienced as a child.

As a teenager, he joined and played in the Wolfe Tone Accordion Band. Around the same period, he joined Na Fianna Éireann. The Hunger Strikes had a major impact on him and from then onwards he knew he would take on a greater role in the Freedom Struggle. In 1983, he made his thoughts known to a senior member of the IRA and joined the ranks of Óglaigh na h-Éireann.

Brendan had a happy-go-lucky nature and keen sense of humour but there was another side to Brendan's personality, and he took his role as an IRA Volunteer very seriously. He was always conscious of the need to protect his own security and that of his comrades. He earned the respect of his comrades for his coolness and efficiency on active service. Lily, his mother, was the Six County Ladies Dart Champion, and in his spare time, Brendan played and watched darts. He also enjoyed going to discos and loved motorbikes. On Wednesday 8th August 1984, Brendan was tragically killed when a hand grenade he was carrying exploded accidentally. His remains were hijacked by the RUC at Craigavon and on the day of his funeral, as predicted, the RUC attacked the mourners in an attempt to remove Brendan's gloves and beret from the coffin.

Brendan is remembered with pride by all his family and friends.

Paddy Brady Sinn Féin

9th March 1949 - 16th November 1984

Paddy Brady was born on 9th March 1949 at 4 Masserene Street in the Pound Loney district of Belfast, one of a family of five brothers and three sisters. Paddy's younger brother Martin was sentenced to eight life terms plus 20 years in England for 'carrying out bombings and conspiring to bomb'. At the age of 15, Paddy left St Comgall's School and took up employment in his first paid job as a butcher's boy. Then he worked as a barman and a bus conductor before eventually becoming a milk roundsman with Kennedy's Dairy in 1974. In 1968, he married local girl Mary O'Reilly at St John's Church on the Falls Road and the couple set up home in the St James's area where much of their political work was centred. They had two children, Patricia and Frances.

The conditions of the prisoners, at home and in England, were one of his chief concerns and he worked tirelessly for both the POW department and the Transport department. During the 1981 hunger-strike, his work as a local organizer was invaluable. It is, however, for his ceaseless local work that Paddy is best remembered. A driving force in the St James's Crescent Community Centre, he strove to improve conditions in the area. Through festivals and sports, clubs and educational courses, he encouraged the youth to shake off the destroying effects of social and economic deprivation.

Paddy was a man of great vitality and energy who combined a deeply-felt concern for the working class with an instinctive grasp of local politics. On Friday, 16th November 1984 Paddy and a 14 year-old helper drove the short distance from his home to Kennedy's Dairy on the Boucher Road, close to the loyalist Village area.

As Paddy was locking the passenger door of his white Volvo, a brown coloured Cortina drew level with him. Several shots rang out and, within seconds, Paddy Brady lay dead on the roadside. His UDA assassins sped off in the direction of the Village.

Óglach Ciaran Fleming

25th October 1959 - 2nd December 1984

Ciaran Fleming was the youngest child of Maud and Paddy Fleming. Brought up on a loyalist estate in the Waterside, he experienced at first hand the bigotry and triumphalism of the Orange state. Arrested and imprisoned at an early age he spent his formative years in the H-Blocks of Long Kesh at the height of the Blanket protest and the Hunger Strikes.

His quiet easygoing nature belied a fierce and dedicated commitment to the Republican cause. Having played a major role in the Great Escape of 1983 he returned at once to the forefront of the armed struggle. When the families of Danny Doherty and William Fleming, along with the Republican community of Derry, gathered at the Republican plot in Creggan to lay their loved ones to rest, they were not to know that William's cousin Ciaran (26) was missing, having failed to return to base after an engagement with British covert forces near the Fermanagh/Donegal border.

On December 2nd, four days before the Gransha ambush, another IRA unit were engaged in preparing for an attack on British forces when they encountered a British undercover unit. A gun battle ensued and one of the Volunteers, Antoine MacGiolla Bhrighde (27) was fatally wounded, as was a British soldier.

Under heavy fire the IRA unit retreated across the swollen river Bannagh, when tragically, Ciaran, a non-swimmer, was swept away and drowned. His body wasn't recovered until December 21st.

On Christmas Eve 1984, despite vicious attacks on the funeral cortege by the RUC, Ciaran was laid to rest by his comrades with full military honours.

Óglach Antoine MacGiolla Bhrighde

29th August 1957 - 2nd December 1984

Antoine (Tony) was the eldest child of Frank and Nora MacBride from Desertmartin, County Derry. In search of work Frank took the family to Belfast in 1964. Living first at Knock Road, Nora was helped to look after the young family by her mother, Nora, who came from a Republican family. She introduced Tony to Republicanism with tales of the Tan war and family exploits. Ignoring politics, the family moved to Killowen Street in Loyalist East Belfast, where they were targeted after the outbreak of the troubles. Attacks graduated from window breaking to attempted bombing and culminated in Frank and Tony being shot. Frank, already ill, never recovered from the 12 bullets that hit him and died 17 months later. Tony made a full recovery and took over as head of the house.

Moving to Newtownards the family again faced sectarian conflict. During this time Tony joined the Free State Army where he excelled, receiving a bravery commendation. Following the death of Frank, the family returned home to South Derry where Tony became deeply involved in the struggle. He was involved in numerous operations and gained the respect of comrades. Captured at Strabane the RUC were unable to identify him initially. After his sentence, he again became active. Having made friends in Norway he travelled there and spread the Republican message.

Returning from Norway in November 1984 he became involved in his last operation. On a night of freezing fog, he and his comrades were ambushed by undercover British soldiers. Tony was captured, interrogated and shot. His comrade Ciaran Fleming drowned and a British soldier was killed. Despite the massive British security at his funeral where mourners were attacked, Tony was buried with dignity in Coolcalm at the foot of Slieve Gallon.

Óglach Danny Doherty

23rd September 1961- 6th December 1984

As a schoolboy, Danny had a great love of animals, always bringing stray dogs home to the consternation of his family. He was also proud of his pigeon loft on which he lavished so much attention.

When he was arrested, Danny was serving his time as a joiner. He also did some casual work at Derry docks like his father and grandfathers before him. He played football for the local Sean Dolan's GAA club, which he loved.

When he was 14 he joined Na Fianna Éireann and then at the age of 17 he lied about his age to join the IRA. A short time later he was imprisoned in Portlaoise Jail for membership and possession of explosives and spent three years and ten months there. The conditions in Portlaoise at that time were very bad and at one time he had no visits for three months. There were beatings and strip searches and the visits themselves were terrible. We have been told that Danny was well liked and respected while he was in prison and during his time there two more brothers, a sister and his father also spent time in prison.

On his release he was more determined than ever to carry on the struggle and reported back to his local command. He married Julie and they have a son Kevin Barry.

Danny was killed, on December 6th 1984 along with Volunteer William Fleming by undercover British soldiers in the grounds of Gransha Hospital. On the day he died his parents were up in Long Kesh visiting his brother John and didn't know about Danny's death until they came home. Although they heard it on the radio, it wasn't until they actually stopped outside their house that it hit them.

Óglach William Fleming

23rd March 1965 – 6th December 1984

William was 19 years old when he and Danny Doherty, a comrade from the Creggan were ambushed and shot dead by a British Army undercover unit in the grounds of Gransha Hospital on the outskirts of Derry's Waterside area, early on Thursday morning, December 6th 1984.

It was in the Top Of The Hill area of the Waterside, that William was born and reared. Sixth of seven children and youngest of Leo and Betty Fleming's four sons, three of William's brothers are former PoWs. William grew up in the midst of a conflict that took its toll on his community and his own family.

Bloody Sunday, Annie's Bar, Internment and the Hunger Strikes all impacted on many young people from the Nationalist/Republican areas of Derry and William was no exception.

When old enough William joined Na Fianna Éireann, and subsequently moved into the ranks of Óglaigh na hÉireann when he reached seventeen.

A tall, quiet, jovial lad, he worked as a barman and enjoyed participating in several sporting activities and listening to rock music in his spare time, which he didn't have much of, considering his commitment to the IRA.

Despite his age, his comrades in the Army saw William as an enthusiastic and reliable asset to the Republican struggle.

Óglach Sean McIlvenna

4th April 1951 - 17th December 1984

Sean 'Maxie' McIlvenna was born on 4th April 1951 in Belfast's Docks area. Shortly after his birth the family moved to Fortwilliam Park, before eventually settling on the Antrim Road. He had one brother, Neil, and two sisters, Jean and Rosario. He was a pipe-fitter by trade.

In 1970 he married his childhood sweetheart, Pat. They had met at their local youth-club. Joining the Republican Movement in 1971, Sean soon showed that he was an intelligent, dedicated and extremely security-conscious Volunteer.

The RUC became suspicious of him due to an informer and he was forced to go on the run in 1972, settling in the Twenty-Six Counties. Up home anyone who new Sean could testify to his sincerity, integrity and dedication, whether as a friend or as a comrade. He loved all kinds of sport. Sean and Pat had seven children. Pat had given birth to twins, Fiona and Sean, just three months before Sean's death. Their other children Cathy, Sinead, Ciara, Sara and Patricia, ranged in age from 14 to three years at the time of his death.

On Monday morning, 17th December 1984, Sean and several other IRA Volunteers ambushed a UDR mobile patrol on Lisbofin Road on the outskirts of Blackwaterstown, County Armagh. They exploded a huge culvert bomb under one of the passing UDR landrovers. Seven of the soldiers inside were injured, two seriously, and the vehicle was devastated. As Sean and one comrade withdrew across fields to an adjacent road, they were spotted by a passing RUC patrol.

The heavily-armed RUC opened fire and Óglach Sean McIlvenna was shot dead.

Óglach Mick Timothy

4th August 1948 - 26th January 1985

Mick Timothy was born in Manchester on 4th August 1948, into a family with a strong Irish identity and a great awareness of their Irish ancestry. His grandparents were born in Ireland and the family have connections in Mayo, Roscommon, Galway and Newry, County Down. Mick was educated at St Bede's College, Manchester, and took an economics degree at Manchester University.

He joined the republican movement in the early 1970s and was an active member of Sinn Féin in Manchester speaking at public meetings and lectures and becoming deeply involved in organisational work. He left Manchester in January 1975 to escape imminent arrest for his republican activities and came to Dublin, he married Alice in August 1975. Mick started working for An Phoblacht in December 1975 in his capacity as a qualified accountant, and stayed on the administrative side, becoming manager of the amalgamated An Phoblact/Republican News until 1980. He had been combining administration with writing for the paper for some time, but concentrated on editorial work from 1980 onwards.

It was 'Burke at the Back' that most reflected Mick's personality. Written in his own wry style, the column humorously but ruthlessly exposed the hypocrisy and arrogance of the establishment North and South. Mick was co-opted onto the Ard Chomhairle in 1983, an appointment he took seriously, contributing consistently and incisively to the debates and business of that body. He gave unstintingly of his time to the committees he was appointed to, in spite of his already heavy commitments. Mick was a devoted husband and father to his wife Alice and his children Ciara, Fiachra and Fionan, and despite pressures from his republican activities he never failed to be a conscientious and loving husband and father, who spent as much time with his family as possible.

He died suddenly of a heart attack on 26th January 1985 and is buried in Palmerstown Cemetery.

Óglach Charles Breslin

5th September 1964 - 23rd February 1985

Volunteer Charles Breslin was from Strabane's Head of the Town area and was the youngest boy in a family of eight. He developed his political views at an early age and was an avid reader of Irish history. At the age of fifteen he became a member of Na Fianna Éireann before joining the local unit of the IRA where he proved to be a daring and committed volunteer who worked hard to perfect his technical knowledge.

He was an easy going individual with a great sense of humour who was a victim of constant harassment at the hands of the British army and R.U.C. On one occasion he was taken to Castlereagh interrogation centre and was badly beaten by members of the R.U.C. who then placed a plastic bag over his head until he lost consciousness. He spoke little of his ordeal for fear of upsetting his family.

Charles Breslin died in one of the most notorious 'shoot to kill' operations conducted by undercover British forces during the 1980s.

Eyewitnesses were adamant that no warning had been heard before the final shots that sounded the execution of Charles and his two comrades.

He was 20 years old when he was killed in a British Army undercover operation in Strabane on 23rd February 1985.

Óglach David Devine

28th October 1968 - 23rd February 1985

David Devine was one of six children who grew up in the Strabane area of West Tyrone. A pupil of St Colman's High School, he was regarded as a quiet but clever student. He joined the local Fianna Éireann when he was fourteen years old and worked energetically to assist the local IRA unit before becoming a Volunteer in Óglaigh na hÉireann about six months before his death.

His eldest brother Hugh was a former POW who died within a few short months of his release in 1983 and it is widely believed that a severe beating received at the hands of British soldiers was a contributory factor in his death.

Volunteer David Devine was one of the youngest IRA Volunteers to be killed during this phase of the campaign. He was sixteen years old when, alongside his brother Michael and comrade Charles Breslin, he was shot dead in one of the most notorious 'shoot to kill' operations conducted by undercover British forces during the 1980s.

The sacrifice of the Devine family is testimony to the commitment and resolve of not just individuals but whole families who have endured so much in our quest for national determination.

Their family, friends and comrades in West Tyrone remember the Devine brothers with pride.

Óglach Michael Devine

26th October 1962 - 23rd February 1985

Michael died together with his brother David and comrade Charles Breslin in one of the most notorious 'shoot to kill' operations conducted by undercover British forces in modern history.

Over one hundred rounds were fired by the British, this alone would suggest that no attempt was made to arrest the trio. Indeed witnesses have recounted that the three had surrendered before a burst of automatic fire was heard.

The Volunteers' bodies were left on the hillside for seven hours after their murder, a priest was denied access to them and the Devine family were not informed of the deaths of Michael and David until their home was raided later that day. Volunteer Michael Devine (22) from Strabane, joined the IRA early in 1984 and rapidly proved himself to be a dedicated and capable Volunteer. A former Irish snooker champion, Michael was well known in Strabane and well liked by all who knew him. Extremely security conscious, he discussed his deeply held political beliefs only with his comrades. Thus to local people his tragic death and revelations of his Republican involvement came as a total surprise.

Michael was a fully committed Volunteer for whom no task was too great or too small. He rapidly won the respect of his comrades, as a careful planner who always did his utmost to ensure the safety of other Volunteers. As well as actively participating in operations against the Crown Forces he displayed great ability in Intelligence work.

Óglach Tony Campbell

1948 - 4th August 1985

Tony spent his early years living in the New Lodge area of Belfast. He joined the Republican Movement in 1968 when he was twenty. He played his part in the defence of North Belfast during the pogroms of 1969. Tony like many of his generation witnessed events in Derry and came on to the streets in solidarity.

He worked as a milk delivery man and was well known throughout Belfast. He had a keen interest in aviaries and was an excellent cook. Many volunteers recall that they enjoyed being in Tony's house, as they were guaranteed a first class meal.

In the seventies he was interned in Long Kesh. In Long Kesh Tony was remembered as a quiet lad and someone who took a keen interest in Irish history. After he was released he married his long time girl friend, Sheila, from Riverdale, and they moved to a house in Nansen Street. He also returned to active service and was a capable and dedicated Volunteer.

He fell ill and was diagnosed as having a form of skin cancer. Initially the treatment appeared to be successful but unfortunately this was not the case. The cancer had spread and his health slowly deteriorated. Tony died peacefully in his own home on 4th August 1985. Tony was a devoted family man and the fact his wife and children were with him when he passed away would have been a great comfort to him.

Tony was buried, draped in the National Flag, and there was a large attendance from across Belfast, which is testimony to Tony's standing in his community. Tony was 37 years of age at the time of his death.

Óglach Charles English

26th July 1964 - 6th August 1985

Charles English came from Cable Street in the Bogside and is survived by his parents Michael and Maureen, sisters Pauline, Michelle, Stephanie and brothers Mike and Keith. Charles' oldest brother Gary was murdered by British soldiers on April 25th 1981.

Volunteer Charles English, a highly experienced active service Volunteer was only 21 years old when he met his death during an engagement with crown forces on Tuesday 6th August 1985. Charles joined Óglaigh na hÉireann in 1982 along with his friend Volunteer Richard Quigley, who was killed on active service at Easter 1984.

On April 19th 1981 Charles lost his brother Gary and his friend Jim Brown when they were murdered by the British Army who deliberately drove two landrovers at high speed straight into a crowd of youths standing in Creggan Street. Although he was known locally as a great gamesman, having won many accolades for football, running, swimming, table tennis and snooker these activities were always second, Charles was also an avid reader and political activist, his commitment to struggle and people came first.

Charles English died as his unit attacked an enemy patrol in Abbey Park. As shots were fired at the RUC patrol there was a loud explosion, caused by the misfiring of a disposable rocket launcher. Charles was fatally wounded suffering severe body injuries. The RUC would not allow anyone near his body for four hours.

About four thousand gathered in Cable Street on Friday morning to accompany the coffin on its short journey to St. Columba's Church for Requiem Mass. Volunteer Charles English was laid to rest beside his brother, Gary.

Óglach Réamonn MacLochlainn

8th August 1951 - 9th September 1985

Réamonn was born in Buncrana in 1951. Like many young people from his area he emigrated to England at the tender age of 15. It was while in England that Réamonn joined the IRA and with his comrades took the war to British soil.

In November 1974 Réamonn was captured in an operation which claimed the life of his comrade James McDade in an accidental explosion at the Coventry Central Telephone Exchange. He was later sentenced to 12 years imprisonment. Throughout the period of his imprisonment in top security prisons across Britain, he resisted the British prison establishments' attempts to dehumanise and criminalise him. Along with his comrades he took part in roof-top demonstrations and pitched battles in prison wings. He played a leading role in the famous Hull prison riots of 1976.

He was released from prison in December 1983 after serving over 9 years of his sentence. Some months later, his brother Colm was arrested and spent time in Long Kesh and Magilligan. Réamonn wrote a book, "Inside an English Jail", on his prison experiences. He immediately re-engaged in the struggle both as a political organiser and an IRA volunteer, but had to go on the run after ammunition was found in a car he was travelling in.

He remained on the run for several months until his death on 9th September 1985 in a drowning accident, at a swimming pool in Shannon. Co. Clare, while holidaying with his Wife Mary and son Padraig. Gerry Adams delivered the graveside oration surrounded by a massive contingent of Special Task Force, Special Branch men and scores of Gardai riot squads. Prior to his funeral they had unsuccessfully attempted to raid the MacLochlainn family home, having been prevented from doing so by the mourners. Their menacing presence at his funeral was a testament to Réamonn's political life.

Óglach Tony Gough

13th June 1961 - 22nd February 1986

Tony was the oldest of six children born to Peggy and Paddy. He had three sisters, Deirdre, Vivienne Rhona and Carol, and one brother, Brian.

Tony was a shy person until he got to know you and then he'd be full of craic and devilment when out for a drink. He was a keen fisherman and a member of Foyle Anglers' Club, fishing the Faughan river. A snooker player and Everton fanatic, he worked as a fitter turner for Molins in Campsie. Tony once used his engineering skills to repair the firing pin of a dysfunctional Bren gun, before returning it to his QM. He loved his bike, a 650 Yamaha Custom and most of his closest friends were bikers.

Even at school, Tony was always republican minded. The Blanket protest and hunger strikes were defining moments in his life. In the IRA, he was very security conscious, and very few of his friends had any idea that he had been an active Volunteer for over five years.

Tony was shot dead by British soldiers of the Royal Anglian Regiment on Culmore Road on 22nd February 1986 after a gun attack on Fort George. Unknown to Tony and his comrade, three British army foot patrols were hidden in positions in Troy Park directly opposite the garage forecourt where the attack was launched on Fort George. They opened fire within seconds of the attack. In total over 100 Brit rounds were fired at the car hitting Tony and his comrade. Over 70 shots entered the car resulting in Tony's death from multiple gunshot wounds. His comrade was wounded and arrested.

Óglach Tom Magill

4th December 1919 - 28th February 1986

Active in the republican movement for over 60 years, Volunteer Tom Magill was extremely well respected throughout republican circles. He had joined Fianna Éireann at the age of seven, and volunteered for active service with Óglaigh na hÉireann when he was seventeen.

He was arrested in Birmingham in 1938 during the IRA bombing campaign, and sentenced to ten years imprisonment. Released in 1945, he married Sadie Malone, herself a dedicated republican from the Springfield Road area.

Tom continued his active service involvement, and was arrested once more on St Patrick's Day 1958 and was interned for four years. In 1969 he underwent a serious operation, and despite his steadily deteriorating health, Tom remained totally committed to the republican cause.

Volunteer Tom Magill died after a long illness at his Turf Lodge home, in the early hours of Friday 28th February 1986. His tricolour draped coffin was escorted on its journey to the family plot in Milltown Cemetery. His wife, Sadie, who had also given years of service to the Republican Movement, died after a long illness in January 2002.

Óglach Seamus McElwain

1st April 1960 - 26th April 1986

Seamus Turlough McElwain was born on 1st April 1960 into a strong republican family from Knockascullion, near Scotstown, Co. Monaghan. From an early age he was determined to play a role in the struggle for Irish freedom, joining Na Fianna Éireann when he was aged 14. When Seamus was 16 a relative in America offered him the opportunity to study there. Seamus refused stating "no one will ever be able to accuse me of running away". It was at this time that he joined the ranks of Óglaigh na hÉireann. By the time he was 19 Seamus was playing a leading role in the Army in Fermanagh. His comrades recall that he possessed great qualities of leadership and yet he was very unassuming, to the point of being shy.

In 1981 Seamus was arrested with a group of Volunteers in a house near Roslea and sentenced to life imprisonment. While he was imprisoned Seamus stood as a candidate in the Cavan/Monaghan constituency formerly held by Hunger Striker Kieran Doherty, receiving 4,000 first preference votes. In September 1983 he, along with 37 comrades, escaped from Long Kesh. It was Seamus' innate sense of direction and the countryside that led six of the escapees to freedom.

On 26 April 1986 Seamus was assassinated by undercover soldiers after his capture on active service near Roslea. In an Easter message in 1985 he stated that "those of us who suffered the hardship of gaol and being on the run know that it is only a matter of strong organisation that will get the British out. The Republican Movement - combining Sinn Féin and the IRA is the only organisation that can do this. We the active IRA Volunteers, will take every risk and play our part. We ask you to do yours."

Óglach Philip McFadden

5th August 1957 - 31st May 1986

Vol. Philip ' Fadgie' McFadden died tragically on 31st May 1986 while fishing on a trawler off the cost of Galway. Fadgie was drowned when the boat hit a rock and sank and more lives would have been undoubtedly lost only for the bravery of Fadgie raising the alarm and alerting the other crew men.

Although quiet and unassuming in his public life, Fadgie was a committed and determined republican and his dedication and steely resolve came to the fore in his time as an active republican.

Fadgie was a Creggan man, brought up with three brothers and three sisters. His oldest brother Larry was forced to leave home and go on the run at an early age and was eventually imprisoned. This, along with the house raids and daily harassment, had a big influence in Fadgie joining the ranks of Óglaigh na hÉireann.

Forced to go on the run himself, Fadgie moved across the border to Donegal, where he continued to be an active IRA Volunteer.

On June 3rd 1986 Fadgie was buried with full military honours. His funeral will be remembered by all who were there, for the massed RUC presence, who bullied and beat the mourners on the route to the City Cemetery.

Óglach Brian Dempsey

31st March1961 - 25th June 1986

Brian was born on the 31st March 1961, the youngest of three sons and lived with his parents in Mayo Street in the loyalist Woodvale area. In the late 1960s Brian's family moved to the relative safety of Cawnpore Street, in the Clonard area, where they lived at number 78. He attended St Finian's Primary School on the Falls Road where he was a popular student and passed his 11+ before moving to St Mary's Grammar School, on the old Barrack Street site and later on the Glen Road.

It was around this time that his interest in Irish history and culture drew him towards the Republican Movement when, at the age of fourteen, he joined the local Slua of Fianna Éireann. He enjoyed the comradeship of Na Fianna and was an enthusiastic participant in the history and training lectures. A tall young man he was often chosen to take part in the Colour Party at Republican parades and was honoured to carry the national flag.

Like most Fianna boys he could barely wait until he was old enough to join the IRA. A quick learner, who carried out his responsibilities with a great zeal, he quickly progressed into the ranks of Óglaigh na hÉireann. At 6ft 4in, he kept himself fit by attending the local leisure centre, and with dark hair and brown eyes he definitely considered himself, tall, dark and handsome, a fact that was hard to argue with given his success with the ladies! He enjoyed a pint with his mates in the Clonard GAC and the nightspots in Ardoyne and West Belfast. A talented snooker player he was often seen carrying his prized cue around with him.

A dedicated and determined Volunteer, when he was forced to go on the run Brian immediately reported for active service with his comrades in the border counties. On the 25th June 1986 Brian was killed in a road traffic accident and respecting the wishes of the Dempsey family, his funeral was private. Hundreds of mourners joined the cortege as it left the family home.

Óglach Patrick O'Hagan

5th January 1954 - 9th August 1986

Patrick, "Pudger" as he was fondly known by all his friends was born in Derry in 1954. He spent his youth in Rinmore Drive, Creggan.

He joined the Fianna and later moved in to Óglaigh na h-Éireann. He was active in the Free Derry area in 1971 and 1972. After Operation Motorman he was based in Donegal where he was also active and helped organise training camps.

He was arrested on the Derry/Donegal border and was imprisoned in Magilligan. He was only there a short time when he escaped. He set up home in Buncrana, Co. Donegal with his wife, Evelyn and their young family.

During this time he continued to stay active in the Republican Movement. Pudger worked hard in the building trade to support his two sons and two daughters. He was a kind and generous man much loved and respected by everyone in the republican circles and by his friends and neighbours in Marian Park.

While building a new home for his family Pudger suddenly became ill and died on 9th August 1986. Pudger was laid to rest in Cockhill Cemetery, Buncrana.

Óglach Jim McKernan

28th January 1957 - 14th September 1986

Jim McKernan attended St. John's Primary School and later St. Thomas's Secondary School. Always cheerful and active, Jim, or 'The Dog', as he was affectionately known, was always in the 'thick of things', whether it was in school activities or later in the ranks of the Republican Movement.

When the present phase of the struggle broke out Jim joined the Gerard McAuley slua, Na Fianna Éireann, and was often seen selling An Phoblacht or Republican News. He also played a major role backing up the Volunteers of Óglaigh na hÉireann on operations.

Despite his youth, Jim had developed into a totally committed and dedicated activist. He joined Óglaigh na hÉireann at the age of seventeen, a very punctual and efficient Volunteer, always professional in his approach, despite the dangers.

He married his childhood sweetheart Margaret Walsh, and was a devoted father to their young family.

Volunteer Jim McKernan was shot dead by British occupation forces while on active service on the Andersonstown Road on 14th September 1986. In accordance with his family's request there were no military honours at his funeral. His family and comrades nevertheless were subjected to brutal treatment by the RUC and crown forces as they attempted to bury this young soldier of Ireland.

Jim McKernan's memory, his strength and commitment will always serve as an inspiration to all who knew him.

Óglach Gerard Logue

2nd January 1961 - 22nd March 1987

Gerard and Nuala Logue had a large family, of which young Gerard was sixth in line. "Bogie", to his many friends, was one of the most affable, genuine and considerate people you could ever hope to meet.

Brought up in the Top Of The Hill area of Derry's Waterside he quickly learned what it was like to be treated as a second-class citizen in his own home town. Having experienced much of what British rule had brought to the streets and to the people of Derry, Bloody Sunday, Annie's Bar, Internment etc., Bogie decided that there was a role for him in the Resistance Struggle, firstly with Na Fianna Éireann and then with the local Active Service Unit of Óglaigh na hÉireann.

Throughout the tragic period of the Hunger Strikes, Bogie was a full time activist and displayed all the qualities which have set IRA volunteers apart, i.e. courage, determination, ingenuity and selflessness.

Bogie was also a keen advocate of all things to do with the Irish language and music.

In September 1982 Gerard married Eilish Maguire and soon had the first of their three sons, Gavin, Tomas and Sean. Despite the added responsibilities of raising a family, Bogie remained an active and key operator with the Army.

Tragically, on the evening of March 21st 1987, while Gerard was returning an assault rifle to a dump after an aborted operation, the rifle accidentally discharged and he was fatally wounded.

Óglach Laurence Marley

24th July 1945 - 2nd April 1987

Larry Marley was an active Volunteer since the beginning of this phase of the struggle. He was first imprisoned in the cages of Long Kesh in 1972, and in March 1975 he was one of the ten Republicans who escaped from Newry Courthouse while appearing on charges related to another escape.

He was recaptured in Belfast in 1977 and charged with possession of weapons during his time on the run and sentenced to another ten years in jail. He was released in 1985 after serving eight years. On Thursday night, 2nd April 1987, UVF gunmen sprayed shots through the front door of the Marley home in Ardoyne, fatally wounding Larry. Within hours of the tragic murder the Marley family began to experience what was to become a week of ghoulish intimidation by the RUC. Hundreds of RUC poured into the area clearly intent on disrupting the funeral. The first attempt to bury Larry Marley took place on Monday morning. Scores of RUC landrovers and a large force in full riot gear attacked the funeral, forcing the Marley family to abandon attempts to bury their father.

Tuesday morning saw the RUC double its presence outside the Marley home. Vicious hand to hand fighting broke out as baton wielding RUC men attempted to force their way through the mourners. Once more Lawrence Marley jnr and his mother emerged from the house to tell waiting mourners that they again had to postpone the funeral for a further 24 hours.

Shortly before 10am on Wednesday morning, the Marley family carried the Tricolour draped coffin from their Ardoyne home, where it had lain for six days. As on previous days a huge force of baton wielding RUC surrounded the Marley home, intent on disrupting the funeral. However, mourners infuriated by two days of provocation were determined to bury the IRA Volunteer with honour and dignity. After seven hours of sporadic and fierce fighting, bitter arguments and determined resistance by thousands of mourners, Larry Marley was finally laid to rest.

Óglach Finbarr McKenna

30th October 1953 - 2nd May 1987

Finbarr McKenna joined the Republican Movement at the age of 15. During the violent loyalist pogroms in the Kashmir Road area of West Belfast in 1969, 'Finn' (a schooldays nickname) along with his father: (Ben, interned on the prison ship Al Rawdah for six years in the IRA's 40's campaign) and local people, actively assisted in defending the homes and lives of families, using makeshift weapons to push back heavily-armed loyalists led by the notorious B-Specials. Following the introduction of internment in August 1971 'Finn' who was constantly harassed by the crown forces was arrested on his 18th birthday on October 30th. He was taken to Palace Barracks and brutally and mercilessly tortured.

Undaunted by this treatment Finn held strong, as was his manner, and kept morale high amongst his fellow Republican prisoners. On his release Finn was again an active volunteer in the Belfast area, always conscious of the need for keeping up pressure, always considerate of his comrades' welfare and the safety of civilians. In 1974 he was arrested and detained for 3 months on fabricated charges. During this period of detention, members of the RUC's Special Branch took him to the isolated Shaw's Bridge area one night. They dragged him into a ditch, held a gun to his head and threatened to shoot. A passing lorry driver however, unnerved the RUC who instead took him to Springfield Road Barracks where he was again tortured. On this particular night an 'X' was scraped on his forehead, a warning that he was marked for assassination by crown forces. Those actions only made Finn McKenna a more determined and committed Volunteer.

In the following years Finn was arrested and tortured many times. Yet his spirit never waned. He was barely out of Long Kesh 10 months when he was killed on active service on 2nd May 1987. An hour before his death he had met his sisters not far away from where he was killed. He gave no indication that he was about to engage the enemy and joking with them said he would see them all later. That was his way. Unassuming, confident and unafraid. That was Volunteer Finbarr McKenna.

285

Óglach Declan Arthurs

28th October 1965 - 8th May 1987

Declan Arthurs from Galbally was born on 28th October 1965, the fourth child of six to Paddy and Amelia. A very close family, Dec couldn't wait to leave school and work with his father, an agricultural contractor. A common occurrence was Declan and Paddy Snr coming home covered head to foot in oil, trying to make it to the shower without leaving an oil slick in their wake.

When Declan started earning he bought a car, quickly followed by a motorbike. He loved going up the mountain on the bikes. At weekends he enjoyed an active social life with brothers and friends. Dec got involved in the Republican Movement at an early age. Along with his family he attended the torch light vigils in 1980 and the funerals of the hunger strikers in 1981. At the funeral of Martin Hurson, also from Galbally, Dec was photographed sitting in a hedge speaking into a radio and it wasn't long until the crown forces started harassing the family. At Christmas 1986, Dec was held in Gough Barracks for seven days, released on the Saturday and re-arrested on the Monday for another seven. This continued into the New Year with Dec having only seven days out of Gough during the month of January despite never being charged with any offence.

Volunteer Declan Arthurs died at Loughgall on 8th May 1987. He is buried in St. John's, Galbally with Volunteer Seamus Donnelly, in death as in life, by his side. His brother Brian writing from 'the Crum' in 1993 said, "It was a very sad day for the Republican Movement, and a very great loss to us all. I had a bond with our Declan which was more than being brothers and best friend. It is a bond I will never forget because his death killed off part of me."

From a close and loving family, Declan Arthurs died aged 21. He had two great loves in his life, his daughter and freedom.

Óglach Seamus Donnelly

11th January 1968 - 8th May 1987

Seamus Donnelly was 19 when he was killed at Loughgall. The fourth eldest of eight children, he had joined the I.R.A. at 16. Growing up in Aughnaskea, Galbally he loved and lived life as any teenager. Galbally is a tight knit community and the Donnellys a close-knit loving family. Family, community and county were devastated by the deaths at Loughgall and the loss of Seamus.

As was customary in the rural areas, where one went all went. At the weekends when Declan Arthurs' car couldn't hold any more, a convoy would head for Cookstown, Omagh or Monaghan for the night out. This was a result of the great comradeship, but it also serves as a good security precaution. In the February before he died the U.D.R. stopped Seamus at a checkpoint. They put a gun to his head and pulled the hammer back, Seamus remained totally calm. He had no fear of them. Only for a witness Seamus might never have left Kilnaslieve that night. His only fear was for the safety of his family. In Gough Barracks the R.U.C. showed him a detailed map of the family home and indicated his bed. Typically Seamus was more concerned for his younger brother, with whom he shared the room than for himself.

Volunteer Seamus Donnelly died at Loughgall on the 8th May 1987 in an ambush by British undercover forces. With him, seven comrades from the East Tyrone Brigade, four were from the Galbally area. They are all greatly missed. Seamus was a caring and thoughtful son, and a loving brother, who it was good to be around. He tried to make a better life for his family.

At the graveside of Seamus and his comrade Declan Arthurs, who were buried together in St. John's Galbally, Martin McGuinness spoke,
"Those young men who were there, with guns in their hands had every right and every justification to be there. They were there for us. And those people who laid in wait, the people who murdered them, they are the terrorists."

Óglach Tony Gormley

17th September 1962 - 8th May 1987

Tony Gormley was the first of the four Volunteers from Galbally, who died at Loughgall to be buried. He is interred in St. Patrick's, Aughnagar, Galbally, a mile from the family home.

The second eldest of six children, Tony was a happy go lucky young man but like his friends, Declan and Seamus, he suffered repeated harassment, and was arrested on numerous occasions and questioned in Gough Barracks, Armagh.

Tony was always a hard worker and he earned a reputation as a reliable and considerate employer. He was an engineering sub-contractor and had 12 men working for him. He was a forward thinker and good strategist. This was evident in the manner in which he would plan every operation meticulously, with attention to all foreseeable eventualities. Always putting himself to the fore, Tony is remembered as highly reliable and dedicated.

The friendship between Tony, Seamus, Eugene and Declan is also remembered. The craic and general "messing" that went on between them reminds us of how young they were and of how much we miss them.

At the time of his death Tony was a highly respected member of the East Tyrone Brigade. He died with his friends at Loughgall on 8th May 1987. They are often thought of and are always missed.

Óglach Eugene Kelly

5th July 1961 - 8th May 1987

In accordance with his family's wish, Volunteer Eugene Kelly, 25, was laid to rest in a private ceremony in Altmore Cemetery, Cappagh. In the 5 years that he had been a member of the IRA he had distinguished himself by his unqualified commitment to the struggle. His decision to join the Army was taken after long and serious consideration, but once made he was dedicated and no task was too small.

Eugene knew the geography of Tyrone and Armagh like the back of his hand. He knew the shortcuts through the country roads like no one else and, on more than one occasion, is remembered for having spirited comrades and weapons past check points. Reliable and courageous he was a well-respected volunteer.

Eugene came from a family of four sisters and two brothers. He was extremely conscious of his own security and feared most for the effect his involvement might have on his family, whom he loved deeply. Like other young republicans from the areas the RUC and British army frequently harassed him, and he spent several 7 day spells in Gough Barracks in Armagh.

He died at Loughgall on the night of Friday May 8th 1987. He, like his comrades, is sorely missed. Eugene is remembered with love and pride by all who knew him.

Óglach Patrick Kelly

19th March 1957 - 8th May 1987

Patrick Kelly, from Dungannon, was 30 when he died at Loughgall on 8th May 1987. As his father Vincent said, "It was the R.U.C.'s beatings that made Paddy a Volunteer." He had the highest respect for his comrades, and is remembered for his exceptional leadership qualities; he gave his whole hearted commitment and his life to the struggle for Irish freedom.

The eldest of five children, Paddy Kelly, was born in the staunchly loyalist town of Carrickfergus. Although from a fourth generation republican family, Paddy Kelly needed no one to tell him about the discrimination and harassment suffered by republicans. He witnessed it at first hand, initially in Carrickfergus, but then when the family moved to his father's home town of Dungannon, like many young men he was routinely stopped, searched and questioned. Once when he objected, he was viciously beaten and from that point confrontations became a part of Paddy's daily life.

In early 1982, he and seven others were arrested on the uncorroborated word of Patrick McGurk. Paddy, industrious as ever, spent his time on remand learning the Irish language. He was acquitted at a fifteen minute trial but the experience made him more determined than ever. His father explains, "No true Irishman can accept the status quo. Nobody likes to see the killings, but it's a war situation, and it happens. Gangsters and criminals are not willing to die for their country. Patrick was not a bad boy. He was a true Irishman who had every thing to live for. He had his wife, their children. He knew the risks but he loved his country."

His wife, Kathleen, was expecting their fourth child the week he was killed. Volunteer Patrick Kelly is buried in Edendork Cemetery, two miles from his Dungannon home. The Kellys say they have some solace, for though they miss Paddy, they see him in the eyes of his oldest son.

Óglach Jim Lynagh

13th April 1956 - 8th May 1987

When Jim Lynagh was not on active service it was because he was in detention or in gaol. His reputation as a revolutionary soldier, a leader of a highly active I.R.A. unit and his warm, intelligent and generous nature made him much loved wherever he went. Equally all this made him hated and feared by both the Gardaí and the Northern state forces.

Born in Monaghan on April 13th 1956, Jim's life was spent in the service of the people. Joining the Army as a teenager he operated mainly in East Tyrone. In 1973 he was seriously injured in an accidental explosion. Captured after this incident he was sentenced to ten years in Long Kesh. On the day of his release, he reported back to his unit - even before he went home. In 1979 he was elected to Monaghan Urban District Council as a Sinn Féin councillor. This did nothing to stop the daily harassment of Jim and his family, which was as intense as their fear of Jim himself. If a passing Garda car saw Jim, or even one of his family they were known to stop traffic to get out to beat him. Jim continued to live among the people of Tyrone and Armagh, and is remembered for his helpful involvement when stating no job was too great or too small if it needed doing.

The R.U.C. would repeatedly raise his name in Gough Barracks and checkpoints. They offered bribes that wouldn't have fitted on the cheque for him to be set up for assassination. No one would have considered it, not through fear but out of love. Jim Lynagh had time for everyone and everyone liked him. He was humble and dignified and under no illusions that he was invincible. Volunteer Jim Lynagh died during the attack on Loughgall barracks on 8th May 1987. All who knew him were saddened at his death and still feel the loss, but the memory of his smile, and stories and wise cracks can't help but bring on a smile.

Óglach Padraig McKearney

8th May 1987

Padraig McKearney was educated at local primary schools in Collegeland and The Moy, and went on to Dungannon Academy but left school after he was first arrested in 1972. He suffered a severe beating and spent six weeks on remand, the charges were dropped when the bruising healed. In December 1973, he was arrested and later sentenced to seven years for possession.

He was in prison when his 18 year old brother, Vol. Sean McKearney was killed while on active service. He was released in 1977 but only to have 3 years of freedom. In August 1980 he was sentenced to 14 years. He served only 3 of them before escaping in the mass break out in September 1983.

A friend remembers that, "When Padraig was 17 and on remand charged with blowing up the Post Office in The Moy, his granny on his father's side told him that his great, great uncle had blown up the same Crown Building, nearly 100 years before." The republican blood of the family runs deep on both sides, with Padraig's maternal grandfather having fought in the Tan War.

Having evaded capture Vol. Padraig McKearney was killed on 8th May 1987 during the attack on Loughgall barracks which also claimed the lives of his seven comrades. At his funeral the McKearney family thanked all those "who took him into their homes and their hearts."

Even his niece, aged 9 at the time of his death, remembered him as, "A brilliant soldier, a great uncle and he was always cool"

Volunteer Padraig McKearney was buried in his hometown, The Moy thirteen years to the day after his brother Sean died on Active Service.

Óglach Gerard O'Callaghan

8th January 1959 - 8th May 1987

Gerard O'Callaghan was the baby in a house of 11 children and grew up in the loyalist area of Benburb. At his funeral in the Church of the Immaculate Conception, Tullysaron, mourners heard the local priest Fr. Campbell explain how, "nationalists have been the victims of gross injustice in the partitioned North." Gerard had joined the I.R.A. when he was 17 in an effort to change this.

He was a quiet lad and at times enjoyed his own company more than that of the crowd. He wasn't one to express his opinions openly but he held a determination that the root of all wrongdoing in Ireland lay with the British presence. The comrades who knew him spoke of his unshakeable courage and quiet determination.

In 1980, he was captured, with Vol. Pádraig McKearney and sentenced to six years for possession of weapons. They were held in C-Wing in the Crumlin Road Jail, during which time they both went on the no-wash protest. On his release he reported back to his unit and resumed activities along the border. On active service, he was sharp, calm and utterly reliable, holding the complete trust of his comrades. Gerard is remembered for always making sure that the operation was carried out to its full as a conscientious individual.

Gerard O'Callaghan died on Active Service at Loughgall on Friday 8th May 1987. His coffin, draped with the National Flag and flanked by a military guard of honour was led by a lone piper from his home in Tullymore, Benburb on the afternoon of Tuesday 12th. He is fondly remembered by all who knew him.

Óglach Margaret McArdle

27th January 1958 - 7th June 1987

Margaret McArdle was born in Belfast in 1958, the eldest of a family of six, four girls and two boys. She was very popular with her many friends, always full of life and laughter. She was always kind and considerate towards others. She was a loving and wonderful daughter and sister, always helping out in whatever way she could. If there was a problem, Margaret would try to solve it, she was a great person with a big heart.

Margaret grew up in the troubles when injustice towards Catholics and Nationalists was commonplace. She felt deep down that she should confront these injustices, and in becoming an Irish Republican she did just that. Margaret's decision to become actively involved in the struggle for Irish Freedom resulted in her being arrested in July 1983 and charged with possession of explosives, along with her father, the well-known Belfast Republican Eddie McArdle (R.I.P.) Though eventually acquitted of these charges in April 1985, 4 other IRA volunteers arrested at the same time, were convicted and sentenced to jail terms of between 6-7 years.

Margaret loved to travel and was fascinated by the way people lived in other parts of the world. Her many trips abroad are recorded in the hundreds of photographs she took while away. Later, when developed, these photos were carefully placed in albums, each with a little note penned on the back. Margaret's ambition was to visit all five continents, something she eventually achieved on her last, and final trip. It was in India on the 7th June 1987, at the age of 29, that Margaret died, unable to survive an extreme heat wave that struck New Delhi during her visit.

Fifteen years on, Margaret's loss is still deeply felt, not only by us - her immediate family, but also by her dear friends and comrades, many of whom still visit her grave in Shelagh churchyard in Hackballscross, County Louth. We will always treasure her memory. We will continue to be inspired by her, and above all, we will always be proud of her.

A Thiarna dean trócaire uirthi

Óglach Paddy Deery

11th November 1955 - 28th October 1987

Paddy Deery was a member of a well-known and respected family from the Creggan estate. The Deery family had an early introduction to the brutality of the British in Ireland when their mother Peggy was seriously injured by British Paratroopers on Bloody Sunday in January 1972. Paddy and his brothers and sisters also had to endure daily harassment and intimidation from the British Army and RUC.

These experiences added to Paddy's resolve to play his part in the fight for freedom and he was soon putting his local knowledge of the streets of Creggan to good use on active service with the IRA. Despite having lost an eye at the age of 15 to a British soldier's rubber bullet, Paddy became an accomplished and skilful driver for his active service unit.

When not on active service or on Óglaigh na h-Éireann business, it was hard to get a serious word out of Paddy, with his constant joking and mickey-taking. He was very popular with his comrades even when some of them were the butt of his wise cracks.

Paddy was married to Colette and they had three children, Patrick Junior, Gavin and Shauna. They were a great support to Paddy even though they had to suffer the daily hardships encountered by a volunteer's family. Paddy paid the ultimate price for his commitment to the struggle when he and his friend and comrade, Eddie McSheffrey were killed in an accidental explosion while on active service. Paddy died on the streets of his beloved Creggan on the 28th October 1987.

The funeral cortege was attacked by the RUC in order to prevent Óglaigh na h-Éireann burying their comrades as volunteers. The RUC attacks failed and Paddy was buried with full IRA honours.

Óglach Eddie McSheffrey

7th August 1958 - 28th October 1987

Eddie McSheffrey was a member of a highly respected family of republicans in Derry. Eddie's family suffered more than most in the cause of republicanism. From the early days of the conflict the McSheffreys were victims of persecution by the British. His father was arrested numerous times and imprisoned on several occasions. In November 1972 the McSheffrey family had a fortunate escape in an explosion which killed two IRA volunteers and destroyed their home in Meenan Drive.

Eddie was a born leader and moved steadily through the ranks of the Fianna and joined the IRA when he came of age. Eddie became a highly respected member of Óglaigh na hÉireann and was known as a fearless Volunteer while on active service. He was also an articulate speaker at IRA meetings and at every opportunity he represented the views of the Volunteers on the ground.

Eddie paid the price for being a republican activist. He was harassed daily, his home was raided on numerous occasions and he was severely wounded and imprisoned after an operation in which his young comrade Charles English was killed.

Eddie married Mary in 1980. They had two children, Charles and Aisling. Mary was very supportive of Eddie's commitment to the movement in spite of the hardships the family had to endure. The suffering of the McSheffrey family came to a tragic climax on the 28th October 1987 when Eddie and his comrade Paddy Deery were killed in an accidental explosion in Creggan.

The funeral cortege was attacked by the RUC who also fired plastic bullets at the mourners. Despite this, Eddie and Paddy were given full military honours.

Óglach Peter Rodden

7th December 1987

The only son of John and Teresa Rodden, Kilrea, Co Derry, Peter was educated at Glenullin Primary School and St Paul's Secondary, Kilrea. Highly political, Peter was one of the first and one of the staunchest members of Kilrea H-Block/Armagh Committee, and attended marches and rallies all over Ireland.

After the Hunger Strikes ended in 1981, Peter joined Sinn Féin in Kilrea and was a highly respected member. However, he was to resign after 18 months due to 'other commitments'. These 'other commitments' were his by now full time role, as a Volunteer in Óglaigh na hÉireann. Also, as a security measure, Peter went from being a member of Sinn Féin in South Derry to being an I.R.A Volunteer in the North Antrim Brigade. During his time as an I.R.A Volunteer Peter was to take part in many actions, and proved himself to be both brave and resourceful. He was to see two of his comrades, Volunteers Henry Hogan and Declan Martin murdered by British undercover agents in Dunloy on the night of 21st February 1984. He himself was lucky to escape death on one or more occasions.

On the night of December 7th 1987 Peter was returning from a night out with his girlfriend. Also in the car was one of Peter's comrades, Liam Casey, and his wife Geraldine. Used to constant harassment, house raids, and spells in Castlereagh it was not surprising that when seeing a R.U.C roadblock in Toomebridge they took a side road to avoid it. On the wet, narrow, and unfamiliar road, disaster struck when their car left the road and plunged into the icy waters of the River Bann. Peter then aged 26, and his friends and comrades, Liam and Geraldine Casey, all lost their lives in this tragic accident. In his last moments, however, Peter pushed his girlfriend Cynthia to safety through an open window allowing her to be rescued.

A massive Police cordon swamped Kilrea on the day of Óglach Peter Rodden's funeral and at one stage heavily armed D.M.S.U.s came into the graveyard insulting and threatening mourners. Volunteer Peter Rodden is buried in St Mary's Drumagarner, Kilrea.

Óglach Brendan Burns

9th February 1958 - 29th February 1988

Brendan was born on the 9th February 1958, the first born of Lillie and Peter Burns. He often looked after his younger brother Joe and his four sisters, Yvonne, Ann, Mary and Attracta. He went to Cregganduff Primary School, then St Joseph's High School, Crossmaglen and finally Newry Technical College. Brendan liked to be in the middle of the craic and enjoyed nothing better than a bit of slagging. He joined Óglaigh na hÉireann at 16 years of age and from the outset he was impatient to become fully operational on active service.

He radiated a confidence, and his determination and commitment during many of the well-planned attacks throughout the South Armagh area, inspired his comrades and instilled fear in the British forces based in the area. By 1984, Brendan, who was on the run from the North was arrested by Gardai Special Branch on foot of extradition orders.

He spent over two years in Portlaoise Prison, and eventually beat the extradition case. On leaving the court he was followed by the Special Branch but, true to form, he slipped through their fingers by jumping on to a motorbike and driving away. From then on, Brendan was on the run, but he refused to allow any danger to stop him seeing his family. Many times he had narrow escapes as the British Army came looking for him.

His coolness typified the kind of man he was and this among other outstanding personal qualities, led him to be held in the highest esteem among the people of South Armagh, who opened their doors and hearts to him without hesitation. This was shown again by the massive number of people who attended Brendan's funeral despite the intimidation of the over-bearing British Army presence.

Óglach Brendan Moley

25th January 1958 - 29th February 1988

For many generations the Moley family have lived in the Dorsey, near Cullyhanna in South Armagh with the first recorded families dating back to the 1600s. At the time of the present phase of the struggle, Brendan's parents, Michael and Mary were living there on a small farm with their nine children. Brendan, the fourth child and eldest son was born on the 25th January 1958. He attended Dorsey Primary School and later went to Crossmaglen Secondary School, where he met and formed a lifelong friendship with Brendan Burns.

With a keen interest in Irish history and politics, from an early age he questioned the British presence and interference in Ireland and at 16 years of age he joined Na Fianna Éireann before quickly progressing into the ranks of Óglaigh na hÉireann, where he became a full-time active service Volunteer. He was arrested several times by the Crown forces and on one occasion a naïve Special Branch man attempted to bribe him with a large amount of money in return for his "co-operation", an attempt that was rejected with contempt.

Brendan was a trusted and respected member of his community whose advice was sought by many. He was involved in some of the most dangerous and daring attacks carried out by the IRA in South Armagh and, typical of his character, he would never ask Volunteers to do anything that he wasn't prepared to do himself.

He had the ability to deal with whatever situation arose while on active service, dealing with the most difficult problems calmly and logically. Brendan was killed on active service on 29th February 1988 and his death was a great loss to his family, friends and comrades in South Armagh.

Óglach Mairead Farrell

3rd March 1957 - 6th March 1988

Mairead Farrell was born in Belfast on 3rd March 1957. She was educated at Rathmore School and was a brilliant student who excelled at exams. But Mairead had already thought deeply on the path her future was to take and at the age of 18 she joined the IRA.

It wasn't long before Mairead was imprisoned but her intelligence and ability quickly ensured that she was to become the Officer Commanding the sentenced women prisoners. On December 1st 1980 Mairead Farrell, Mary Doyle and Mary Nugent went on Hunger Strike alongside their fellow prisoners in the H-Blocks of Long Kesh.

It was while in the hospital wing on the night of December 18th that Mairead and her comrades first heard that the Hunger Strike in the H-Blocks was over. Only after confirmation from their O/C on December 19th, Mairead and her comrades decided to call off their Hunger Strike.

Mairead was a tireless worker and Volunteer and it was while on active service in Gibraltar that she and her fellow comrades, Dan McCann and Sean Savage, were summarily executed in broad daylight on Sunday 6th March 1988.

A major campaign of disinformation ensued, orchestrated by the British but despite their lies and hypocrisy the truth slowly emerged that the three Volunteers were in fact unarmed and were gunned down by undercover British soldiers.

She was buried with full military honours.

Óglach Dan McCann

30th November 1957 - 6th March 1988

Dan McCann was born on 30th November 1957 into a much loved and well-respected family from the Clonard area of West Belfast. He began his schooling in St. Gall's Primary School and later moved to St. Mary's Grammar School on Belfast's Glen Road.

In 1973 Dan's studies were cut short when he was sentenced to six months for 'riotous behaviour'. That same year he joined Óglaigh na hÉireann. Dan was to experience prison on three further occasions as well as loyalist and British Army death threats. In January 1979 he was arrested and convicted for the possession of a single detonator. He was sentenced to two years in prison, which he spent on the blanket and no-wash protest. On his release in January 1981, he resumed active service but his spell of freedom was to be short lived. In May 1981 Dan was to find himself again in prison, on this occasion he was to spend four months on remand for alleged possession of a weapon.

Back again on active service by September, Dan was free for only three months before he was again arrested. The spurious charge against him was dropped after he had spent six months in prison. Dan's last spell in prison was in July 1982, the victim once more of internment by remand. He was arrested on the word of a witness, and blackmailed by the RUC. When the charges were dropped Dan and three others were released. Ironically one of the three was Sean Savage.

On Sunday, March 6th, Dan was gunned down in Gibraltar with his two comrades, Mairead Farrell and Sean Savage. He was murdered by the same British gunmen whose sordid presence he had spent his short but full life attempting to remove from the land he loved.

Óglach Sean Savage

26th January 1965 – 6th March 1988

Sean Savage was born on 26th January 1965, in the Kashmir area of Belfast. He was only 4 years old when 'Paisleyite' inspired mobs launched the 1969 pogroms, which left the small streets of his neighbourhood a smouldering pile of rubble. Educated first at St. Gall's Primary, then St. Paul's Secondary School on the Falls Road, Sean proved to be a promising scholar. He was taking 8 'O' levels when his efforts were cut short by his arrest.

Sean was a quiet and single-minded individual who neither drank nor smoked and rarely socialised. He was solitary by nature but by no means shy or withdrawn. He was deeply articulate with deep political convictions, which he would readily debate with vigour.

At 17 years of age Sean joined Óglaigh na hÉireann. He showed early leadership qualities, which he was to bring to bear during his short but full years of active service. His dedication to the struggle was total and unswerving. To his fellow Volunteers he was a strong, steadfast comrade, whose sharp and incisive judgement was relied on in delicate situations. To his family he was a devoted and loving son and a loving and loved brother. Sean was gunned down with his two comrades, Dan McCann and Mairead Farrell, in cold blood, in broad daylight and in front of witnesses on the streets of Gibraltar, on Sunday 6th March 1988.

The British soldiers, who carried out the murder, were acting on precise and clear instructions from their political wing, the British cabinet, once again demonstrating to the world the chilling and brutal nature of Britain's dirty war in Ireland.

Óglach Kevin McCracken

22nd June 1956 - 14th March 1988

Kevin McCracken grew up in Turf Lodge in Belfast, the eldest of five children. One of his sisters, Deirdre, served a sentence in Armagh Womens' Prison between 1975-76.

Young Kevin was so deeply affected by the suffering of the people, that he joined Fianna Éireann in 1972 when he was 15 years old. Three years later he had joined Óglaigh na hÉireann, and was soon at the forefront of IRA attacks in West Belfast for the following two years. Arrested in April 1977, he was sentenced to 13 years for IRA membership, and incendiaries.

During his time in Long Kesh he took part in the 'blanket and no-wash' protests for political status. On his release in November 1985, he immediately reported back to Óglaigh na hÉireann and was actively involved in broadening the republican base in Turf Lodge.

Volunteer Kevin McCracken was shot dead by a British soldier on Monday night, 14th March 1988. He was preparing to launch an attack on the crown forces that had saturated the area in an attempt to intimidate the family of Volunteer Sean Savage who lived nearby.

Kevin McCracken lay mortally wounded in the pathway at Norglen Crescent for fifteen minutes after local people had called an ambulance. Kevin died before he reached the hospital.

Volunteer Kevin McCracken is buried with his comrades in Milltown Cemetery, Belfast.

Óglach Caoimhín MacBradaigh

25th October 1957 - 16th March 1988

Volunteer Caoimhín MacBradaigh, who so heroically gave his life along with two other nationalist youths, in an attempt to prevent certain slaughter for countless people in Milltown Cemetery on Wednesday, 16th March 1988, was a quiet, versatile and dedicated revolutionary soldier. He had so much to offer his country, and was never found wanting in that regard.

Caoimhín was the youngest in a family of four boys and three girls. His parents were fluent Gaeilgeoiri, and raised their family in their native tongue.

Caoimhín was an adaptable revolutionary activist who could, and did, fulfil a variety of roles within the movement. He was as effective in public, political work as he was on active service. In 1975 at the age of 17, Caoimhín joined Óglaigh na hÉireann. He was seriously injured in a car accident in 1976 and was inactive for a period. As soon as his health returned, he was back on active service.

Always maintaining a close relationship with his imprisoned comrades, Caoimhín was a regular visitor to the prisons throughout Ireland. He built deep and lasting friendships and commitments. His death itself was like his life - one of selfless concern for others.

Volunteer Caoimhín MacBradaigh was buried in Milltown Cemetery, Belfast.

Óglach Hugh Hehir

21st November 1950 - 6th May 1988

Hugh Hehir was born on 21st November 1950, the third eldest of seven children. A plumber by trade he was politicised during the Civil Rights period in 1968 and joined the IRA in the aftermath of the August pogroms of 1969.

Hughie operated in many parts of the border area and knew other Volunteers from the 26 counties who had also gone north, such as Tony Ahern and Dermot Crowley from Cork.

In early 1974 he was arrested in Belfast's New Lodge Road area along with Joe Doherty and charged with possession of explosives and IRA membership. While in Crumlin Road jail on remand, he and Joe attempted to escape but were caught. He served his sentence in the Cages of Long Kesh where he made many friends and when he was released in November 1979 he immediately reported back to the IRA.

Hughie lived in Clarecastle, Co. Clare with his wife Anne and their three children, Hugh, Séan and Fiona. Their other daughter Tara died in a car accident four years before Hugh was killed.

On Friday 6th May 1988, Hugh, was shot by a member of the Gardai while on active service. He was taken to Ennis General Hospital before being transferred to Cork General Hospital where he died. Hughie is buried at Cnoc an Claire Cemetery, Ennis, Co. Clare.

Óglach Seamus Woods

13th January 1965 - 7th July 1988

On the 7th July 1988 Volunteer Seamus Woods from Limehill, Pomeroy was engaged in a mortar and gun attack on the Pomeroy R.U.C. barracks. Seamus had taken responsibility for carrying out one of the most dangerous aspects of the operation - driving the mortars, positioned on the back of a tractor, to within yards of the heavily fortified barracks. He was killed while withdrawing from the mortars. During a subsequent search by the crown forces at 8a.m. the next morning, his body was found in a field at Edenbank Road.

On Friday the 8th, Volunteers from the East Tyrone Brigade secured a position in the Pomeroy area and fired a sustained volley of shots over his beret, gloves and the Flag in a simple tribute to their comrade. The volley was timed to coincide with the release of his body from Craigavon Hospital. In a statement the Army said this was their final tribute and took away any pretext for the Crown Forces to harass either the Woods family or mourners, as had been the case at previous wakes and funerals in the area.

The second youngest in a family of six boys and two girls, Seamus was an electrical engineer by trade, a trade he put to good use in the engineering department. Joining the I.R.A. in 1985, he was a highly active Volunteer, committed to whatever he was asked to do. Volunteer Seamus Woods was the first Volunteer to be buried in the Republican Plot in Pomeroy. His coffin, draped in the Tricolour was carried into the Church of the Assumption, Pomeroy as every movement of the mourners, who were surrounded by the R.U.C. was videoed by Special Branch.

Seamus Woods was a well respected, dedicated and intelligent Volunteer who was liked by everyone who knew him.

Óglach Brendan Davison

14th February 1955 - 25th July 1988

Brendan Davison was born and raised in Joy Street and spent his life in the small closely-knit Markets area of South Belfast. Brendan, or 'Big Ruby' as he was more commonly known, came from a well known republican family in the area and like many of his peers he joined the ranks of the 3rd battalion of the Belfast Brigade.

Brendan joined the IRA in late 1971 and within a few short months he was arrested and sentenced to 15 years for a gun attack on British soldiers.

He was released in 1980 and again within a few short months he was back in prison during the infamous 'Supergrass' era of the early 1980s. This time he spent over two years on remand in Crumlin Road jail before he was finally released and, like the first time he was released, he immediately reported back for active service.

Standing over six feet tall 'Big Ruby' stood out in a crowd. An affable and easy-going person the long years of imprisonment had ensured he remained youthful in his outlook on life.

An active Republican he was targeted by loyalists, and in 1987 he was shot and wounded while standing in a bookmakers shop in Cromac Street in the Markets area. A year later loyalist gunmen, dressed in R.U.C. uniforms, returned and shot 'Big Ruby' dead in his own home.

Óglach Brian Mullin

21st December 1962 - 30th August 1988

Born on 21st December 1962 and christened on Christmas Day, Brian was the sixth in a family of seven boys and three girls born to Michael, who died in January 1984, and Cissie Mullin. The family lived on a farm in Foremass, Sixmilecross and were known locally as the 'Bard' Mullins because their grandfather had been a poet. Brian was educated at Altamuskin Primary School and later at St. Ciaran's in Ballygawley.

While still in primary school Brian saw the first of many British Army raids on his home. His eldest brother Patrick, who died in May 2001, was arrested, tortured and beaten and served a three year prison sentence in Magilligan. He later served a life sentence in Long Kesh, where he endured the barbaric and brutal conditions of the H Blocks.

Brian was a hard working bricklayer who was big in stature, who enjoyed life and who had a great future ahead of him with his lovely girlfriend Eileen. He was a tireless worker for the Political Status campaign and a frequent visitor to the jails. He was also an extremely dedicated and courageous Volunteer in the IRA.

The Mullin family were no strangers to harassment, roadside beatings, house arrests and spells in Gough Barracks. On two occasions Brian's father uncovered British Army dugouts on the family farm.

Brian was killed in an ambush, by a British Army undercover unit, alongside his brother-in-law Martin Harte and Martin's brother Gerard, at Drumnakilly outside Omagh on 30th August 1988. Brian was a loving son and great friend to all who knew him. It is the courage of volunteers like Brian that has kept the 'Flame of Freedom' alight.

Óglach Gerard Harte

7th April 1959 - 30th August 1988

Gerard Harte was born on 7th April 1959 in the townland of Striff near Loughmacrory in Co. Tyrone. He was the third eldest in a family of six and at the age of sixteen he trained to be an architect, a career which he pursued until his untimely death. He was married in 1986, exactly two years before his death. Gerard had one young son, Colm.

A highly respected member of his local community, Gerard occupied many key roles both as manager and player with his local GAA club, Naomh Treasa. One of his many achievements was a Tyrone junior championship medal, which he won while playing corner forward with the Loughmacrory side in 1980. Gerard also formulated and spearheaded a successful youth programme and managed many underage teams to success during the 1980s.

His greatest love however, was his country. He had an acute knowledge of the history of British oppression and the struggle of the Irish people. This conviction led Gerard to join the ranks of Óglaigh na hÉireann at an early age. As a Volunteer, he fearlessly participated in countless actions against the British forces of occupation and their agents in this country.

On Tuesday 30th August 1988 Gerard, along with his brother Martin and Brian Mullin moved into action against a member of the enemy forces in the townland of Drumnakilly outside Omagh. As the Volunteers approached their target in a commandeered vehicle, British undercover soldiers riddled their car with hundreds of bullets. People from the area then heard three single shots which was the coup de grace.

Óglach Martin Harte

3rd October 1966 - 30th August 1988

Martin Harte was just 21 when he was shot dead close to his home at Drumnakilly on Tuesday 30th August 1988. Martin was married with a young son Declan. A joiner by trade, he was, like his brother - a skilled Gaelic footballer. He captained Saint Teresa's team at the time of his death and was the holder of the club's player of the year award - a title that he inherited from the previous year's holder, his brother Gerard.

Holding the position of centre halfback, Martin was arguably one of the best footballers in the county and no doubt had his footballing career not been prematurely cut short, he would have represented Tyrone at Senior County football level.

However Martin's passion was his country and its people. This passion led Martin to become active in the H-Block campaign and resulted in his arrest on numerous occasions and the continual harassment of himself and his family. Martin's republican ideology and his experiences at the hands of the crown forces convinced him that joining the ranks of Óglaigh na hÉireann was the only effective way to address the situation and ultimately achieve the reunification of his country - an ideal which he held in high esteem.

It was this commitment, passion and ideology, which led Martin along with his brother Gerard and brother-in-law Brian Mullin, to pay the ultimate sacrifice in the cause of Irish freedom.

Fuair siad bás ag troid ar son saoirse na hÉireann

Óglach James Joseph Connolly

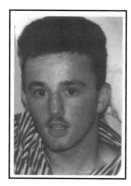

19th August 1968 - 6th February 1989

Josie, the eldest son of Joe and Annie Connolly, excelled at his trade of bricklaying and was a keen sportsman. He had earned numerous trophies for boxing, including an Ulster Junior Championship. Josie was also a keen footballer and played for his local team, St Eugene's G.A.C.

Josie's grandparents had deteriorated in health over the years prior to his death. Constant attention was needed at their farmhouse and here Josie put his shoulder to the wheel. Typical of his devotion to both his natural and Republican families is the story of how Josie left his grandparents' wake on Easter Sunday to attend a local commemoration at the graveside of Volunteer Seamus Harvey. He was buried in the graveyard to which Josie made his final journey on 9th February 1989.

Shortly after 11pm on February 5th 1989, a bomb detonated prematurely in the village of Drumquin. As Crown Forces personnel arrived, they found a seriously injured young man. Conscious and aware, he refused to give any information or even his identity.

The following day the young man died from his injuries. The man was James Joseph Connolly from Castlederg (20). The IRA confirmed that he was a Volunteer deployed on active service.

Josie Connolly was described as 'one of the most popular lads in the parish'. He was respected by all and a well-known figure through his sporting achievements. His loss to his family, friends and the Republican Movement is immeasurable.

Óglach John Davey

1st May 1927 - 14th February 1989

John Davey was a native of North Antrim where many of his family reside. John was a former Volunteer and was interned in the '50s campaign. John moved to South Derry with his wife Mary and three children and lived in Gulladuff.

John was again interned on August 9th 1971 and he suffered serious head injuries when British soldiers beat him during his arrest. On release from Long Kesh, John helped to build Sinn Féin in South Derry and worked tirelessly for prisoners and their families and was a great source of help and comfort at the time of the H-Block Hunger Strike Campaign.

John's strong Republican beliefs and leadership qualities earned the respects of everyone, even those people who didn't share his Republican beliefs. John was arrested, assaulted and harassed by the RUC, UDR/RIR and British Army almost on a daily basis and became a target of a pro-British death squad. In 1985 John was elected to Magherafelt District Council where Unionists in the chamber physically assaulted him.

John worked tirelessly for the people of his area and confronted discrimination wherever it arose. John survived a murder bid in 1988, later claimed by Michael Stone.

On 14th February 1989 John was murdered on his laneway, returning from a council meeting in Magherafelt. John's wife Mary and three children, family and friends suffered further when the RUC cordoned off the South Derry village of Gulladuff and harassed mourners attending John's wake and funeral.

John Davey is buried at St Mary's Graveyard, Lavey.

Óglach Gerard Casey

10th August 1959 - 4th April 1989

Gerard was born the fifth child of Hugh and Kathleen Casey's eight children. Gerard found work as a joiner with his father in the family building trade, quickly earning a reputation as a craftsman. Gerard had an active interest in the GAA, playing football for Rasarkin.

He was a member of the North Antrim Brigade Óglaigh na hÉireann and as such was the victim of constant harassment by the Crown Forces, being arrested on numerous occasions. His last arrest took place in October 1988, when his house was raided in the early hours of the morning. Among items taken from the home were family photographs and a legally held shotgun, while those involved in the raid drew maps of the interior of his home. While being interrogated he was told by his captors that he would never be back in the interrogation centre because he would be shot and his killing would be claimed by Loyalists.

On the night Gerard was killed, a local couple were held hostage and had their car taken by the death squad who were made up of five to six men with English accents. Gerard was shot dead in his bed, in front of his wife and child. The killing was claimed by the UVF. There is little doubt, however, that Gerard's murder was the product of collusion between his killers and the Crown Forces. Mourners at his wake and funeral were subjected to the same harassment that Gerard had been a constant victim of. Gerard Casey lies in St. Mary's Graveyard, Rasharkin.

Óglach Seamus Twomey

5th November 1919 - 12th September 1989

Seamus Twomey was born in Marchioness Street in Belfast's Lower Falls. He joined Fianna Éireann in 1936, and Óglaigh na hÉireann the following year. During the Second World War, Seamus and his future wife, Rosie McCotter, were both interned, Seamus on the Al Rawdah and in Crumlin Road, while Rosie was held in Armagh Jail. They married after their release, and in the late 1950's moved to Andersonstown.

He was arrested in October 1973. Within three weeks, along with J.B. O'Hagan and Kevin Mallon, Seamus made a dramatic escape from Mountjoy Jail in a commandeered helicopter.

He resumed his role in the IRA in 1975 and oversaw the most effective and long lasting re-organisation in the movement's history. Seamus was re-arrested after a high-speed car chase through Dublin in December 1977, and sentenced to 8 years. By this time he was in his late 50s. He was released again in 1982 and continued his active involvement with the struggle.

Despite a terrible illness, he remained a very forceful and dedicated Republican up to the end. Volunteer Seamus Twomey died on Tuesday 12th September 1989, and is buried in the family plot in Milltown Cemetery, Belfast.

Óglach Liam Ryan

19th February 1950 - 29th November 1989

Liam was born on the 19th February 1950, the third in a family of twelve, to Willie and Sally. Liam's mother came originally from Gola Island, Donegal. She was a native speaker and her great uncle Pat McGinley was one of the gunrunners of the Asgard Rising. As with many boys of his time, school and sport dominated Liam's early and teenage years. From St. Peter's in Moortown, he moved on to Cookstown and then Dungannon Technical Colleges, pursuing a career in electronics. Liam was an all round athlete, enjoying hurling and boxing.

In 1969 he visited America for his sister's wedding, and opted to stay and did not return until 1972. He became a bailiff on Lough Neagh, employed by the Fisherman's Society. In 1976, however he decided to return to America.

Using his technical training he found employment with Con Edison Electricity Co., remaining with them until his return home in 1985. Intending to stay home, Liam bought "The Battery Bar", and returned to America to tidy up his affairs. While in America he was arrested and charged with buying firearms with false documents. At his trial in New York in December of that year he was handed down a suspended sentence of four years and a $10,000 fine. From his return home until his murder by the U.V.F. on 29th November 1989, Liam was under constant surveillance and harassment by the Crown Forces, but it was also a happy time. he married Geraldine and their son, Declan was born in the September of '89. Declan was little over a month old when his father was murdered in "The Battery".

It is a measure of his sensitivity and generosity, that since that night many people have told of the help and assistance he gave to those in trouble. Liam never would have mentioned it himself. His friends miss him very much indeed.

Volunteer Liam Ryan is buried in Ardboe.

Óglach Sam Marshall

18th September 1958 - 7th March 1990

Sam was a well-known republican activist in Lurgan. At the age of 18 in March 1976, he was arrested and subsequently sentenced to 7 years. Sam immediately joined the Blanket Protest. He refused to be broken in his resolve to be treated as a POW. He was to serve six of those seven years, most of them on protest. Sam was released in April 1982. He rejoined the Republican movement in Lurgan where he was prominent in political and cultural activity. Sam had become a keen language enthusiast in the H Blocks.

Sam was to experience another brief period in prison when he and two friends were charged with possession of ammunition. They eventually got bail and it was signing weekly bail conditions at Lurgan RUC Barracks that enabled the RUC/Loyalist death squad to target the three friends. In one of the most blatant examples of RUC-Loyalist collusion, the three men were followed by the RUC to and from the barracks until the loyalist death squad emerged to launch their attack. Sam's two friends made it to cover but Sam was caught in a burst of gunfire and died immediately.

Sam was survived by his four sisters, his brother and his mother Alice. He is buried in his family plot in St. Colman's, Lurgan.

Óglach Sean Bateson

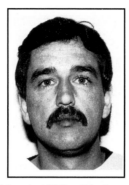

28th March 1956 - 7th June 1990

Sean Bateson came from a tight-knit community in the Bone area of North Belfast. Sean was educated first at St. Columbanus Sacred Heart Boys' School and then at St. Gabriel's Secondary.

Traumatised like most of his generation by the renewed onset from loyalist death squads in 1968/69, Sean quickly came to see that his people's only chance was to organise for resistance. He became an active member in Fianna Éireann and shortly after his 16th birthday he joined the IRA.

Later that year British soldiers arrived at the Bateson home in the early hours. Both Sean and his father John were taken to Long Kesh Internment Camp. Sean spent two years in Long Kesh. After his release in 1974, he resumed his involvement in the Army. During this period he survived a loyalist assassination attempt.

Sean Bateson was arrested in 1977 and taken to Castlereagh Interrogation Centre. He arrived there on May 3rd and was subjected to gruelling and brutal interrogation techniques used to force false confessions from suspects. Sean became another victim - of the many - processed on the infamous conveyor belt of Castlereagh/Diplock/H-Block. He was sentenced to five terms of life imprisonment and given a recommendation that he serve a minimum of 30 years.

On Thursday 7th June 1990, Volunteer Sean Bateson died from a heart attack in Long Kesh, aged just 34. He had served 15 and a half years and he had spent all his adult life serving the cause of Irish freedom.

Óglach Dessie Grew

9th October 1990

Dessie was the second eldest in a family of seven girls and four boys born to Kathleen and Patrick Grew. Dessie's schooling was first at Knocknaconey and then at the Christian Brothers, Armagh where he gained excellent grades in both 'O' and 'A' levels. He had a love of all things Irish, and was a fluent speaker. In his youth he had been a keen footballer, playing for both his school teams.

Living in a predominantly loyalist area, the Grew family suffered sectarian attacks. First in 1972 when the family home was burned down and again in 1975 when the new family home on the outskirts of Charlemont was bombed, six of the Grew children being physically injured in the second attack.

Dessie was no stranger to the harsh realities of life and in the early 1970s he joined the Republican Movement. Before his murder on the 9th October 1990 by undercover British Forces in an ambush at Loughgall, he had served four terms of imprisonment in Portlaoise and Long Kesh, a total of 12 years in all. His final release was June 1988.

In life and in death, Dessie Grew was an inspiration to others. He was tireless in his work and harboured no grand illusions. He knew that the struggle was bigger than any one individual and was big enough to offer a place to anyone. A few weeks before his death, Dessie had spoken of what should be done in the event of his death, a friend remembers how he asked to have "no marble tombstone over him, only a tree which would spread and grow strong."

He is buried in Armagh City Cemetery.

Óglach Martin McCaughey

24th February 1967 - 9th October 1990

Gerard Patrick Martin was the oldest son of Bridget and Owen McCaughey from Aughnagar in Galbally. A great ceili house, you were always sure of good company, good conversation, a wee drop in your hand and even breakfast the next morning should you not make it home. Martin had many close friends, including Declan Arthurs, Seamus Donnelly, Tony Gormley and Eugene Kelly who had been killed at Loughgall. All the local Volunteers were the closest of friends, travelling to dances, discos and football matches together.

Martin was an excellent player, and played for Galbally Pearses, going on to be selected to play for the Tyrone Minor Team. He was also a skilled bricklayer and could have chosen his own workplace, but Martin chose instead to become a full time Óglach. Although only 16, Martin impressed local republicans with his understanding of the situation and his unromantic outlook on the risks and responsibilities of membership and he was accepted into his local unit. Harassment was part and parcel of growing up in Galbally, but before long Martin held the distinction of being the most arrested man in the country. Injured in a shoot out with British troops in Cappagh, Martin recovered and continued his role.

He stood for election as a Sinn Féin Councillor, the youngest in Ireland at that time. For Martin there was no difference in armed action and political mobilisation, both being needed to achieve the 32 county Republic he fought for. Volunteer Martin McCaughey died at Loughgall, on the 9th October 1990, with him was his friend Volunteer Dessie Grew. He is buried in Galbally Cemetery.

Martin left behind a heart-broken fiancée, a grieving but proud family and a community that still mourns his loss.

Tommy Casey Sinn Féin

9th May 1933 - 26th October 1990

On the 19th September 1990 the U.V.F. fired over thirty shots into the home of Tommy and Kathleen Casey. In the adjacent house a former Sinn Féin councillor, his wife, and their five children also escaped the murder attempt, as the same gunmen riddled their home with machine gun fire. Members of the two families had been threatened by U.D.R. patrols that they were to be targets.

On the 26th October 1990, just five weeks later, Tommy Casey arrived at a neighbour's house, when he got to the back door three men approached and he was shot several times dying instantly. Kathleen, who had been waiting in the car was dragged out and thrown to the ground beside him. Several members of the U.D.R. were arrested and questioned about the murder but released without charge.

Four years after Tommy's murder the R.U.C. came to inform Kathleen that Tommy's details had been found in a loyalist dump and that he should take all necessary security precautions.

Tommy was the father of eleven children, eight girls and three boys. He had worked tirelessly for Sinn Féin throughout his life and both he and Kathleen were known for their generosity and hospitality to all.

Kathleen Casey died on 18th November 1996. They are both greatly missed.

Óglach Fergal Caraher

12th April 1970 – 30th December 1990

Fergal Caraher was born in Annaghmare, Cullyhanna, and was the fourth son of a family of nine to Peter John and Mary Caraher. Fergal attended St.Patrick's P.S. Cullyhanna and St Colman's College, Newry where he took his 'O' Levels before starting work in a meat factory. Fergal had an easygoing, funny personality; he was good-natured, popular with his friends and had a good sense of humour. He was always quick with a witty remark and a laugh.

His main past-times were football and playing the bass drum in St Patrick's Youth Band Cullyhanna. Fergal had a deep love for his family and his country and he lived near the family home with his wife Margaret and son Brendan. At the age of sixteen, having seen the need to free his country, Fergal joined the I.R.A. Even at this young age, he played as full a part as possible in many of the operations that took place in his area.

He was ever willing and keen to participate in the struggle whether politically or militarily. He had a strong loyalty to his beliefs and upheld those beliefs at every opportunity. On several occasions he found himself in dangerous situations with the enemy and in one particular instance, after an intense gun battle, Fergal's intimate knowledge of the area and coolness under pressure prevented the capture of several Volunteers as he led them from the scene.

Sadly, on 30th December 1990, in an extension of the British shoot-to-kill policy, a group of British Army soldiers opened fire on a car in which Fergal and his brother Miceál were travelling, killing Fergal and seriously injuring Miceál. The manner of his death shocked the entire community as was evidenced by the thousands that attended his wake and funeral. As the British cover-up attempt began, the shock felt by the community quickly turned to anger and a quiet determination to expose their lies. This encouraged many young people to join the I.R.A. in an effort to achieve the goals for which Fergal fought and died.

Óglach Patrick Sheehy

2nd January 1991

Patrick Sheehy was born and reared in the small West Limerick village of Ballysteen with his parents Patrick and Marita, and his brothers Michael, John, Noel and Liam, and his sisters Eileen, Annette and Birdie. An extremely popular young man in his native area, Packie came from a hard-working and very well respected Ballysteen family. His father Patrick worked a small farm and his mother, Marita Sheehy, is well known for her voluntary work in Ballysteen. Packie attended Ballysteen National School and Askeaton Secondary School and played football with the local GAA club. On leaving school, Packie trained as a plasterer and became an expert in his trade. His plastering skills were highly admired and his work is to be seen in many homes around the West Limerick area.

Packie joined the Republican Movement in the early 1980's, being attracted to republicanism by the self sacrifice of the H-Block hunger strike martyrs. He joined the West Limerick Brigade of Óglaigh na hÉireann. Packie was regarded as an exceptional Volunteer by his comrades. He was very dedicated to the republican ideal and was courageous, loyal and dependable. Life became very difficult for Packie in the years before his death as the British media accused him of involvement in many IRA operations in Britain. His photograph was featured on the front pages of British newspapers several times and Packie was forced to live life on the run.

Patrick died in tragic circumstances on 2nd January 1991 and is buried in Beagh Cemetery in West Limerick.

Óglach Noel Wilkinson

9th September 1967 - 2nd March 1991

"I joined the I.R.A. to soldier. I never wanted glory or to be known. … I joined to fight as a soldier. I'm at the end of the road now. I have only minutes, hours to live, but I'm not afraid to die. The most important thing now is my wife and family. I don't want to be taken alive and a British bullet will never pass through me."

Volunteer Noel Wilkinson (2.3.1991)

Until shortly before his tragic death Noel Wilkinson had been an unknown, a clean soldier. He was first class at his job, an excellent volunteer in every sense, very security conscious and incredibly professional. Close to the end, after two stints in Gough Barracks, he knew he was now a target. The state policy at that time was one of assassination and not arrest. He had been told that he was next and he knew that it was about to happen.

Noel loved his family. His priority at all times had been for their safety. He knew that the enemy had no regard for the welfare, safety or lives of his family. Noel had worked and fought to create a better life for his mother, father, sister, and then for his young wife and beautiful daughter. He would not allow the enemy to endanger their lives.

Volunteer Noel Wilkinson died on the 2nd March 1991 and is spoken of with respect and with love by all.

He is buried in Ballinderry Graveyard, Ardboe.

Óglach John Quinn

13th June 1968 - 3rd March 1991

John Quinn was born on 13th June 1968 and was the second youngest child of Pat and Peggy. John had four sisters and threes brothers, two of whom died in infancy. The family home is a farm of 45 acres at Cranogue, Cappagh where John often worked with his family. Educated at St. Joseph's, Galbally and St. Patrick's Intermediate, Dungannon, John later did woodwork at Beechvalley Training Centre. The items he made are still in the family home.

John could not find a suitable job; he worked just about anywhere to earn money. He had an interest in motorbikes and was a talented pool player, winning a number of trophies.

John joined the I.R.A. in 1987 after his friends were killed at Loughgall, and was soon to be involved in many operations in the Tyrone area, utilising his engineering skills. John always said he would never send anyone out to do something he was not prepared to do himself and was well respected in the Tyrone area. The doors were always open to him and his comrades, and not only in Tyrone.

John was shot dead as he approached the entrance of the local pub in Cappagh on the 3rd March 1991; two of his comrades were killed with him in the car. Another man died in the pub when the killers shot in through a window in an attempt to maximise casualties. They were killed by the U.V.F. acting in collusion with British Forces.

John his buried in Altmore, Cappagh, Co. Tyrone.

Óglach Malcolm Nugent

10th November 1970 - 3rd March 1991

Malcolm Nugent was born in 1970 into a family of six children in the Cappagh area of Co. Tyrone. After the tragic death of his mother, Malcolm was reared by his Granny. Coming from a close-knit family and community he enjoyed to the full his early years and was often to be found working in and around the family farm. Shortly after leaving school he began work with a local firm as a welder and as with any young lad he enjoyed his game of pool and a pint at the weekends.

The murder of his cousin Martin McCaughey in a British Army undercover ambush at Loughgall in 1990 had a profound effect on Malcolm. Having given the situation every consideration, he left his job in order to devote all his time and energies to the Army.

A comrade in jail wrote of him,

"Our memories of Malcolm may differ, but he will act as an inspiration to us all. We will miss Malcolm's smile, his craic and mostly his company as a friend and comrade. We have our precious and warm memories of him and these are what sustain us. That and the belief that he fought for a just cause.

Cappagh, Galbally, indeed all the areas that make up East Tyrone are resilient. There is a belief in the right and just fight, a pride in remembering, a sense of humour in the face of terrible abuse and overwhelming loss that keeps the spirit alive. The craic, the nights out, the loves and the losses continue. People remember and talk about what went before with pride, with love and with sorrow, but it is never the same."

Volunteer Malcolm Nugent is buried in Galbally.

Óglach Dwayne O'Donnell

27th July 1973 - 3rd March 1991

On the 3rd March 1991, Dwayne O'Donnell along with three other local men, John Quinn, Malcolm Nugent and Tommy Armstrong was murdered at Boyle's Bar in Cappagh. Dwayne was 17 years old. They were shot when the U.V.F., aided and assisted by British Forces, attacked the local pub. Dwayne, John and Malcolm had just pulled up in the car when the attack began. A civilian Tommy Armstrong was killed when they fired blind in through the pub window.

Born on the 27th July 1973, Dwayne Michael O'Donnell was the eldest son of Briege and Brian, in a family of five children, four boys and one girl. As a youth he attended St. Patrick's Secondary in Dungannon where he was mannerly and attentive. On leaving school he pursued a career as a fitter welder with Masterscreen, a local engineering firm.

During his young life he was keenly interested in current affairs and enjoyed reading, especially books on Irish history. He also played the whistle and would head to the Fleadh when he got the chance. While not an active participant, Dwayne enjoyed football. He was a member of the Tír Eoghain Freewheelers Club, and along with his brother and accompanied by blind cyclists, he did a 400 mile trip from Cork to Malin Head in Easter 1987.

A quiet and modest child by nature Dwayne was always ready to help those in need. Dwayne lived his young life in an area where there was much trauma, sadness, death and destruction. As a member of the community he himself was being continually harassed. On the night of his death, he and his friends were meeting up with others to travel the short distance to the disco. Young people travelled in groups to minimise the level of abuse endured at checkpoints.

Volunteer Dwayne O'Donnell is buried in Galbally.

Óglach Colum Marks

11th June 1961 - 11th April 1991

Colum was born on the 11th June 1961 the second child in a family of three boys and three girls. His parents, Gerry and Roisin, lived in an old house in Kilkeel for a number of years before moving to Newry. They failed to be re-housed in Kilkeel because of the council's religious bias towards Catholics.

At fourteen years of age Colum was arrested by British soldiers for throwing stones. He attempted to avoid arrest by hiding in a tree. From then onwards he was constantly harassed and was arrested on several occasions and spent a period on remand in Crumlin Road Jail.

He moved to Downpatrick when he was 27 years old and was immediately active with the local IRA unit in the town. On the 11th of April 1991 Colum was on active service when he was ambushed by an undercover R.U.C. unit who had been lying in wait. They fired flares and opened fire and Colum, who was unarmed, was hit several times and badly wounded.

Despite his wounds he was handcuffed and dragged across the field to a nearby entry where he was interrogated for over half an hour before being taken to Downpatrick Hospital, less than two minutes away. On arriving at the hospital Colum was able to give his name but died soon afterwards.

He died as he had lived, a dedicated IRA Volunteer, remembered with pride by his family, friends and comrades in South Down.

Óglach John O'Rawe

1st April 1922 - 4th May 1991

John O'Rawe came from Belgrade Street in Belfast's Lower Falls, a home that was to become a centre of republican activity for many years. John joined Fianna Éireann in 1938 and in November of the same year was arrested with 18 other members while training and spent a month in Crumlin Road prison. After the outbreak of the Second World War, John joined the IRA, and moved quickly up through the ranks.

In the period leading up to the execution of Volunteer Tom Williams in 1942, John helped to organise, and participated in many operations from his home. By the end of September 1942 John was back in prison again. When he finished his sentence for possession of ammunition, he was re-arrested and interned.

John helped to revive the Republican movement in the 1960s and with Jimmy Steele, Seamus Twomey and others, helped to form the Roddy McCorley Society, and worked tirelessly for the National Graves Association.

On 9th August 1971, John was among the first arrested in the internment swoops, and remained in prison until December 1973. On his release he reported back to the IRA, and was a member of Belfast's 1st Battalion. John O'Rawe remained an active and committed republican until his sudden death on 4th May 1991.

Volunteer John O'Rawe was buried in a family plot in Milltown Cemetery, Belfast.

Eddie Fullerton Sinn Féin

26th March 1935 - 25th May 1991

Eddie, the eldest of sixteen children from Sleadrin, Buncrana, Co. Donegal, was born on 26th March 1935 to John and Maria Fullerton. He attended the local school until the age of 13 and most people said that there was little point in him staying on as he could teach the master a thing or two.

A gifted amateur footballer and boxer, he worked with his father until the age of 18 when, despite his opposition to emigration, he left Ireland for Scotland in search of work. After working on the tunnels for two years, he moved to Birmingham where he lived with his wife Diana and their six children.

In the early 70s, Eddie became involved in political work in Birmingham, selling An Phoblacht around the bars and clubs, where the bantering, bearded Irishman became very popular. Returning to Ireland in 1975, he set up the Gaughan/McDaid Sinn Féin Cumann, the first in Buncrana, and until his death Eddie was the biggest seller of An Phoblacht in Ireland.

In the Buncrana local and county election in 1979, Eddie stood as a Sinn Féin candidate. The rest, as they say, is history. Eddie Fullerton was a tireless, popular and hardworking councillor and one of his greatest achievements was The Pollan Dam, a multi-million pound dam project situated several miles outside Buncrana, and now named The Fullerton Pollan Dam.

Eddie Fullerton was gunned down in his own home in the early hours of 25th May 1991 by UFF gunmen. People turned out in their thousands to pay their respects to the popular Sinn Féin councillor, the local Irish lad from Buncrana. He was 56 years old.

Óglach Tony Doris

4th January 1969 - 3rd June 1991

Anthony Patrick Doris was born in Coalisland on the 4th January 1969. He attended the local Primate Dixon and St. Joseph's High School, where he showed great promise as a footballer. His height and general physique were invaluable to the school and local Fianna G.F.C. teams and he could well have become an excellent senior player but his ideals took him down another path. As a teenager he was very headstrong and when his mind was set on something he would determine to see it through to the end. When asked by his family of his involvement he was always elusive.

As he began his teenage years, the Hunger Strikes unfolded and Tony began to form very strong political opinions. He begged his mother to take him to a march in support of the Hunger Strikers and from then he took part in every march and attended every funeral.

On leaving school there was little opportunity to gain permanent employment and Tony saw government training schemes as exploitation and cheap labour. He was interested in driving and had applied for his H.G.V. licence.

Before Tony was killed, his daughter Róisín was born. He and his fiancée, Brigid could not have been happier but it was to be that only three months later on 3rd June 1991, that Tony and his two comrades Volunteer Pete Ryan and Volunteer Lawrence McNally were to be shot on Coagh Main Street by British Forces.

Tony was the first to be buried in the Republican Plot in Coalisland but before a year would pass his friends and comrades, Barry O'Donnell and Séan O'Farrell would be laid to rest by his side.

Óglach Lawrence McNally

20th November 1951 - 3rd June 1991

Lawrence McNally was 38 when he was murdered by British forces in Hanover Square, Coagh on the morning of 3rd June 1991. Originally from Ballinderry, he had a long and distinguished history of involvement in the Struggle. Interned during the 70s Lawrence made many friends in the Cages, one being Jim Lynagh with whom he would later operate. Lawrence was a very popular figure, well liked and well respected and all who met him trusted him. The state forces on both sides of the border regularly harassed Lawrence. Hated and feared by the Special Branch he was once kidnapped by them, severely beaten and then dumped in Monaghan. He won his case against them in court but it did little to deter further attacks. Along with Jim Lynagh and Pete Ryan, Lawrence was recognised by the states forces as a serious threat to them. They attempted to restrict his movements, harassing him and his family at every turn.

Lawrence had settled in Monaghan and had a daughter but continued to operate North and South. On the morning of June 3rd 1991 the British ambushed Lawrence and his comrades, Tony Doris and Pete Ryan as they drove through Coagh. Local residents said they heard sustained gunfire for at least 10 minutes. The ferocity of the gun attack caused the petrol tank to explode and the car crashed into a parked vehicle and was engulfed in flames. There had been no attempt made to stop the car or to arrest the men at any point. All three men died at the scene. A local man who heard the shooting said his first reaction was an instinct that no one could have survived. An estimate at the time put the number of rounds fired into the car at two hundred.

Lawrence's brother Phelim had been murdered by loyalists in November 1988 and the family had suffered harassment and attack for many years and the vicious murder of Lawrence devastated the McNally family. A dedicated and long standing, highly respected member of Óglaigh na hÉireann, Volunteer Lawrence McNally was buried in Tyholland in Co. Monaghan.

Óglach Pete Ryan

6th July 1955 - 3rd June 1991

Pete was the fourth born to Arthur and Kathleen Ryan in a family of eight boys and two girls. He was born on July 6th 1955 at "The Harbour" on the Lough shore in Ardboe. He was christened Michael James but the pet name his father gave him, Pete, stuck to him through his short but full life.

Pete experienced normal boyhood trials. He first attended Mullinahoe P.S. and then St. Patrick's in Cookstown and although he was a bright pupil he did not pursue an academic career. In the evenings after school, he worked as a farm hand. On leaving school he went to work with Malachy McElroy attending plasterers. Around this time he had his first experience of harassment. He soon became aware of the British occupation of his country and decided to do something about it.

In 1972, Pete was forced to go on the run when the car he was travelling in was fired upon. The driver was killed and Pete helped a wounded comrade to safety. He came home for a while to work in the family bar, The Battery and outwitted the British when they raided the family home looking for him. Pete showed his I.D. of Michael James Ryan. Unfortunately it was time for Pete to go again as they would not make the same mistake twice. He was eventually captured at Drumullan in Cookstown shortly before Easter 1980. While on remand he and seven other prisoners escaped. Monaghan became his second home, but in 1982 he was sentenced to ten years in Portlaoise. In prison he stayed mentally and physically fit, learning Irish language and history and working out. Upon his release he again volunteered in East Tyrone. The murder of his cousin, Liam at the family bar increased his determination and Pete was prepared for all eventualities.

On 3rd June Pete, Tony Doris and Lawrence McNally were ambushed at Coagh by British undercover forces. He is buried in the Old Cemetery at Ardboe Old Cross, right on the lough shore.

Óglach Danny McCauley

8th March 1957 - 3rd June 1991

Volunteer Danny McCauley, a member of the West Tyrone Command Óglaigh na hÉireann died of natural causes on 3rd June 1991, brought on as a direct result of Active Service.

Danny was a committed political and military soldier, who first joined the ranks of the IRA in 1971/2 and became renowned for his ingenuity and leadership. He saw the Volunteers of the Strabane unit through their most successful and effective era until his arrest in the 26 counties in 1982. Prior to this Danny actively worked on the ground politically to obtain a fusion of the political and military elements of the struggle, and was an ardent H Block campaigner and political activist.

Danny died as he had lived, an inspiration to all who knew him, a proud yet humble soldier. In his death the Republican Movement lost a leader who had left the movement stronger than he had found it.

Danny, the revolutionary had a second cause that drove him forward, namely his wife and children. His dedication and love for his family did not play a secondary role in his life. Indeed it was due to this great love and aspirations for his family that Danny saw the need for freedom and social justice.

Where there is a struggle for justice, the desire for freedom and resistance to exploitation there will always be a Danny McCauley. We salute you comrade, onwards to victory.

Pádraig O'Seanacháin Sinn Féin

11th August 1958 - 12th August 1991

Pádraig O'Seanacháin's 33rd birthday was spent bailing hay on the family farm, amid the green sloping hills of Aghnahoo, Aghyaran. Pádraig had refused to leave the family homestead despite long term intimidation. The next morning less than a mile from the farm near the village of Killen, loyalists in conjunction with their allies in the RUC/UDR shot him dead.

At the time of his death he was employed as a driver by the DoE and provided assistance on the family farm.

Harassment and death threats from the UDR/RUC were a constant feature of Pádraig's life. Despite a long reign of terror and threats against him and his family, he refused to move and would never apologise for his Republican beliefs.

Pádraig was an active member of Sinn Féin, having joined the party during 1980. He contributed much during elections and always participated in the local Easter Commemoration, where he took great pride in leading prayers for the fallen in his native tongue.

Pádraig was a member of Comhaltas Ceoltoiri Éireann and will be forever remembered for his love of Irish dancing, which he practised and taught at cultural gatherings throughout Ireland.

The circumstances surrounding his death, and the farcical inquest that followed, gave rise to the formation of the Castlederg/Aghyaran Justice Group, who organised an informal inquiry chaired by Judge Andrew Somerville. The group and Pádraig's family continue to lobby for justice and have recently taken Pádraig's case to the European Courts of Human Rights.

Óglach Tommy Donaghy

21st January 1953 - 16th August 1991

Tommy was born on 21st January 1953, the son of John and Mary Donaghy, Gortnacrane, Kilrea, Co. Derry. He was to devote his entire adult life to the struggle for Irish freedom. Only 4 years old the first time he witnessed the B' Specials, including his own neighbours, raiding the family home, he would, years later, see this exercise repeated many times by the RUC, UDR and British Army.

Already a victim of poor housing and discrimination, Tommy was deeply affected by the murder of 14 Civil Rights marchers in Derry on Bloody Sunday, one of the many injustices that led him as a teenager, to join the ranks of Óglaigh na hÉireann. Interned without trial in 1974, he was one of those who revolted and burnt Long Kesh to the ground in 1974, and the following month he took part in the foiled tunnel escape which ended with the murder of Hugh Coney by British soldiers. Released in October 1975, Tommy rejoined his unit in Kilrea, but following constant house raids, harassment, death threats and finally an assassination attempt he went on the run in July 1976 in South Derry. Captured on Holy Thursday 1977, following a gun battle at Slaughtneil, Tommy was taken to Maghera RUC station, where bound and blindfolded, he was almost beaten to death by uniformed and Special Branch RUC men.

Taken to Castlereagh Holding Centre he was to suffer six more days of torture. When finally charged with possession of the weapons he was captured with, he had a burst eardrum, kidney damage and it was one and half years before he regained the use of his hands. Sentenced to 19 years, he spent three and a half years on the Blanket Protest until it ended, and was eventually released on 3rd July 1988. On his release he became a member of Sinn Féin and the P.D.F. However, 3 years of constant harassment and death threats from the RUC and the UDR were only to end in one way. On 14th August 1991, members of the then legal UDA, working with state force collusion, gunned Tommy down as he arrived for work at Portna Fishery. After his death the uniformed wing of Loyalism took over, as the RUC taunted and harassed mourners during the wake and funeral.

Tommy Donaghy is buried in St. Mary's, Drumagarner, Kilrea.

Bernard O'Hagan Sinn Féin

12th September 1953 - 16th September 1991

Born on September 12th 1953, in Belfast, Bernard grew up in Newington, with his three sisters and five brothers, attending Holy Family Primary School and then St Patrick's, Barnagheeha. When his school days were over, he worked for two years as a lorry driver, then a bar man among other things, before heading to England to train as a teacher in Newman College, Birmingham.

It was there that he developed further his interest in politics, becoming involved in the trade union movement and organising student protests against cuts in education funding. In his fourth and final year at college he met Fiona his future wife, they married in 1980 and settled for a couple of years in Birmingham, bringing their only daughter Nuala into the world. Bernard, however, never intended to remain in England, always longing to be back in Ireland to help out in some way. He had become a member of Sinn Féin whilst in Birmingham assisting with the Troops Out Movement and attending prison protests and Hunger Strike rallies.

On returning to Ireland in January 1986, he took up his post as a lecturer in Computer Studies at Magherafelt Technical College, Co Derry. In May 1989, Bernard was elected as a Sinn Féin councillor in Magherafelt, working tirelessly for the people of the area whether their problems were big or small.

One sunny Monday morning, September 16th 1991, on arriving at work, he was mercilessly gunned down by the UFF, leaving behind his grieving wife Fiona, daughter Nuala and two sons Finbar and Malachy.

He always knew the risks, but argued that he had a lot to do and a lot to give.

Thank you Bernard

Óglach Patricia Black

28th November 1972 - 15th November 1991

Patricia Black was born in Belfast on 28th November 1972, the second eldest in a family of four. She was educated at St. Oliver Plunkett Primary School, and St. Genevieve's Girls Secondary School. Patricia left school at sixteen and, at eighteen she joined the ranks of Óglaigh na hÉireann as a member of the Belfast Brigade.

She very quickly earned the respect and admiration of her comrades, who were inspired by the determination and dedication of this young woman. Her work as a Volunteer was intelligence gathering and full time operational involvement, which she hid from all around her. In fact few knew of her work, even in the ranks of Óglaigh na hÉireann.

The youth, beauty and smile of Patricia didn't die in a foreign street, when she was killed alongside her comrade Frank Ryan. In the hearts and minds of her friends and comrades it will inspire and strengthen our resolve. We cannot replace for her family the gift that was Patricia, we can only say, in a lonely cell, in silent streets, and many homes, a sad tear was shed. Her gentle smile will be with us forever.

Volunteer Patricia Black was killed in an accidental explosion while on active service in England, on 15th November 1991. Her comrade, Volunteer Frank Ryan died with her.

Patricia is buried in a family plot in Milltown Cemetery, Belfast.

Óglach Frank Ryan

23rd September 1966 - 15th November 1991

Frankie Ryan was born of Irish parents in Harlow, Essex, on October 23rd 1966. The eldest of a family of three, it was in England that he was educated, and spent the greater part of his life. However, he developed an understanding of Ireland and the struggle of the Irish people to achieve freedom from British rule.

In 1985 he came to Ireland and very soon became involved in the Republican Movement. After six years in Belfast, Frankie joined the Irish Republican Army. He immediately earned the respect of his comrades for the enthusiasm and dedication towards the struggle.

Frankie was very security conscious, and although his family and friends were aware of his Republican sympathies, they only learned of his involvement with the I.R.A. after his death.

Volunteer Frank Ryan died alongside his comrade, Volunteer Patricia Black, in an accidental explosion while on active service in England on November 15th 1991.

He was buried with full honours in Milltown Cemetery, Belfast.

Óglach Damien Brolly

27th September 1961 - 30th December 1991

The sudden and untimely death of Volunteer Damien Brolly caused widespread shock throughout the entire communities of Strabane and his native Castlefin in County Donegal. One of eight children, Damien was 30 years old and living with his partner and their two young children at the time of his death.

A modest and unassuming young man who always had a smile on his face, he was always helping someone with something, whether family, friends or comrades.

He was a keen scholar and sportsman who played football for Castlefin F.C. and also Robert Emmett G.F.C., where he was known as a gutsy player who was full of passion and determination; qualities which he also displayed as an active Volunteer in the ranks of the West Tyrone Brigade of the IRA.

A security conscious individual who took great care in protecting his activities - he was never once arrested despite his many years of active service. He inspired confidence and those who knew him were sure that every task he undertook would be carried out to the full.

His family, friends and comrades will eternally remember his sound judgement and unfaltering commitment.

Óglach Proinsias MacAirt

18th April 1922 - 8th January 1992

Proinsias MacAirt first became involved in the Republican Movement when he joined Fianna Éireann as a teenager in the late 1930's. His keen intellect and leadership qualities were quickly noticed and put to use within the IRA. He was arrested as a juvenile in 1940 and served two years of a sentence in Crumlin Road where he remained, after his internment was ordered, until 1945. The next phase of armed resistance to British rule saw him interned again from 1957 to 1960.

Proinsias played a key role in the reorganisation of the Republican Movement in 1970 after the split with the reformist leadership, which later became the leadership of the Workers' Party. He assisted Jimmy Steele in the foundation of the Republican News, of which he served a period as editor himself. He was soon back in Crumlin Road, and on the hunger strike which won political status for Republican Prisoners.

Like other Republicans, Proinsias viewed jail as an extension of the struggle on the outside and he used his time creatively. Being a keen Gaeilgeoir, he taught the language to other comrades. In later years he sought to educate younger Republicans about the history of Ireland and the struggle against British imperialism.

Proinsias MacAirt, life long Republican, died on Wednesday 8th January 1992. In his graveside oration West Belfast MP, Gerry Adams spoke of MacAirt with fondness. "He had a great sense of fun, craic and loved telling stories, mostly against himself. Many of us respect or agree with other Republicans. MacAirt had a unique quality of being liked by all who knew him."

340

Pat McBride Sinn Féin

30th September 1952 - 4th February 1992

"Pat came to our home at the age of 15 years old. He was to stay one year until he found work and a flat. Suffice to say, Pat stayed 26 years until the day of his death. Our own four children were coming along and grew up with Pat being their big brother.

Our only son Malachy looked on Pat as a superman as Pat took him under his wing. Before long Pat took on the mantle of home maintenance man. He had great hands. Papering and painting came to him naturally. He had a great way with him. He made friends instantly. Our house was never empty with Pat's pals calling at all times. Before Pat's death he ran a disco in several venues for kids on the Falls Rd. Pat met Bernie McDaid and soon love was in the air. Some time after, young Patrick Óg was born. At the time of Pat's death, he was making wedding plans. Bernie and Pat Óg visit every week. We lost a great son and father and friend.

Pat was shot to death by a member of the RUC on the 4th February 1992 while he was working in the Sinn Féin office on the Falls Road. Two other people were also killed along with Pat."

John Keenan

Paddy Loughran Sinn Féin

8th May 1930 - 4th February 1992

Paddy Loughran was born in 21 Scotch Street, in Belfast. A friend wrote the following tribute, "Paddy was one great gentleman, husband and father. From a young age his family called him 'Paddy the Irishman'. He and Barbara were well matched; he just lived for her and his eight children of course."

Nothing was too much trouble for him as long as he was helping anyone or anything. Paddy played for Shelbourne F.C. From the age of 14 he was an avid Celtic supporter. He took long walks every day; you would have always met him any place with four of his children. He never took a bus or a taxi in his life. There were no complaints from Barbara for she knew that kept him happy, so she was happy too, until that awful day when he was taken away.

Paddy Loughran was shot dead by a member of the R.U.C. while he was working in the Sinn Féin Centre on the Falls Road. He was a tireless worker and was well known for his courteous manner to all who came into the building.

Óglach Joseph MacManus

23rd May 1970 - 5th February 1992

Joseph MacManus was born the first son of strong republican parents Seán, now a member of Sinn Féin's Ard Chomhairle and Lord Mayor of Sligo, and Helen MacManus, in Willesden where his father was living in May 1970. He also has a brother, Chris, who was elected as a councillor in 1999 to Sligo Corporation. The family moved back to Ireland when Joe was six years of age and he attended Scoil Ursula and St John's National Schools in Sligo and Summerhill College where he sat the Leaving Certificate in 1988. He went on to Sligo RTC to follow a business studies course, which he eventually left to devote himself more fully to the national liberation struggle.

Joe was very active in the field of sports and had won medals with St Mary's Gaelic Football Club, Sligo at all junior levels and shortly before his death had received a medal with Coolera Gaelic Football Club. He played a lot of soccer as well and played at senior level for both Collegians and Corinthians.

Joe was an avid reader of history and politics and his understanding of Irish Republicanism was deep and clear-sighted. He was involved in local Sinn Féin activities in Sligo for several years before his involvement with the I.R.A. Joe's reading of Irish history, his awareness of the turbulent situation in the occupied Six Counties, only a few miles up the road from his native Sligo, his knowledge of Irish Republican philosophy, but above all his inherent integrity led him to throw himself fully into the fight for national liberation.

Joe was killed in action in Fermanagh, on 5th February 1992. He is buried in the Republican plot in Sligo Cemetery.

Óglach Sean O'Farrell

20th September 1969 - 16th February 1992

Sean O'Farrell was born on 20th September 1969 one of a family of two sisters and three brothers, one of whom was his twin, Austin. The family home was in Coalisland. Sean was educated at the local primary school and later at St. Joseph's Secondary. When he left school he took employment as a fitter welder, later moving on to start work with a local building suppliers, but still continuing his trade. Sean enjoyed life to the full with a particular interest in music and Irish culture. He was a familiar and popular face at the local sessions, giving a tune himself in the back room of McGirr's. He had an active social life attending many dances and discos.

He spent his time in the company of his close friends, many of whom were later to become his comrades. From a young age, Sean had shown a keen interest in the political situation developing around him, and he was determined that one day he would play an active part in the struggle. When the day came that he joined Óglaigh na hÉireann, he did so in the company of his friend Barry O'Donnell. He was 18, and from then until his death at the age of 22, Sean saw many successful encounters with the enemy, something that did not go unnoticed, as he was to suffer tremendous harassment and arrests.

In May 1991 Sean and Barry were arrested on a charge which was later dropped. He immediately returned to active service on his release from gaol, undeterred and more committed than ever. In a matter of weeks he was to see his friend and comrade Tony Doris killed on Active Service, something which had a profound and lasting effect on him. Less than eight months later, on 16th February Sean was to lose his own life in a British undercover ambush at Clonoe Chapel, along with three comrades.

Volunteer Sean O'Farrell was laid to rest in the Republican Plot in Coalisland alongside his comrades and life long friends Tony Doris and Barry O'Donnell.

Óglach Barry O'Donnell

24th March 1970 - 16th February 1992

Kevin Barry O'Donnell was born on the 24th March 1970. He was the third in a family of seven, having three brothers and three sisters. Christened Kevin Barry on an Easter Sunday by his parents, Jim and Celine, he was always known as Barry to his family and friends. Barry attended the Primate Dixon Memorial School in Coalisland and then St Patrick's Academy in Dungannon. After 'O' Levels he attended Loughry Agricultural College in Cookstown and then was accepted to Harper Adams Agricultural College in Shropshire, England. At school Barry was interested in Irish and he spent many summers in the Gaeltacht in Donegal to practise and improve his spoken Irish. He was a fluent Irish speaker who would often use his cúpla focail. Barry enjoyed a game of football and played for Coalisland Fianna and later with Stewartstown Harps. He also played for the Loughry team who reached the All-Ireland Agricultural Colleges Final.

Barry was only a child when the O'Donnell house was raided for the first time. During his teenage years harassment became a routine to him and many of his friends. The massacre at Loughgall was to have a big impact on him. When he was 18 Barry and many of his closest friends joined the I.R.A. It was in May 1990 that Barry was arrested after a car chase through London with two A.K. rifles in the boot of his car. The following month Barry and Sean O' Farrell were arrested in Coalisland and spent a month on remand in Crumlin Road Jail, before all charges against them were suddenly dropped. At this stage the level of harassment from both the RUC and the Gardaí in Monaghan intensified, as did the death threats. Barry was devastated when his close friend and comrade Tony Doris was killed in action in June 1991. This made Barry and his comrades more determined to continue the fight.

On the 16th of February 1992, Volunteer Barry O'Donnell was killed on active service in Clonoe with his comrades Sean O'Farrell, Peter Clancy and Patrick Vincent. He is buried in Coalisland Republican Plot with his comrades Sean and Tony.

Tá muintir agus mac s'aige Ruairí croíbhriste go fóill agus beidh go deo na ndeor. *Níl cara ag cumha ach cuimhne.*

345

Óglach Patrick Vincent

17th July 1971 - 16th February 1992

Patrick Vincent was the second oldest in a family of four. He had two sisters and one brother. Patrick grew up on the outskirts of Dungannon in a predominantly loyalist area. He attended St. Joseph's High School, Coalisland where he was very popular with all his classmates. After leaving school he became a crane driver, which was to be his occupation until the time of his death.

Patrick joined the Army in 1991 and was an active member during his time. His security consciousness was extremely high, so much so, that at the time of his death his family were completely unaware of his involvement. The state forces had also no idea of his activities, allowing him and his comrades to move freely.

Patrick, or Paddy as he was called by his friends, was well known for his love of the craic at the weekends and his ability to have a joke with anyone. He was game for a laugh at anytime.

It can only be said that Paddy is missed by everyone who knew him, none more so than his family.

Volunteer Paddy Vincent was killed at Clonoe on 16th February 1992. He is buried in Edendork Graveyard, between Coalisland and Dungannon.

Óglach Peter Clancy

31st October 1970 - 16th February 1992

Peter Clancy was born on the 31st October 1970. He was the youngest of six boys. Having been schooled at Aughamullan and then St. Joseph's High School in Coalisland, he took a job with Masterscreen International, where he was popular with his fellow workers. An active participant in all sports, especially gaelic football he was a life long member of Clonoe O'Rahilly's, G.F.C. Members of the club formed a Guard of Honour at his funeral.

When Peter was six years old, raids on the family home by the state forces were a common occurrence. Later when he himself started going to dances he was frequently stopped and on one occasion when going on holiday he and his friends were stopped and detained for almost the full day.

Peter was, from an early age educated enough to know the struggle in which he chose to become involved was morally right and justifiable, and he had no illusions about what joining the I.R.A. might entail. Whilst recovering from a serious injury sustained on Active Service, Peter re-dedicated himself becoming a more powerful person from within. All those he came in contact with held him in high regard.

On the 16th February 1992, Volunteer Peter Clancy along with his friends and comrades, Barry, Sean and Paddy was shot after an attack on Coalisland R.U.C. station. They were ambushed by British Forces in the car park of Clonoe Church. No warning was given and no attempt made to arrest them. The British waited until they were dismantling their weapons and then shot them.

Peter is buried in the cemetery adjacent to Clonoe Chapel.

Óglach Brendan Seery

19th March 1948 - 19th February 1992

Brendan Seery was born on 19th March 1948 and was from Ballinalack near Mullingar in County Westmeath. He was serving an eight-year sentence with three of the years suspended, in Portlaoise prison. The Special Court sentenced Brendan on arms charges in 1991. Brendan was one of the most colourful characters in the jail and was well liked by his comrades, who came from all parts of the country. He was affectionately known as 'Cen Fáth'.

With a wide experience of life, ranging from service in the Congo with the United Nations to hard graft on the roads, he had a vast supply of humourous and not so humourous anecdotes.

In mid February 1992 Brendan, whose family had a history of heart trouble, complained of chest pains and was taken to the hospital. The prison and hospital authorities were well aware of his family history yet within a few short days, he was transferred back to the prison having been told that he was suffering from indigestion.

Two days after his return to Portlaoise Prison he died, aged 44, of a heart attack - a victim of gross medical neglect. He is buried in Rathaspic Cemetery, Co. Westmeath.

Danny Cassidy Sinn Féin

23rd December 1952 - 2nd April 1992

Danny Cassidy was born on 23rd December 1952 and was educated at Movanagher P.S. Kilrea. The eldest of seven children he worked mainly as a driver.

While still in his teens Danny became involved in the Republican Movement and was a Volunteer in the Kilrea unit in South Derry.

During the 70's and into the 80's Danny remained faithful to the republican cause and during the Hunger Strikes he was a committed member of his local H.Block/Armagh Committee.

After numerous arrests Danny was remanded in custody in 1983 and subsequently released. The British Army then began a campaign of harassment against him. At this time Danny was a member of the local Sinn Féin Cumann.

In March 1992 the RUC told Danny that he would be dead in a week and on 2nd April 1992 Danny was shot dead by the UFF, yards from his home.

Danny was 40 years old when he was shot, he was married with four young children. He is buried in St. Mary's Drumagarner.

Óglach Christy Harford

4th December 1934 - 5th May 1992

Christy Harford was from Walshestown, Co Dublin. He attended the Bog of the Ring National School not far from the family home. On leaving school he served his apprenticeship as a carpenter in Walshes of Balbriggan. He was regarded as a very good neighbour especially by older people, who he was always ready to help out. He had a fondness for animals and birds and is described by family and friends as having a good sense of humour. He had a deep love of Irish traditions, especially traditional Irish music and he played the tin whistle and mouth organ.

He had an abiding interest in the local history of his country about which he read avidly. In his trade as a carpenter he worked all over the country but in the mid-1950s he was forced to emigrate to England. Shortly after his return to Ireland in the spring of 1970 he joined the ranks of Óglaigh na hÉireann. It was a time when northern nationalists had begun their uprising against the Orange State and conflict was erupting in the Six Counties. Christy was dedicated and unflinching in his republican activities and deeply respected by his comrades.

In 1984 he was arrested by 26 County State Forces and when he got the chance he went on the run. From that point on he was permanently on active service with Óglaigh na hÉireann until his death on 5th May 1992 at the age of 59. He is buried at Hollywood Cemetery in north County Dublin.

Sheena Campbell Sinn Féin

17th November 1962 - 16th October 1992

Sheena Campbell was born Sheena Teresa Fagan in the townland of Ballinagarrick, Gilford, Co. Down on the 17th November 1962. When she was ten years old the family moved to Ardowen, Craigavon. She left school in 1978 and went to work as a machinist in a local stitching factory. A devoted mother her proudest moment was when her son Caolan was born in December 1981.

From her early teens Sheena was active in Republican politics, assisting in fundraising, distribution of leaflets and selling An Phoblacht. With the onset of the H-Block protest and the resulting hunger strikes her political role increased and she founded a local Youth Against the H-Blocks group. She became a tireless campaigner on behalf of Republican prisoners and aged 16 she worked at an administrative level for her local Cumainn Comhairle Ceantair and An Cuige Ulaidh.

In her 20s Sheena represented Sinn Féin overseas and in the late 1980s and early 1990s Sheena was instrumental in developing an electoral management strategy for Sinn Féin that became the blueprint for fighting elections. Despite her heavy workload with Sinn Féin, she remained active in community politics, serving on the committees of several community groups. In 1989, in keeping with her conviction that we should strive to better ourselves in order to help others, she managed to find time to go back into academic education and took up a course in law at Queens University, Belfast. In the words of the Marge Piercy poem read at her funeral service, Sheena was 'A Strong Woman'.

Her bubbly personality, smiling face and zest for life made her popular and loved wherever she went. But despite her unquenchable desire to do all in her power to improve the lot of her people, her first love and first responsibility was as a mother to her son Caolán, and to her partner, Brendan. Sheena was gunned down by loyalist paramilitaries as she sat in the York Hotel, in the Botanic area of Belfast on the 16th October 1992.

Óglach Pearse Jordan

12th December 1969 - 25th November 1992

Pearse Jordan was born on 12th December 1969 in the lower Falls area of Belfast. He was born at a time when large areas of the Falls were under attack from loyalist mobs. Many streets were barricaded and there was daily riots as the nationalist community attempted to defend both their lives and their homes.

When Pearse was six months old he was almost killed when British soldiers flooded the area with CS gas canisters. A close neighbour who promptly rushed the injured and unconscious child to the hospital undoubtedly saved Pearse's life. Pearse would suffer the side effects from this incident for the rest of his short life.

Later the family moved to Roden Street, which was a mainly Protestant area. The family had to eventually leave their home after having to endure almost eight months of sectarian attacks. The day after the British Government adopted a policy of interning nationalists the Jordan family moved into New Barnsley. This is where Pearse was to spend the rest of his life. Pearse attended St Aidan's and St. Thomas' School on the Whiterock Road and on leaving school he began to work with his family in the catering business.

On 25th November 1992 Pearse was murdered by the R.U.C while driving down the Falls Road. Pearse's car was rammed by the R.U.C. and on staggering from the car he was shot in the back three times, from a range of only three yards.

On the day of Pearse's funeral, the customary ring of steel was thrown around the cortege, but the R.U.C could not intimidate the throngs of people who came out to pay their respects to this brave young Irishman.

Óglach Malachy Carey

29th September 1956 - 13th December 1992

Malachy was the fifth son of Don and Bridie, a native of Buncrana. As a youth, Malachy attended St. Anne's Primary School, Corkey, and spent his teenage years at Our Lady of Lourdes. After his secondary education he began a career in the building trade as a bricklayer. Malachy was deeply committed to his local community and hurling club, Loughgiel Shamrocks G.A.C. He had a genuine passion for the Irish language. Malachy played hurling for his local club Loughgiel. On the field Malachy never quite made the impact his brothers Paddy, Sean and Martin made as they enjoyed success as All Ireland club medalists. A fitting tribute in memory of Malachy has been erected at the Loughgiel Shamrock grounds. His words echo encouragement to the hurlers of the Loughiel club.

Malachy lived in a generation where there was continuous, unprovoked harassment and intimidation from the British Armed Forces. This was the catalyst that lead to his decision in becoming a Volunteer of the North Antrim Brigade. Arrested in 1977 he spent his first five years in jail on the blanket protest until it ended. During his time in jail he shared a cell with Bobby Sands. On his release in 1984, Malachy joined his local Sinn Féin Cumann and ran as a Sinn Féin candidate in the 1989 local government elections. On 12th December 1992, Malachy was fatally wounded at the corner of Victoria and John Street. Members of the UDA tried to force him into a nearby vehicle. During a struggle Malachy was hit once on the body. He was rushed to Coleraine Hospital and in the early hours of Sunday morning, lost his battle for life after having undergone emergency surgery. There was definite evidence of state collusion in his murder.

Large numbers attended Malachy's funeral. On Tuesday 15th December 1992 Malachy's remains left on their final journey. His coffin was draped with a tricolour and a lone piper led the cortege as it made its way to St. Patrick's Graveyard, Loughgiel where he was laid to rest in the adjoining graveyard. In his oration Pat McKeown, a former comrade of Malachy's paid tribute to a gallant friend and soldier.

Peter Gallagher Sinn Féin

27th June 1947 - 24th March 1993

Peter Gallagher was a lifelong nationalist and supporter of the Ancient Order of Hibernians. He first became involved in Republicanism through the anti-H-Block campaign in the 80s and was a faithful attendee at all protests and rallies. He was deeply moved by the sacrifice of the Hunger Strikers, attending all of their funerals. He assisted in fund raising activities for the local PDF and was always a willing worker whatever task he was given, whether ticket selling, doing the door or car parking duties.

"Big Peter" with his fiery red hair and disarming smile became known far and near. He assisted in Sinn Féin's first foray into electoral politics in the 1983 Westminster election and shortly after joined the local Sinn Féin Cumann in Toome, on whose behalf he often attended Ard-Féisenna and conferences up and down the country. Peter fully backed Sinn Féin's electoral strategy and was a regular feature sitting in the local polling booth at election times, thinking nothing of taking the day off work to do this task, though with his large family he could ill afford to do so. In fact he usually took the next day off as well to attend the counting of votes.

In 1985 when there was a problem finding a candidate for the local government elections, Peter was willing to let his own name go forward, but when another candidate was found, Peter took great pride in assisting the election of the first Sinn Féin councillor to Antrim Borough Council, whom he accompanied to a number of council meetings to lend moral support against loyalist intimidation at these meetings.

Peter was shot dead by a UDA gunman as he opened the gates of his workplace on the Grosvenor Road in Belfast. It is unlikely that his murderer even knew his identity, as Peter was not the usual person to open the gates. Peter was only 45 years old when he died leaving behind his wife and seven children and his first grandson who was born shortly before Peter died.

Peter Gallagher is buried at Cargin Graveyard, Toome.

Óglach James Kelly

10th February 1968 - 25th March 1993

Jimmy was the eldest child of James (Neecie) and Annie Kelly. He had two sisters and one brother. Jimmy was educated at Glenview Primary School and St Patrick's College, Maghera. Through his father Jimmy developed a great love of horses and he spent many happy times riding and driving horses.

Jimmy had a keen interest in the outdoors, and a particular fondness for salmon poaching. When only a schoolboy he was arrested in Dungiven in the possession of long nets. He was brought before the courts and fined heavily for his exploits!

In 1988 he travelled to England for work, but he returned home shortly after, when his 16-year-old brother, Mickey, went missing. Mickey was found brutally murdered in what was a callous sectarian murder. Soon after this Jimmy became a Volunteer in Óglaigh na hÉireann. He proved to be a courageous and able Volunteer, and soon became the subject of attention by the RUC Special Branch. He was a victim of constant harassment. He endured several 5-day spells in Castlereagh Interrogation Centre. On countless occasions the RUC and British soldiers threatened Jimmy's life.

These threats became a reality on 25th March 1993 when Jimmy, sitting along with four of his workmates, was shot dead in a work van in Castlerock. There is no doubt that the RUC colluded with the Loyalist death squad who carried out this attack.

Jimmy was a dedicated Republican and a committed Volunteer who paid the ultimate price for the principles in which he believed. He is sadly missed by his family, friends and comrades.

Óglach Alan Lundy

11th November 1953 - 1st May 1993

Alan Lundy was born in 1953 in the Ardoyne area of Belfast where he was to spend the greater part of his life. On leaving school he trained as a plasterer and he made this skill available to friends and comrades. Alan became involved in the struggle against British occupation as a young man at the age of 17. He was arrested in early 1972 and interned in the Cages of Long Kesh. In 1973 he was taken out of internment, charged with possession of a bomb and remanded in Crumlin Road.

Alan was one of the first to experience the 'justice' of the then newly established Diplock Courts. In 1973 a lone judge found him guilty of possession of a bomb and sentenced him to ten years imprisonment. Alan spent the next five years of his life in the Cages of Long Kesh. Upon his release, in November 1977, he immediately reinvolved himself in the struggle and was known as a man who worked hard for his people, his party and the struggle.

Alan Lundy was 39 years of age when Loyalist killers gunned him down outside the home of his friend Councillor Alex Maskey on Saturday 1st May 1993. The death squad acted with the help of British crown forces, as in the week prior to the killing the RUC stopped Alan and a number of others at the Maskey home. For a number of hours on the day of the killing, large armoured vehicles remained parked in the street and then suddenly left.

In his oration Pat McGeown touched the hearts of all who knew Alan when he said: "All of us will find reminders of Alan all through our lives, because when we meet gentleness and genuineness mixed with good craic and humour, there we will see Alan".

Óglach Michael Motley

22nd June 1957 - 12th June 1993

Michael Motley, son of William and Mary was born on the 22nd June 1957 in Portlaoise Hospital. He was the third of six children. He had one sister, Mary, and four brothers, Billy, John, Tony and Seamus. He attended Mayo National School for eight years and Carlow Regional Technical College, where he sat the group exam. His first job was in a shoe factory in Carlow and then in the Sugar factory, where he worked for a further eight years, before going to Rossmore mines with other members of his family. At the time of his death, he was on a FAS scheme working at a running track in Ballickmoyler.

Michael played handball with St Brigid's handball club; he loved GAA and was an avid follower of the Laois football team. He had a great love for darts and played on Behan's team for fifteen years, winning numerous medals and trophies. When his parents died, Michael took over the family home. His four nieces and two nephews were regular visitors to his home and he loved playing with them. He was a very generous person never forgetting birthdays, Christmas and Easter. Michael was also known for being a joker. His father was a member of the old IRA during the 1950s and he himself became involved in republican politics during the Hunger Strikes in 1981. He started by selling An Phoblacht/Republican News before joining Óglaigh na hÉireann.

Because of his republican politics, Michael suffered extreme harassment from the Dublin government's secret police. Arrested in 1993 he was charged and released on bail, and was forced to sign daily at the Garda barracks in Abbeyleix, 14 miles from his home. The special branch were constantly at his house and followed him everywhere. According to local republicans, the special branch had commented just before he died, that the next time they saw him he would be dead. He died suddenly on 12th June 1993, just days before his 36th birthday. He was given a full Republican funeral and is interred in Mayo Cemetery with his parents.

Óglach Thomas Begley

10th November 1970 - 23rd October 1993

Thomas Begley came from Ardoyne in North Belfast where the nationalist community has suffered more at the hands of loyalist death squads than in any other part of the Six Counties. Born three years into this present phase of the conflict, Thomas Begley was to grow up in a community besieged both by British forces and their loyalist death squad allies.

It was Irish Republicanism, the desire for freedom, justice and peace that motivated Thomas. He was by no means sectarian. He had worked with Protestants and as a Republican his wish was to see an end to all sectarianism.

Thomas 'Bootsy' Begley joined the ranks of Óglaigh na hÉireann in January 1993 and was immediately recognised as having great potential. He was quick in comprehending the methods and techniques used by his comrades. Bootsy's eagerness and dedication in fighting in the struggle for the Irish people's right to self determination was evident in the many military operations he was involved in against the British Crown forces.

The tragedy in which Thomas Begley and nine civilians died on the Shankill Road, marked another terrible milestone in the present stage of conflict. Part of that tragedy was the misrepresentation in many quarters of the motives of a young man who went out not to commit a sectarian act, but to try to help put an end to the oppression of his community and his country.

Óglach Martin Doherty

11th July 1958 - 21st May 1994

Martin Gerard Doherty was born on 11th July 1958 and grew up in Finglas with his five brothers and six sisters. He went to St Bridget's School and later attended nearby St Fergal's National School, where he played Gaelic football. He also played soccer for the local Dunsink club. He had two sons Martin and Michael.

Martin, known as 'Doco' to his friends, joined the ranks of Óglaigh na hÉireann in the wake of the 1981 republican hunger strikes. He was a Volunteer with the IRA's Dublin Brigade, constantly on active service up until his arrest and imprisonment in 1982, having been set up by a Garda informer, Éamonn Maguire. Released from Portlaoise Prison in 1988, he got involved in the building trade in Dublin, working as a labourer, and also immediately reported back to the IRA's Dublin Brigade, where he resumed active service going to the heart of enemy territory in England. It was during his second period in Britain that he was arrested by British Government forces and charged with IRA offences, but later released due to lack of evidence. Doco returned to Ireland and rejoined his comrades in the Dublin Brigade. He never once ceased his involvement with the IRA up until the time of his death.

On the 21 May 1994, Doco along with his partner Ann O'Sullivan, was running a function for the Sinn Féin P.O.W. Dept. which involved him doing security on The Widow Scanlan's pub in Dublin's Pearse Street. Sensing that something wasn't right, he went out and was faced by a loyalist death-squad. He challenged them, forcing them to abandon a partially primed 18lb bomb in the stairwell. They shot him through the heart and again as he fell to the ground.

Doco's funeral was attended by thousands of republicans. His military guard of honour prompted John Bruton to make begrudging comments in Leinster House, of the heroic actions of this brave IRA Volunteer. Volunteer Martin Doherty is buried in Glasnevin Cemetery.

Óglach Pól Kinsella

11th November 1963 - 13th December 1994

Pól Kinsella came from a republican family that experienced all of the ravages of British rule on the streets of Derry. Because of work commitments - care assistant for the elderly in various nursing homes and a worker in Altnagelvin Hospital Geriatric ward - Pól decided that rather than join Óglaigh na hÉireann, he would serve in a civilian capacity.

Having witnessed the arrest of a number of volunteers over a period of time in the area, Pól decided that he wanted to become a volunteer. Pól's wife and young daughter were foremost in his mind when he did make the decision and their commitment to the republican struggle and to his decision to join Óglaigh na hÉireann were evident by their unwavering support for him through the dark days.

Hearing that an operation was in progress, Pól volunteered to use his own car so that other volunteers were not put at risk in the process of hijacking, but the British intercepted his car. Sentenced to eighteen years imprisonment, Pól played a full part in the various prison struggles. It was whilst imprisoned in Long Kesh that Pól was to find out that he had leukaemia. Typically, his only thoughts were for Cathy and Michaela, and how they would cope.

Pól Kinsella, aged 31, died on the 13th December 1994. At the time of his death Pól was still an IRA prisoner, the British establishment having refused to release him, despite the fact that the IRA had already declared a military cessation.

Pól was buried with full military honours.

Óglach Edward O'Brien

18th September 1974 - 18th February 1996

Edward O'Brien was born in Wexford on 18th September 1974. The red haired boy also known as 'the quiet man' lived with his parents, Miley and Margo, sister Lorraine and brother Gary, in Gorey in County Wexford. He attended the local national and secondary schools. He was a member of St Enda's Gaelic Football and Hurling club and of Gorey Rangers Soccer Club. He also was a talented boxer. He was a bakery worker up to the time he left for England.

Eddie joined Óglaigh na hÉireann in 1992 in the full knowledge that his life would no longer be that of an ordinary young Gorey man. Like everything he undertook, he was very serious about his decision and his commitment. While planning or carrying out operations he showed the same seriousness and attention to detail. He was always concerned about civilian safety and several operations were cancelled because the possibility of civilian casualties could not be ruled out. A thoughtful, strong willed young man, he impressed his comrades in Wexford with his determination often travelling miles to meetings and searching for things to do. He spoke of his frustration at not playing a more active role and it came as no surprise when he volunteered for active service in England.

Any volunteer operating on foreign soil is left in no doubt what hardships they face. He was told of the inhumane conditions that exist in English jails, the long suffering of prisoners like the Balcombe Street Volunteers. Eddie had already thought it through. His reasoning was that attacking the enemy on their soil was the role for him and the only thing England would listen to. He always believed that deep down most Irish people were Republicans who wished to see Ireland free from British occupation and interference. Eddie was only 21 when he gave his life for the cause of Irish freedom. He was killed in an accidental explosion on 18th February 1996. Eddie is buried in St Michael's Cemetery in Gorey, Co Wexford. He will always be loved and remembered by his family and comrades.

Óglach Eugene Martin

2nd February 1974 - 8th April 1996

Eugene Martin joined the South Armagh Brigade, Óglaigh na hÉireann at sixteen, and quickly established himself as a courageous and clever Volunteer. Kind and easy-going by nature, Eugene was also known for his steely determination, illustrated in his active sporting interests – boxing and hurling. He also played Gaelic football with Silverbridge Harps and was involved with the Ashling na Tire walking group. He was a coach with the Kilkerley Boxing Club and two of his charges were due to fight for national titles in the week he died.

He earned his living as a self-employed welder which he enjoyed, but the freedom of his country was Eugene's first love. Despite his busy work schedule and sporting life, he was an extremely active Volunteer, playing a role in many notable operations in South Armagh in the years prior to his death. Trusted and liked by all who knew him, or as one comrade said; "You always felt good with Eugene, knowing he would never let you down". Eugene was "a strong and courageous individual with an extremely gentle and kind nature. A wonderful young Volunteer with exceptional leadership qualities".

Eugene was tragically killed in a traffic accident at the age of 22 on 8th April 1996 and thousands of people turned out for his wake and funeral. Indeed, there were 100 men and women acting as pall-bearers walking in lines of four in front of the hearse, as it moved from Eugene's home to the Church of the Sacred Heart, Shelagh.

His massive funeral, with full military honours, was attended by an entire community, and was a fitting farewell to one of Ireland's most notable sons. Eugene will be sadly missed by his comrades and friends, but, even more so by his heart-broken family.

Óglach Malachy Watters

8th April 1974 - 8th August 1996

Malachy Watters was the eldest of a family of five children and grew up with his two brothers and two sisters in a small village called Culloville, just south of Crossmaglen. He attended Clonalig Primary School and St. Joseph's High School, Crossmaglen. Like most young lads his age he was full of craic and was fond of the odd bit of slagging. He was also a keen footballer and played for his local Gaelic Club right up until the time of his death.

Malachy also had a serious side and often spoke of his love for his country and expressed his anger at the effects of British oppression in Ireland. Throughout his life he had heard, read and indeed witnessed at first hand the results of British misrule. He was a strong and determined character, the type of person to stand up for himself and what he believed in.

At the early age of 17, he joined the 2nd battalion of the South Armagh brigade of Óglaigh Na hÉireann, playing an active role in some of the most successful operations carried out by his unit. He was a committed volunteer and was well liked by all who knew him.

The news of his tragic death on the 8th August 1996 shocked the entire parish of Crossmaglen, where he was buried with full military honours after a service in St Patrick's Church. The previous night his comrades delivered their final salute when they fired a volley of shots over his tricolour draped coffin.

Malachy's death was a huge loss not only to his family and his comrades in the Republican Movement but the entire community in South Armagh.

Óglach Jimmy Roe

14th December 1927 - 10th August 1996

Volunteer Jimmy Roe was born in Albert Place, Belfast on 14th December 1927. He was the second eldest of a family of four of George and Amelia Roe. He attended St. Gall's Primary School in Waterville Street. Jimmy followed in his father's footsteps. He had been a member of the IRA in the twenties.

Jimmy had been involved in the G.A.A all his life and had represented Antrim in hurling and football. Jimmy was one of the prime workers in the development of Casement Park, which went on to become the senior venue for Antrim.

In the early years of his life he joined Na Fianna and like most lads he progressed to the ranks of the IRA. In the present phase of the struggle, he was arrested in May 1972 and remained in Long Kesh until July 1975.

On Jimmy's release he reported back to his unit. Jimmy was a tireless worker on behalf of the Green Cross and a long time member of The National Graves Association. Until his untimely death in 1996, he was still involved in all aspects of our struggle.

Óglach Diarmuid O'Neill

24th June 1969 - 23rd September 1996

Diarmuid O'Neill was born and reared in London. He lived there with his parents, Eoghan and Terry, and his sister Siobhán and brother Shane. He had a great love for Ireland and all things Irish. Although culturally and politically an Irishman, his was not a narrow view of nationalism. He would have described himself as a socialist republican and had a broad view of the world - he was always on the side of the underdog. The Basque struggle was probably the next important thing to his heart after family and friends. He visited the Basque country on several occasions and his girlfriend, Karmele, was from the Basque Country.

It was Diamuid's courage and determination as a soldier in the Irish Republican Army that made him a special friend and comrade to all who knew him. He knew when he joined the IRA that it wasn't the Six Counties for him. His theatre of operations was to be in the belly of the beast, the toughest and most difficult environment for an IRA Volunteer to operate in. He never hesitated. He was bright, intelligent, bursting with ideas and ingenuity and always looking for chinks in the enemy's armour.

He was shot dead by British Police in dubious circumstances, during a 4 a.m. raid on his flat, in Hammersmith on 23rd September 1996. He is buried at St Mologas' Cemetery, Timoleague in Co Cork.

Óglach Pat McGeown

3rd September 1956 - 1st October 1996

Pat - or Pat Beag, as his friends and comrades knew him, grew up around the streets of Beechmount and Cavendish Street. Like most youths in his area he experienced intense harassment and was first arrested at 14 years of age. In 1973, whilst travelling to a training camp he was arrested and interned. Released after eighteen months he married his girlfriend Pauline and began a family. They lived in Harrogate Street in the Clonard area.

Arrested once again in 1975 he was physically assaulted for several days before being charged with blowing up the Europa Hotel in Belfast's City Centre. Sentenced to 15 years he had political status until he was caught attempting to escape from the Long Kesh Cages. Transferred to the H-Blocks he immediately joined the Blanket and No Wash protests. Pat became one of the leaders of the protest and in 1981 he replaced Joe McDonnell on hunger strike.

On his 47th day on hunger strike he lapsed into a coma and was taken to Musgrave Park Hospital where he was revived and made a slow recovery, returning to the blocks when the prison protest was entering another phase, wrecking the administration from within, the success of which led to the 1983 escape. Released in 1985 he reported back to the IRA in Belfast. He was among a number of people falsely rearrested in 1988 in relation to the deaths of two undercover British soldiers at an IRA funeral. Whilst in prison Pat's baby Marc and his mother Claire died. All the charges against him were eventually dropped.

Pat, by now suffering heart disease as a result of the hunger strike, threw himself into the political struggle, helping to develop Sinn Féin's peace strategy. He became Chair of Belfast Sinn Féin and was elected to the City Hall as a Councillor for Mid-Falls. He made many, many friends in the Protestant community and in the Loyalist political parties.

Pat McGeown, a soldier, a revolutionary, a thinker and a conciliator died suddenly on 1st October 1996.